Gold Rush Port

The publisher gratefully acknowledges the generous contribution to this book provided by the Valerie Barth and Peter Booth Wiley Endowment Fund in History of the University of California Press Foundation.

Gold Rush Port

*The Maritime Archaeology
of San Francisco's Waterfront*

James P. Delgado

UNIVERSITY OF CALIFORNIA PRESS
Berkeley · Los Angeles · London

University of California Press, one of the most
distinguished university presses in the United States,
enriches lives around the world by advancing
scholarship in the humanities, social sciences, and
natural sciences. Its activities are supported by the UC
Press Foundation and by philanthropic contributions
from individuals and institutions. For more information, visit www.ucpress.edu.

University of California Press
Berkeley and Los Angeles, California

University of California Press, Ltd.
London, England

Library of Congress Cataloging-in-Publication Data

Delgado, James P.
    Gold rush port : the maritime archaeology of San
Francisco's waterfront / James P. Delgado.
        p.   cm.
    Includes bibliographical references and index.
    ISBN 978-0-520-25580-7 (cloth : alk. paper)
        1. San Francisco (Calif.)—Antiquities.
2. Waterfronts—California—San Francisco—History.
3. Harbors—California—San Francisco—History.
4. San Francisco (Calif.)—Commerce—History.
5. Archaeology and history—California—San
Francisco.   6. Urban archaeology—California—
San Francisco.   I. Title.
F869.S347D45   2009
979.4'61—dc22   2008034388

Manufactured in the United States of America

17   16   15   14   13   12   11   10   09
10   9   8   7   6   5   4   3   2   1

The paper used in this publication meets the minimum
requirements of ANSI/NISO Z39.48–1992 (R 1997)
(Permanence of Paper).

*To my family, especially my wife, Ann,
who inspired, guided, and gently nudged
me when needed.*

*To the memory of my mentor,
Dr. Theodore C. Hinckley.*

Contents

Tables

Acknowledgments

A long list of supporters and colleagues have supported my Gold Rush research, both in the field and in the archives. First is Allen G. Pastron, who provided access to *William Gray*, Hoff's Store, *General Harrison*, Hare's shipbreaking yard, and a number of other Gold Rush and early San Francisco urban archaeological sites. Rhonda K. Robichaud worked diligently with the collections, spent many hours in front of microfilm readers to help bring *General Harrison* back to life and coauthored the final report on the ship. Richard Everett, of San Francisco Maritime National Historical Park, persuaded Allen to pick up the phone and invite me to the *General Harrison* dig. A truer friend would be impossible to find. I also would like to thank my friend and colleague James Allan of William Self Associates, who provided invaluable access to information on his firm's excavation of the Gold Rush hulk *Rome* and involved me in the analysis of WSA's excavation of the Hare shipbreaking yard and the remains of the whaling bark *Candace*.

The Archeo-Tec field crew worked long and difficult hours on this project and under trying circumstances, including constantly wet and muddy conditions and the need to work in the midst of a busy industrial construction site with tight deadlines. I thank the field and laboratory crew: Dale Beevers, Matt Calder, Patrick Cave, Jamie Wadell, Andrew Gottsfield, Jonathan Goodrich, Michelle Collins, Anne Olney, Jason Claiburne, Eros Hoagland, Rebecca Sue Johnson, Paul Landgraver, Kasey Hovenkamp, Rebecca Percey, Nora Yolles, Bill Percey, Julie Kirkenslager,

Richard Stradtford, Tom Hirashima, Emily Wick, Yosuf Nashir, Dave Nichols, and Alison Vanderslice.

In 1980 and 1986, I was fortunate to work with other Archeo-Tec field crews at the *William Gray* and Hoff's Store sites. I thank Eugene M. Hattori, Richard Ambro, Bridgette M. Brigham, Jerre L. Kosta, Michael R. Walsh, Janice Narita, Julia Huddleston, Mitsuru S. Watanabe, Dennis P. McDougall, Paula B. Terrey, Stephen G. Botkin, Margaret Brown, Barbara Bucciarelli, Ron Chambliss, Gerald Doty, Robert Sheets, Samantha Walker, William Wihr, Jim Houston, and Tim Shover. My interaction with Richard Ambro, as well as with Archeo-Tec's Julie Kirkenslager and Emily Wick, have continued to the present, and their pointing out the work at 343 Sansome was an invaluable addition to this book. Richard's participation in the early stages of the 343 Sansome Project as well as at Hoff's Store helped clarify the comparisons for me.

Harlan Soeten, the retired curator of the San Francisco Maritime Museum, introduced me to the buried Gold Rush ships, as did the late Karl Kortum, the museum's founder, and museum librarian David Hull. Another guide and mentor was the late John B. Goodman IIII, whose encyclopedic compendium of the Gold Rush fleet that sailed to California in 1848–49 remains a landmark achievement in Gold Rush scholarship. Many a Gold Rush reference found its way to me through the diligence of Robert J. Chandler of the Wells Fargo Bank History Department. Carlos Lopéz Urrutia, naval and maritime historian and expert on Chile's participation in the California Gold Rush, as well as a former Chilean consul, shared his knowledge and rare research materials from his library.

I am also grateful for the support of Cathy and Jerry Solley of Waldport, Oregon. Cathy, a descendant of Joseph Perkins Beach, shared the family archive she has collected through the years, notably Henry Day Beach's letters from San Francisco and Sacramento about the family's storeship, *Apollo*. Cathy and Jerry also graciously hosted a weekend's research at their seaside Oregon home.

The late Raymond Aker and William Avery Baker provided naval architectural advice and guidance, as did Curator Stephen Canright of the San Francisco Maritime National Historical Site. Lines taking and documentation of *General Harrison*'s hull remains was supervised by John Muir of San Francisco Maritime National Historical Park and included a field team of Diane Cooper, Todd Bloch, Mike Jablonowski, and Jason Rucker. Reconstruction drawings of *General Harrison* and *Niantic* were prepared by my friend and colleague John W. McKay. Maps for this book were prepared by archaeological illustrator Jack Scott.

My research in Chile was assisted by Juan Carlos Zalaquett and Melissa Taylor. I enjoyed sharing and debating Gold Rush theory and frontier issues with Margaret Purser. My father, Robert D. Delgado, re-tired assistant chief of the San Jose Fire Department, was an invaluable resource in reconstructing the May 4, 1851, fire.

Analysis of the *General Harrison* collection came through the assis-tance and professional support of Liz Honeysett of Far Western An-thropological Research Group, Annalies Corbin of the P.A.S.T. Founda-tion, Christine Langford of the U.S. Department of Agriculture Forest Products Laboratory, Tim Teague of the Earth and Planetary Science De-partment of the University of California, Berkeley, Harold Harlan IIII of Harlan Associates, Jessica Just of EST Laboratories, and Julie Trosper of the Oakland Museum. I am indebted to the analysis of the *Niantic* as-semblage, led by Mary Hilderman Smith and fleshed out by the many scholars she consulted, and was pleased and privileged to participate in that work.

The following institutions and their staffs were a great help: the Bib-lioteca Nacional de Chile, Santiago, Chile; the Museo Nacional de Chile, Santiago; the Bancroft Library, University of California, Berkeley; the So-ciety of California Pioneers, San Francisco; the Wells Fargo Bank His-tory Room and Archives, San Francisco; the California Historical Soci-ety, San Francisco; the California State Library, Sacramento; the J. Porter Shaw Library, San Francisco Maritime National Historical Park; the Maryland Historical Society, Baltimore; the Peabody Essex Museum, Salem, Massachusetts; the Newburyport Historical Society, Newbury-port, Massachusetts; the W. B. Chung Library at the Vancouver Maritime Museum; the West Vancouver Memorial Library, whose reference staff allowed me hours of use of their microfilm reader/printer; and the United States National Archives, Washington, D.C., and San Bruno, California.

I also wish to acknowledge the guidance and review of my colleagues David Burley, Ross Jamieson, and Warren Gill of Simon Fraser Univer-sity; Jay V. Powell of the University of British Columbia; Margaret Purser of Sonoma State University; Mark Staniforth of Flinders University; and Michael McCarthy of the Western Australian Maritime Museum, all of whom read and reviewed an earlier version of this manuscript, which formed the basis of my doctoral dissertation at Simon Fraser University. My assistant Kathy Smith was another invaluable member of the team as my dissertation became a book. I also thank my editor at the University of California Press, Blake Edgar, and the press's editorial staff and team, notably Suzanne Knott and Adrienne Harris.

Finally, but not last, my gratitude is boundless toward my wife, Ann Goodhart, for her encouragement and support.

James P. Delgado, 2007

CHAPTER I

Introduction

The rapid rise of San Francisco between 1849 and 1856 engaged the attention of contemporary nineteenth-century observers and subsequent historians. In that period, San Francisco grew from a small village of a few hundred to a city of thousands. It also became the principal American port on the Pacific Ocean. Interpretations as to how and why the city grew into this role vary, although all accounts note the role of the discovery of gold in California and the subsequent "Gold Rush" as causative factors (for example, Taylor 1850; Capron 1854; Soulé, Gihon, and Nisbet 1855; Hittell 1878; Bancroft 1888; Eldredge 1912; Caughey 1948; Lotchin 1974; Holliday 1981).

In 1854, E. S. Capron summarized the contemporary view of the events leading to the creation of San Francisco:

> Previous to the year 1848, the wildest imagination could scarcely have conceived that a large and populous city would suddenly arise under the flag of the Union on that remote and alien shore; or that the waters of that silent harbor would be whitened with the canvas of every nation, and be vocal with the restless commerce of the world. But enterprise is not now the tardy nag it was forty years ago; the sentiment *"perseverantia vincit omnia"* is not, at this day, a merely literary flourish or theoretic idea, but is a practical fact; and its truth has never been more signally illustrated than in the history of San Francisco—a history that has no parallel in the annals of the world (122–123).

Capron suggests that San Francisco was an accidental city propelled into greatness by an enthusiastic, international maritime capitalistic response to the discovery of gold in California. He is correct in part, but as I suggest in this book, the rise of San Francisco was far from accidental. Gold was not an instigator, but an accelerant, to development. The remote and alien shore Capron describes was neither. Connected to preexisting Pacific and global maritime trade and commerce, San Francisco was not a frontier in any traditional sense; it was part of a maritime frontier (Gibson and Whitehead 1993).

This book explains the rapid rise of San Francisco; in it, I propose a frontier model based on the concept of an entrepôt, or a zone of free exchange. Key to my thesis is the assertion that although the city's growth was fueled by the economic energy of the Gold Rush, San Francisco had already attracted the attention of capitalist interests in the early nineteenth century as a potential entrepôt. These interests sought to dominate Pacific trade. San Francisco's first historians, participants themselves in the process, maintained in 1855 that the port city, though established by Spain in the previous century, had lain stagnant until the arrival of capitalist interests:

> The Spaniards had scarcely proceeded any way in the great work,—if they had not rather retarded it, when the Anglo-Saxons, the true and perhaps only type of modern *progress,* hastily stepped in, and unscrupulously swept away both their immediate forerunners as effete workers, and the aborigines of the land, all as lumberers and nuisances in the great western highway of civilization. This highway is fated to girdle the globe . . . and there need not be the slightest doubt but that the empire, or rather the great *union* of peoples and nations in the Pacific will soon—perhaps in fifty years, perhaps a century—rival, if not surpass the magnificent States of the Atlantic. Indians, Spaniards of many provinces, Hawaiians, Japanese, Chinese, Malays, Tartars and Russians, must all give place to the restless flood of Anglo-Saxon or American progress (Soulé, Gihon, and Nisbet 1855:53–54).

With the U.S. acquisition of San Francisco Bay during the Mexican War of 1846–48, the way was clear to achieve the ultimate goal, an entrepôt that would dominate not only Asian trade but also that of the entire ocean:

> Not only are Japan and China much nearer to the California coast than India is to England; but with the aid of steam the time for accomplishing the distance is immensely reduced . . . So it was with the English in India; and so it may be with the Americans in China. Just give us *time.* England has not been very scrupulous in her stealthy progress over Hindostan, Ceylon and Birmah. Then neither need America fear her reproaches, if she, in like manner, conquer, or annex the Sandwich Islands, the Islands of Japan, those of the great Malayan Archipelago, or the mighty "Flowery Empire" itself.

A few more years, and a few millions of Americans in the Pacific may realize the gigantic scheme . . . The railway across, or *through* the Snowy and Rocky Mountains, which will bind all North America with its iron arm into one mighty empire, will facilitate the operation. And then SAN FRANCISCO—in the execution and triumph of that scheme, will assuredly become what Liverpool, or even London is to England, and what New York is to the Middle and Eastern states of America—a grand depot for numerous manufactures and produce, and a harbor for the fleets of every nation (Soulé, Gihon, and Nisbet 1855:54–55).

The establishment of American governance and the subdivision of the town's public lands for private sale were the first steps in creating the entrepôt that would facilitate the development of the port.

The discovery of gold in 1848 and the "rush" that began in 1849 abetted and accelerated this process. The Gold Rush provided more than large amounts of gold for capitalization, a requisite aspect of the town and port's development as it constantly rebuilt after a series of disastrous fires. The Gold Rush provided a market and a start-up role for the new entrepôt as it served the needs of the mines and miners who came for gold. Holliday discusses how San Francisco's geographic placement made it the "Great Commercial Emporium of the Pacific" (1999:182). The city's location on the shores of the region's greatest harbor, on a bay into which flowed two major rivers that penetrated deep into the surrounding country, guaranteed its role as the landing place for thousands of passengers and cargoes. By 1850 San Francisco was a port "secure in its monopoly by the luck of geography," its rise assisted "by the driving ambitions of its businessmen, who worked to connect their port with the vast inland mining empire, mother lode to the city's prosperity' (182).

The primary means of supply was by ship, with vessels calling from around the globe. Thousands of vessels arrived at San Francisco between 1849 and 1856, discharging thousands of passengers and more than half a million tons of cargo (Delgado 1990a). A variety of global partners with commercial, not political, interests at stake abetted this trade. The first step toward creating a successful entrepôt was to build a unique waterfront that used ships as floating buildings, wharves as streets, and buildings on pilings into which goods could flow from around the world. On this quickly built waterfront, the entrepreneurs of the time hastened to sell or repackage these goods and transship them to the interior of California and the gold mines.

A major fire destroyed this waterfront on May 4, 1851, but the foundations for a successful entrepôt had been laid, and San Francisco became an established new link in the world's maritime trade: America's New York on the Pacific. Bancroft described the success of the city and port as of 1856:

> Thus lay transformed San Francisco, from an expanse of sand hills, from a tented encampment, to a city unapproached by any of similar age for size and for substantial and ornamental improvements . . . The fluctuating settlement stood now the acknowledged metropolis of the west. . . . and this phenomenal progress was the achievement of half a dozen years, surpassing the wildest of those speculations which had incited, first the entry of the pioneers, then annexation by the United States, and finally city building, and the founding of an empire out of the manifold resources . . . A series of surprises marked the advance of the state as well as of the city—the one a wilderness bursting into bloom, the other a mart of progress purified by many fiery ordeals (1888:787).

This new city, outpost of American ambitions on the Pacific, had not only rapidly evolved, but it had done so in a way that did not fit the traditional frontier process.

The traditional frontier process, as proposed by Turner (1894), was marked by waves of exploration, trapping and trading, and farming and settlement by "men of capital and enterprise" who built villages that finally grew into towns and cities. Later Billington (1956) modified Turner's model of slow and steady westward movement, proposing that as the movement gathered pace, "a standardized zonal pattern" of settlement emerged. The resulting zones were the domains of fur traders, cattlemen, miners, pioneer farmers, and equipped farmers; the "final frontier zone" was one of town and city (3–6). The founding of towns and cities, in Billington's model, came with the arrival of entrepreneurs and opportunity seekers who "chose their homesites at strategically located points in the center of agricultural communities, usually selecting a crossroads, a point in the head of navigation on some stream, or an advantageous spot on a canal or railroad. As more and more concentrated there, a hamlet, then a village, then a town, gradually took shape" (306). However, San Francisco, isolated by the landmass of the continent and the mountain ranges of the Midwest, was not linked to the rest of the United States by land.

Reps, in his study of frontier processes, challenged the Turner and Billington models. Noting the earlier tradition of Hispanic town planning and settlement and the "simple truth . . . that in every section of the West, towns were in the vanguard of settlement," Reps suggested that frontier towns were laid out as planned communities with designs for future growth (1981:2). This framework provides a better one for understanding San Francisco. Reps specifically rejected the agrarian emphasis of Turner and Billington, arguing that a variety of factors induced migration to the frontier, including mining, urban speculation, railroad building, and pioneers' desire to escape religious intolerance.

In this view, Reps followed Paul (1963), who argued that the discoveries of gold and silver in the nineteenth century resulted in a series of detached frontiers. His argument also fits with the theoretical premise of Steffen (1979), who examined processes of settlement and broke down change into two patterns: modal change, a slower, minimal process; and "fundamental" change, a process that significantly disrupts the status quo. These processes created two models in the United States: the "cosmopolitan frontier," a modal change, with a large number of interacting links; and the "insular frontier," a fundamental change influenced by indigenous environments, with few interacting links. The mining activities of the nineteenth century, argued Steffen, did not create a frontier in Turner's sense but a continuity of "national trends that occurred in the decades before the initial rush to California" (110). One of those national trends, beginning in the 1780s, was the American push into the Pacific to seek new avenues of maritime trade. By the nineteenth century, American commercial, military, and cultural interests were flooding into the Pacific and dominating the Pacific Basin's oceanic trades (Gibson and Whitehead 1993:6–9).

I suggest that San Francisco is an artifact of the maritime system at play in the Pacific in the first half of the nineteenth century. Thanks to ships and shipping, San Francisco tied into a web of international relationships and trade to become America's principal seaport on the Pacific and a participant in the global economy. My study of archival sources and the material record of the Gold Rush waterfront of San Francisco in the late spring of 1851 confirms that San Francisco, as Reps suggests, was a planned town. At that time, San Francisco was in transition, evolving rapidly from a small village into a major port and entrepôt, and the waterfront was a carefully planned aspect of that expansion. To the modern eye, the Gold Rush waterfront is a vanished landscape. However, because of a series of catastrophic fires, landfilling, and urban development, the waterfront of 1849–56 survived, albeit as a buried archaeological resource. A number of the ships, wharves, and other infrastructure of San Francisco's Gold Rush waterfront lie buried beneath the streets, sidewalks, and high-rises of the modern city. Indeed, the tide still rises and falls on the beaches of 1849, albeit percolated through a thick matrix of mud, sand, and rubble.

The macroartifact that is the entire waterfront has been discovered during downtown construction and documented through decades of archaeological excavation and investigation. To sample the Gold Rush waterfront, I have participated in the detailed excavation and analysis of a Gold Rush floating warehouse—in contemporary terms, a storeship—*General Harrison.* By comparing the data on *General Harrison* with the results of earlier excavations of other storeships, particularly the neighboring *Niantic,* I have been able to fill in some data missing from the *General Harrison* site. In turn, I have been able to assess the representative nature of the *General Harrison* site and its assemblage within its neighborhood.

A comparison of two other contemporary sites—Hoff's Store and another, unidentified store or stores at 343 Sansome Street—enhances this analysis. The archaeological sites of Hoff's Store, 334 Sansome, *Niantic,* and *General Harrison* are in close proximity, and all four were "destroyed" in the cataclysmic fire of May 4, 1851. Obtaining a precise dating of the archaeological deposit containing all four sites has been particularly important because the next level of analysis, after examining the physical characteristics of each site and their role in the planned development of the town's port, focuses on the material culture (cargo) of *General Harrison.* In this cargo I have looked for evidence of the global patterns of maritime trade.

MARITIME COMMERCIAL INTERESTS AS ENGINES OF GROWTH

San Francisco was not an ideal candidate for future growth: it was hemmed in by tall sand dunes, and its shallow waterfront became an expansive mudflat at low tide. Unlike other Spanish settlements, which began as walled or easily defended citadels, San Francisco began with a plat that laid out streets on an open grid for future commercial growth. This initial plat, created in 1839 and extended by the Americans in 1847 and again in 1849, is a graphic artifact of the triumph of political maneuvering over commercial development. The city's plat, described by a newspaper editorial in 1855 as proof of "the jealous avarice of the city projectors into turning every . . . square [yard] . . . of the site, into an available building lot" (cited in Reps 1981:112) was squares of land for speculation without public spaces. This purely commercial emphasis prompted quick improvisation of an extensive infrastructure. The resulting dynamic urban environment was characterized by frequent change and a hectic pace of life, specifically on the waterfront (Barth 1975:130).

The development of the waterfront defined early San Francisco economically as well as physically, generating an urban, commercial, and
mercantile core that allowed its developers and inhabitants to thrive in
the face of competition and prosper despite the lack of available land,
boom-and-bust economic cycles, and a series of destructive fires. The
founders of San Francisco were capitalists gambling on San Francisco's
becoming a point of transshipment of goods off-loaded from deepwater
oceangoing craft into smaller bay and river craft that could navigate the
bay and its connecting San Joaquin and Sacramento rivers to deliver their
cargo to the mining settlements in the mountains (Barth 1975:139).
Lotchin also cites this creation of a "transportation break" as the key to
San Francisco's success (1974:6). Though maritime in nature, this trans-
portation- and transshipment-based origin of San Francisco is similar in
some respects to the role of the railroad in other frontier settlements, particularly in the development of another "instant city," rail-linked Denver, Colorado (Barth 1975). The story of commercial maritime influences
on San Francisco's creation and ongoing survival complements "the other
great nineteenth century American narrative about the articulation of private commerce, public government, land speculation, transportation technology, infrastructure, power, and transformation of urban form, particularly on some given frontier. . . . [as well as] the story of railroad
development in the country" (Purser 2003a).

INTEGRATING SAN FRANCISCO INTO WORLD TRADE

San Francisco became the city it did simply because of maritime capitalists' desire to tap into global maritime trade. Economic historians Eric
Jones, Lionel Frost, and Colin White note that the first effect of the gold-
fueled rise of San Francisco was "to link the regions of the Pacific Rim
more closely with metropolitan centers in Europe" (1993:66). The development of the city also marked the commencement of a new and expanded pattern of transpacific and coastal Pacific trade. Anglo-American
Pacific trade had previously existed on a smaller scale thanks primarily
to the China trade and whaling. The Gold Rush changed this trade sce-
nario. As Jones, Frost, and White point out, in the nineteenth century,
the center of the global economy "clearly moved from Western Europe
to the United States" (1993:5–6). I believe that the major factor in this
shift was America's ability to dominate Pacific trade thanks to the Gold
Rush and the rise of San Francisco.

The intermingling of mariners in regularly arriving ships and the influx of miners in pursuit of goods, services, or simply respite from the harsh winters of the mountain camps made San Francisco a hub of trade and a core of the communication network. From here, "investment capital, knowledge, and personnel moved into the mountains and dividends, experience, and information about the West returned to the east" as well as Europe (Barth 1975:209). Not coincidentally, also at this time, "oceanic routes integrated the world economy as never before. . . . [worldwide] rapid growth and revolutionary change in transportation and communications increased the output and trading of goods . . . [and] shifting patterns of international trade across the North Pacific further stimulated commerce" (Perry 1994:61).

To tap into this emerging Pacific trade, San Francisco needed quickly to establish a proper zone of commercial maritime exchange on the waterfront. "Wedded to maritime trade," San Francisco's residents, as Barth suggests, spotted the solution to the emerging town by transforming the shoreline into the heart of the business district (1975:210). Barth identifies these resident developers, as a "new breed of speculators, responsive to the hectic pulse of the changing city" (211). Lotchin (1974:9) also describes the quick development of commercial facilities on the waterfront, quoting contemporary journalist Bayard Taylor's observation that whatever advantages San Francisco lacked for success as a transshipment point "will soon be amply provided for by wealth and enterprise" (1974:9).

Those with the means to develop San Francisco were the merchants with strong international ties to maritime trade, most of them commission merchants with preexisting business arrangements in Central and South America, China, the eastern United States, and Europe. Lotchin (1974:52) places them at the top of the economic food chain of Gold Rush San Francisco because they essentially controlled the city's trade through their handling of incoming goods. Their role in building up San Francisco, largely on their own initiative, was abetted by a weak government presence. Vigilantes drawn from the mercantile elite dealt with lawlessness. Lack of coin was remedied by the establishment of private mints, and "solutions to other problems were often provided within a context of free market operations rather than reliance on government" (Jones, Frost, and White 1993:90).

No strangers to the frontier process, commission merchants had played a significant role in developing the Mississippi Valley frontier before the California Gold Rush. In San Francisco, commission merchants had access to an undeveloped waterfront, which, developed to their specific needs, became the locus where goods were quickly off-loaded, safely stored, or rapidly sold and reloaded for transshipment. By tapping into the gold of California, they literally had unlimited means to create such an entrepôt. This circumstance was unusual in world history and was repeated only one other time in North America, in Denver (Barth 1975). However, unlike Denver, the instant city of San Francisco, whose trade links by sea offered a seductive alternative to the vastly more difficult overland routes, did more than draw the American frontier westward. It realigned Pacific and then global maritime networks of transport. This international trade linkage made San Francisco a "cosmopolis" and a "world city" from the start, much like Venice, Amsterdam, or St. Petersburg (211).

Miners came to California from various lands or states, driven by economic or social circumstances to try their hand in the mines. Merchants, nonetheless, were the instigators of settlement and development who maintained the lines of trade as part of an interlinked global network. Merchants tapped the energy of the Gold Rush to create San Francisco, further tying the Pacific into the world system. Despite longstanding American desires to dominate this shift in the focus of trade (Perry 1994), the effort was a global one, particularly demonstrated by the relationships of commission merchant ands their backers with commercial interests in London, Hamburg, Paris, and ports in diverse spots such as Hawai'i, Denmark, Sweden, and Portugal. The internationalism of Gold Rush San Francisco was no accident, and like the city itself, it grew out of the use of maritime trade to transform the Pacific from a peripheral trade zone to a nexus of world trade.

HISTORICAL ARCHAEOLOGY
ON SAN FRANCISCO'S WATERFRONT

Since the 1970s, as historians rejected the Turner model of the frontier and looked in new directions (known as the new western history), the application of historical or text-aided archaeology (Little 1992) has helped create a new model of the frontier. Particularly significant has been Hardesty's argument that a mining community on the frontier was an urbanlike organization "loosely integrated and atomistic, cosmopolitan, male-dominated, marked often by dramatic boom-bust fluctuations in population size, and with economic and political dependencies upon large scale world systems" (1993:5). I propose expanding this model to recognize the role of the global maritime system (a subset of the world system), which had expanded thanks to trade by sea from its fifteenth-century beginnings to well beyond Europe. Maritime trade in the first half of the nineteenth century was rapidly bringing the system to the Pacific Rim, and Gold Rush San Francisco was a key player in that process.

San Francisco provides an archaeological sample within a discrete physical and temporal boundary to assess the rapid adoption of global maritime trade to create an "instant port" by designating the city as an entrepôt. Economic historians have noted that "a settlement located at the intersection of major trade routes, at some point where a change in the mode of transport is required . . . will be well placed to attract investment in transport facilities and commercial activity" (Jones, Frost, and White 1993:134). San Francisco's entrepreneurs saw their raw and undeveloped city as such a place and invested capital to overcome its physical limitations. They also fought off competing port cities on the bay and sought to lessen the appeal of bypassing San Francisco and sailing directly into the heart of the gold fields. To do so, they used their economic and political clout to seize legal status as a government-enforced port of entry for foreign goods, thus creating the business foundation for their entrepôt.

My analysis takes a historical archaeological approach that draws on Hardesty's "features system" (Hardesty 1988, 1993) and on an emergent school of thought that sees the maritime system as a subset of world systems theory (Staniforth 2003; Russell, Bradford, and Murphy 2004) to examine the rise of Gold Rush San Francisco. Such an archaeological assessment is possible because of the decision of San Francisco's founders to construct much of the city's infrastructure over water. The subsequent partial destruction by fire left a rare archaeological matrix, encapsulating the city by deep burial in sediments that provided a wet environment conducive to preservation, even of organic remains. My focus on these inundated and then buried sites with links to maritime activities also fits within the general shift away from the shipwreck and maritime archaeology of recent years toward a more integrative approach that places historical archaeology within the context of world systems theory and new western history.

This matrix is a rich archaeological assemblage of tens of thousands of artifacts. When combined with a detailed archival record that begins with San Francisco's major newspaper, the *Daily Alta California* and continues with other newspapers such as the *San Francisco Daily Herald* and the *San Francisco Bulletin;* contemporary written accounts, including business correspondence; and an amazing array of graphic evidence, including maps, plans, drawings and photographs, the total data set offers an impressive amount of material for study. Both sets of data more than adequately meet Deetz's (1977) highest standards for "visibility" and "focus"—offering abundant physical remains and the potential to read and clearly interpret the remains.

My field and archival research has spanned thirty years. I have presented some of the results in earlier publications, presenting a historical model that argues for a maritime-oriented frontier process (Delgado 1990a, 1990b). Here I build on that work, following Deetz's and Hardesty's suggested format of study by integrating oral, written, and material sources to interpret the Gold Rush waterfront of San Francisco and by extension, to examine the ways in which this Pacific Rim "frontier port" fits the theoretical model of a global maritime system. This hypothesis of a maritime-driven Pacific context for the world system will no doubt be relevant to other ports and sites, especially those where commercial interests built "new towns" on "made land" for better functioning of the port (as in Valparaíso, Hong Kong, Sydney, and Seattle).

I draw archaeological data from four sites, two piling-supported stores and two storeships that commission merchants converted from floating vessels into warehouses in the heart of the Gold Rush waterfront. The ships were part of a fleet of several hundred vessels that arrived at San Francisco during the Gold Rush years of 1849 and 1850. Close to five hundred were laid up, some permanently and others turned temporarily to other uses. Over two hundred fifty were converted into floating or mud-moored buildings, most of them warehouses, linked by pile-supported wharves and structures to create the necessary infrastructure for the commission merchants' transshipment business and commercial exchanges. Without those ships, the rapid rise of San Francisco would have been different and perhaps impossible.

The storeships, controlled by the commission merchants, tapped into and focused on the output of an international production sphere, with goods flowing in from around the world. They created a sphere of distribution and economic exchange in the nine-square-block area on the waterfront where they docked. The storeships are the quintessential Gold Rush San Francisco artifact. By intensively studying their preserved cargoes to determine their functions and activities, we can improve our understanding of the city's role in global maritime trade, particularly its interaction with the world system as an entrepôt. Moreover, we can glimpse the workings of the European modern world system as it reached the Pacific in the nineteenth century by looking at these global patterns of maritime trade.

These data enable me to address the critical importance of storeships in the emerging economy of the port, specifically the role of the commission merchants. Study of the Gold Rush waterfront sheds light on the more typical aspects of the capitalist world system, especially core/ periphery production, supply relationships and trade patterns, and the shipment of market goods (see Russell, Bradford, and Murphy 2004). As such, the waterfront is similar to Hardesty's view of mining frontiers: "Mining colonies were financed, manned, supplied, from the urban centers of America and Europe. Despite their geographical remoteness and small size, the colonies were linked into a vast transportation, communications, demographic and international scale" (1988:1).

Drawing from approaches of maritime archaeologists and anthropologists such as Murphy (1984, 1997) and Staniforth (1997), I center much of my theoretical analysis on the concept of the maritime system. I support these scholars' underlying tenet that a maritime-system approach accounts for integrated maritime activities for an event like the Gold Rush. It incorporates all aspects of a maritime world, from ships, shipyards, and waterfronts to activities (Russell, Bradford, and Murphy 2004:101). It looks at interconnectivity, not specific sites or isolated events, and it fits well with the current direction in maritime archaeological studies.

As a maritime archaeologist, I have participated in the excavation and analysis of numerous Gold Rush waterfront sites in San Francisco. Reanalyzing these data, including my more recent analysis of the material culture and historical connections of the *General Harrison* site, has led to my thesis that San Francisco does not fit the traditional pattern of frontier development in the United States. In the chapters that follow, I lay out the theoretical perspectives that have guided my assessment of the creation of San Francisco. I then offer a historical summary of the development of the city and port, paying special attention to the role of the commission merchants. The development of archaeological methodology and field techniques in the excavation of the material record of San Francisco—the subject of chapter 6 and an aspect that has not hitherto been presented—is critical to understanding the historical archaeology of San Francisco's waterfront and understanding why, without *General Harrison*, the amount of data provided an insufficient sample to develop and assess my thesis. With this foundation, I summarize the material record and then draw my conclusions about the maritime world system's role in San Francisco's creation.

CHAPTER 2

Theoretical Perspective

As a maritime archaeologist, I am generally in accord with a number of my colleagues in applying aspects of world systems theory to my work (Staniforth 1997, 2003; Russell, Bradford, and Murphy 2004). However, a variety of theoretical perspectives and approaches, practiced both in urban and mining archaeological sites, are pertinent to this book.

WHAT KIND OF SITE?

The site at the heart of my study, the San Francisco waterfront, grew up as part of a "new town"—in an urban context and on a mining frontier—yet it is maritime in its raison d'etre. This mixed urban, mining, and maritime identity poses a challenge to scholars: how to select an appropriate approach for studying the site and how to reconcile the theoretical debates within each of the three areas of study.

Despite the site's urban setting and roots in the California Gold Rush, the San Francisco waterfront is foremost a maritime rather than an urban archaeological site. Typically, maritime sites are discrete entities, such as shipwrecks, their associated cargoes, and other contents. Here, however, I assess more than one ship and a several-block area of associated waterfront and infrastructure, in keeping with the view that "maritime archaeology is concerned with all aspects of maritime culture" (Muckelroy 1978:4). In this view, maritime archaeology should focus not just on technical matters but also on social, economic, political, religious, and other contexts and include within its study "all aspects of seafaring" (4). Thus, in my study of the Gold Rush waterfront, I examine the landscape of wharves, docks, beached ships, waterfront buildings, and their associated assemblages, including stowed cargoes, discarded or lost merchandise, and even the landfill used to reclaim land from the sea.

THEORETICAL PREMISE

I suggest that San Francisco's Gold Rush waterfront grew up as part of the worldwide development of capitalism—a position that is in general accord with a growing group of fellow maritime archaeologists who have adopted elements of the *Annales* school and world systems theory. This premise also is in accord with the school of new western history, which views the West as a site of European conquest, colonization, exploitation, development, and expansion of the world market (Limerick 1987, 1991; White 1991; Gibson and Whitehead 1993; Nugent 1994; Robbins 1994).

My role, then, is to assess how the maritime system as a subset of world systems theory explains the development of the San Francisco waterfront and entrepôt.

WORLD SYSTEMS THEORY

Trading systems often have what is almost a life of
their own. . . . They extend widely, over the boundaries
of many politically independent societies. But sometimes the different parts of a widespread trading system
of this kind can become so dependent on each other
commercially that one can no longer think of them as
independent entities.

(Renfrew and Bahn 1996:336)

This quotation summarizes Immanuel Wallerstein's argument for a modern world system. His "world system" did not encompass the globe, because such an economic (as opposed to political) system "is larger than any juridically-defined political unit" (Wallerstein 1974:15). Rather he originally conceptualized a series of world systems that encompassed discrete geographical entities—such as the Mediterranean, the pre-Columbian Americas, Asia, and Europe—and that existed in different periods and dated back some 5,000 years (Wallerstein 1974:16–18; Frank and Gills 1993).

Only in the more modern era, post–1450 A.D., did a more global economic system evolve. This period witnessed the rise of a world economy and the spread of capitalism from Europe to create an interconnected global system of commodity exchange. Wallerstein's premise, inspired by both the *Annales* school and the work of Fernand Braudel (1980), saw that rise occurring in the *longue durée*, in which change was "slow, a history of constant repetition, ever-recurring cycles" (Wallerstein 1974:20). These cycles were marked by periods of contraction and expansion that when charted through decades, show a wavelike pattern of peaks and troughs. These so-called Kondratieff waves, or K-waves (Kondratieff 1979), reflect the alternation of periods of economic stagnation and depression with booms. The booms coincide with actions to integrate new geographic areas and their commodities into the world system.

The proponents of world systems theory see it as a unifying, "albeit diverse, stream of world history" of interrelated processes that offer "a powerful antidote to Eurocentric or Western-centric distortions of history . . . as well as to Sino-, Islamo-, Afro-centric and other parochial alternatives to Eurocentrism" (Frank 1994:1). Adherents to this view see the process of capital accumulation as the motor force of history, playing the central role in the world system for several millennia (Gills and Frank 1991; Frank and Gills 1993).

The world systems approach posits a series of zones of exchange, with peripheral zones supplying raw materials to core zones that are politically and economically dominant. Within the world system are long and short economic cycles of both ascending and descending phases, with changes in the center and periphery following the same cycles in K-wave patterns (Frank 1994:2). For example, Liu points out that postmedieval changes in trade affected sites of accumulation, specifically in the Indian Ocean and Asia, where "the shift of trade routes caused the rise and fall of these cities as effectively as warfare or other political crises" (1988:178).

Because this book assesses San Francisco's waterfront within Wallerstein's world systems perspective, a review of his basic premise is in order. In setting forth his concept of world systems, Wallerstein cites three critical dates, 1500, 1650, and 1800 A.D. (1980:7). Beginning with 1500, Europe expanded beyond the Mediterranean, taking a series of actions that created "a capitalist world-system." The year 1650 marked the emergence of the first capitalist states of the Netherlands and Great Britain.

Finally, by 1800, the role of industrialism had become the crucial agent of change.

> The modern world-system took the form of a capitalist world-economy that had its genesis in Europe in the long sixteenth century and that involved the *transformation* of a particular redistributive or tributary mode of production, that of feudal Europe (Braudel's "economic *Ancien Régime*), into a qualitatively different social system. Since that time the capitalist world-economy has *(a)* geographically expanded to cover the entire globe; *(b)* manifested a cyclical pattern of expansion and contraction. . . . and *(c)* undergone a process of secular transformation, including technological advance, industrialization, proletarianization and the emergence of structured political resistance to the system itself—a transformation that is still going on today (7–8).

The world economy remained the same between 1500 and 1750, expanding after 1500 to encompass the Caribbean (Wallerstein 1980:9). Wallerstein analyzes changes in the boundaries of the world economy in Europe during this period, examining shifting economic, political, and cultural patterns. He also singles out one commodity from the Americas that made the modern world system possible: bullion, "a necessity for the expansion of the European economy" (1974:45). Bullion would also play a role in the establishment of San Francisco as an entrepôt.

Of particular interest in my work is Wallerstein's assessment of the role of maritime transport in the development of the world economy and world system. Other scholars, notably Hugill (1993), see ships and maritime trade as the connective links of the global system of commodities exchange. Wallerstein also emphasizes the role of entrepôts in the mercantilist origins of the modern world system. In assessing Dutch hegemony in the world economy of the seventeenth century, he identifies the critical factors for hegemony: "Marked superiority in agro-industrial productive efficiency leads to dominance of the spheres of commercial distribution of world trade, with correlative profits accruing both from being the entrepôt of much of world trade and from controlling the 'invisibles'—transport, communications, and insurance. Commercial primacy leads in turn to control of the financial sectors of banking (exchange, deposit, and credit) and of investment (direct and portfolio); these superiorities are successive, but they overlap in time" (1980:38). Wallerstein believes that Dutch seafaring efficiency was first manifested in the herring fishery of the early seventeenth century. Combined with the creation of the polders, the successful growth of agriculture, and the rise of the textile industry, this herring industry eventually developed into a substantial shipbuilding industry for the Dutch and helped the Netherlands establish maritime dominance (1980:40–45).

By the last quarter of the seventeenth century, Dutch shipping dominated the world's carrying trade, growing tenfold between 1500 and 1700 (Wallerstein 1980:46). The creation of the Vereenigde Oost-Indische Compagnie (VOC) in 1602 and its subsequent domination of the spice trade were key to Dutch hegemony. Through the VOC, the East Indies became a peripheral zone to the capitalist world economy, albeit one linked solely by maritime transport (47). In that world economy, Amsterdam was its greatest entrepôt because of its commodity market and its role as a shipping center and capital market (Wallerstein 1980:55; 1974:212). Wallerstein' attributes the success of the Dutch and their entrepôt and the superiority of their "commercial organization" largely to a network of commission agents (Wallerstein 1980:56).

Dutch hegemony led to competition, particularly from England and France. The availability of work in these new powers encouraged the emigration of skilled Dutch shipwrights, who enabled England and France to build up their navies, and in the case of England, to launch the East India Company to compete with VOC (70). A century and a half of struggle ensued between the three would-be powers, culminating with the rise of England as the new hegemonic power after 1763 (240). English success included the acquisition of the key Dutch entrepôt of Nieuw Amsterdam, in the semiperipheral area of Middle Atlantic North America (236).

Once in English hands, the renamed entrepôt of New York played an important role in English maritime trade, especially the triangular trade of slaves, molasses, lumber, tobacco, and manufactured commodities between Africa, the Caribbean, British North America, and England. Wallerstein notes that the significance of the trade was not in movements of ships but in flows of commodities (Wallerstein 1980:238). Interestingly, an effort by Scottish capitalists to create a "major entrepôt of world trade" on the Isthmus of Panama at the end of the seventeenth century failed because "neither Amsterdam or Hamburg merchants would invest the necessary capital," and the venture collapsed (253). As we will see, a similar effort by American capitalists to establish a major entrepôt of world trade on the Pacific, at San Francisco, succeeded one hundred fifty years later with the support of investors from New York, London, Amsterdam, Hamburg, and elsewhere, because of the need for a maritime mercantile foothold on the Pacific and the boon of California gold.

Wallerstein acknowledges the role of maritime trade in the seventeenth-century rise of England, crediting the nation's focus on "new transport infrastructure," such as ports and ships, and "the entrepôts of Atlantic trade," such as London (1989:59). He also notes that although European protectionism kept British ships from reaping large profits, Britain's more extensive colonial holdings brought greater success. Not only did Britain have a far larger colonial market than France, but it was able to "penetrate extensively the markets of other colonial powers" (68). Britain's aggressive overseas trade policy, backed by a navy to protect that trade, expanded the British Empire to India in 1757 and Canada in 1763. These colonies added new peripheral zones to an increasingly British world system that the French characterized as a "despotic power over the high seas" (71). The final struggle for hegemony was the wars of 1792–1815, in which Britain prevailed (112).

The rise of English hegemony was consolidated economically and militarily through Britain's acquisition of maritime bases around the globe. Between 1763 and 1815, Britain acquired Trinidad and Tobago, Saint Lucia, Bathurst, Sierra Leone, Ascension, Saint Helena, Tristan da Cunha, and Gough Island in the Atlantic/Caribbean region; the Cape Colony, Mauritius, the Seychelles, the Laccadive and Maldive Islands, Ceylon, Penang, and the Andaman Islands in the Indian Ocean region; New South Wales, New Zealand, the Macquarie and Campbell Islands, Auckland, Lord Howe Island, and Chatham Island in Australasia; and Malta and the Ionian Islands in the Mediterranean region (Wallerstein 1989:123). At the same time, because of maritime trade, commercial commissions, and remittances from the colonies, Britain became the financial center of Europe. The world economy centered on the port of London, which had become the world's greatest entrepôt.

The spread of Britain across the globe by sea did not keep other maritime nations from expanding their own trade. In the eighteenth and nineteenth centuries, the burgeoning European world economy added new peripheral zones such as India, the Ottoman Empire, Russia, and West Africa. As trade increased, the production processes in the zones became integral to the commodity chains because of "market conditions" (1989: 129–130). The key to incorporating the new zones was the use of effective decision-making bodies that could control production and merchandising decisions, one model being the plantation system of grouping primary production in large units. More relevant to my thesis is the model that would ultimately be used in San Francisco, in which merchants— "what the French called *négociants* as opposed to *traitants* or *commerçants*" (153)—stationed themselves at bottlenecks to adjust production to respond to market demands or to limit the flow of goods to create demand. Examples of the goods these bodies controlled include Indian opium, Chinese silk, Indonesian spices, California gold, and Middle Eastern oil.

Wallerstein also points out that the incorporation of India introduced Central Asia and China into the European world system as an external zone—a point that is relevant to the rise of the port of San Francisco. Britain subsequently developed a triangular maritime trade of goods between India, China, and Britain that began with silver, moved to cotton, and finally shifted to opium (1989:167–168). Unfortunately, Wallerstein did not more fully develop his perspective on China's incorporation because "that is another story" (168).

Wallerstein did address the role of the United States in the world economy, stating that at the end of the eighteenth and in the early nineteenth century, the newly independent nation's economy and trade was largely in the hands of the British because Britain's entrepôts were strong and offered inexpensive commodities, and U.S. merchants had "long established commercial connections with them" (1989:228). Initial efforts of the United States to expand its trade, according to Wallerstein, were in the Caribbean (230). Next came westward expansion, which would play out in the nineteenth century as the United States joined other economic rivals in the further development of a world system that would be "far more organized, systematic and self-conscious" (256).

A large body of scholarship adopts, challenges, and refines Wallerstein's basic frameworks, especially those who reject a Eurocentric view of history. For example, Wallerstein viewed Asia as a peripheral zone. However, Frank argues that China, the Ottoman Empire, India's Mughals, and Persia's Safavid Empire dominated the world system of Asia and Europe until the period of 1750–1850, making Asia the world's strongest core zone (1994:11–12, 1998). Wolf specifically challenges Wallerstein's and Frank's separation of mercantilism from capitalism and argues that a truly capitalist world system did not emerge until the industrial age and the global movement of mass-produced commodities and labor to extract those commodities(1982:296–353).

Hugill (1993), writing from the perspective of historical geography, offers a well-argued examination of the interaction between environment, geography, and technology in the creation of the world system. He also makes extensive note of the role of ships and shipping in the diffusion of capitalism and discusses the role of maritime commerce and trade in the development of the modern world system (105–158). Hugill also carries the world systems model forward into the twentieth century by assessing the role of new technologies, such as steam power, containerization, and automobiles, aircraft, and telecommunication.

The circum-Pacific region, also relegated to peripheral status because Wallerstein's studies terminated around the 1840–50 period, was by itself part of a world system. As we will see, that system merged into an emerging Anglo-American world system beginning in the late eighteenth century and dramatically so after 1849 (Gibson and Whitehead 1993). In this process, San Francisco became an important locus of accumulation, and the entrepôt built for it on the new city's waterfront is a significant artifact of that process. Thus, San Francisco was a regional center that both influenced and was influenced by this global phenomenon.

Since the late 1970s, archaeologists have adopted Wallerstein's theoretical model to examine intersocietal interactions. Trigger specifically notes that Childe's 1928 studies of interactions between a Near Eastern core and Europe "anticipated world-system theory in many important aspects and have no doubt predisposed European archaeologists to accept Wallerstein's approach" (Trigger 1989:333). Kohl (1978, 1979, 1987) has used world systems theory to assess Southeast Asian, Central Asian, and Near Eastern sites, whereas Ekholm and Friedman (1979) have used it to look at ancient systems. Blanton, Kowalewski, Feinman, and Appel (1981) have adopted it for economic interpretation of Monte Alban and its region. Renfrew and Shennan (1982) have used it in assessing early Europe. In the 1990s, Kohl remained a vocal advocate for world systems theory, as did Peregrine (1992) in Mississippian sites, Kristiansen and Jensen (1994) in Bronze Age studies and La Lone (1994) in Andean archaeology. More recently, Groover (2003) has used world systems theory as an interpretive tool in the analysis of an Appalachian farmstead to "explore capitalism's structuring influence on rural households . . . during the 19th century" (21).

Other archaeologists, however, argue that world systems theory has no use in archaeological interpretation and suggest that a better approach is to look at interregional interaction systems such as Cohen's (1971) trade-diaspora model or Stein's (1999) distance-parity model. Frank (1999) takes issue with these models, arguing that world systems theory does work for archaeology, and though it is occasionally abused, it is a valuable theoretical approach. It is especially useful in assessing the extent of world systems beyond Wallerstein's European model of the past five hundred years.

Wallerstein's world systems theory has been accepted by some maritime archaeologists, including me, who consider the global maritime trade of the eighteenth, nineteenth, and twentieth centuries to be the main driver of expansion of a global world system. In turn, I argue that San Francisco during the Gold Rush played an important role in expanding the Anglo-American world system into the Pacific and Asia.

THE DEVELOPMENT OF THEORY IN MARITIME ARCHAEOLOGY

Maritime archaeology—also termed *nautical, underwater,* or *marine archaeology*—developed with the application of archaeological methods to submerged environments in the early 1960s. The seminal events in the development of the field after the initial work of George Bass (1966, 1972, 1988) were the publication of *Maritime Archaeology* by Keith Muckelroy (1978) and a 1981 colloquium organized by the School of American Research, whose proceedings were published under the editorship of Richard Gould (1983) as *Shipwreck Anthropology.*

Muckelroy defined maritime archaeology as the study of all aspects of maritime culture and humanity's interaction with the sea and other waters. He proposed a three-tier hierarchy: (1) the archaeology of shipwrecks; (2) the archaeology of ships, which includes ships as closed communities; and (3) the archaeology of maritime cultures, which considers nautical technology, naval warfare, maritime trade, shipboard societies, and incidental contributions by maritime sites to archaeological inquiry.

In the 1980s, maritime archaeologists began to embrace a regionalized approach to study, assessing the types of craft that happen to wreck within specific geographical areas, or ship traps (Murphy 1997; Gould 2000). At the instigation of the U.S. National Park Service's Submerged Cultural Resources Unit, Gould organized the colloquium on maritime archaeology at the School of American Research in 1981 (Gould 1983). At the meeting, Gould himself made perhaps the most salient statement about the seminar's contribution, pointing out that it had introduced

a new willingness to posit generalizations about past and present human behavior based upon shipwreck remains. For some of us, shipwreck archaeology is viewed as part of social science. What makes it a science is not the use of scientific techniques or apparatus, but an organized process of reasoning based on the application of certain rules of science, such as the testing of alternative hypotheses, the principle of parsimony, the need for repeatability of results, and the ability to extend the results from a particular case to the realm of general propositions about the nature of variability in the behavior of the human species in a convincing manner (22).

Following the publication of *Shipwreck Anthropology*, the focus of maritime archaeology broadened, particularly in the ranks of the National Park Service. The agency had a mandate to survey for and assert management control over significant cultural resources both within and outside the National Park System, particularly through the National Register of Historic Places.

In more recent years, Gould has joined the argument for expanding maritime archaeology into maritime infrastructure. Though he has limited his focus to the development of ancient ports and one modern technological approach (a floating dry dock), his reasoning is valid (2000: 299–315). In the same vein, McCarthy (1999) has emphasized the importance of maritime landscapes, a concept originally developed to explain maritime sites in Scandinavia (Westerdahl 1992) and subsequently adopted by archaeologists who see its application to sites throughout the world. McCarthy specifically examined the shoreline resources of Oakland, California, on San Francisco Bay. McCarthy was studying individual features "to understand the Oakland waterfront as a maritime cultural landscape worthy of scrutiny, the way in which that landscape connects to the greater San Francisco Bay Region, the role of human choice and responsibility in the making of landscapes, and the historical context within which decisions about landscape modification have been made" (1999:11). Esser (1999) presented a similar argument in her study of the terrestrial-maritime landscape interface at Montezuma Slough at the confluence of the Sacramento and San Joaquin rivers.

In addition to the work in the United States, the greatest amount of published shipwreck research and theoretical debate in maritime archaeology that is pertinent to this discussion has come from the United Kingdom and Australia. Of course, outstanding nautical archaeological work has taken place in other regions, especially the Baltic and the Mediterranean, but my focus here is on the broader theoretical perspective. U.K. researchers have wedded archaeology more closely to history than to anthropology, but they have produced useful regional and thematic surveys. In particular, the work of Peter Marsden (1994, 1996), who has focused on the rise and development of the port of London, is relevant to this book.

Marsden's work has spanned the past three decades, and only recently has he summarized it in two comprehensive volumes. He points out that though maritime trade made London "one of the leading financial centers in the world, . . . nothing was known about the early waterfronts that formed the gateway through which so much of this wealth passed"

(1994:11). Merchants from the continent founded London around 50 A.D. to serve as a provincial capital. However, "its importance lay in the trading process," with much of its wealth "no doubt derived from maritime trade" (11). In his study of the London waterfront, Marsden first assessed a series of more or less intact wrecks and then expanded his inquiry into broken-up ships, some of whose parts were recycled to construct waterfront bulkheads; quays and wharves, as well as excavated berths; environmental reconstruction of the riverfront and its once-tidal banks; and spilled or broken cargoes.

In his second volume (1996), Marsden provided more extensive examples from the next several centuries. Marsden's study of the London waterfront is a theoretical and methodological analogue of the study of Gold Rush San Francisco's waterfront. However, San Francisco took only a decade to create what London took seventeen centuries to do. Coinciding with Marsden's work, Milne (1992) added to the model of maritime landscape. Among other things, these studies extend the maritime landscape to incorporate timber building techniques and shipyards. Milne's work (1998, 2003) also assesses vessel types in the ship graveyard on the River Medway in Kent, viewing it as an analogue to the London site, and he reconstructs the port of medieval London.

URBAN ARCHAEOLOGY'S INTERSECTION WITH MARITIME ARCHAEOLOGY

Both historians and archaeologists have long been interested in the rise of the city, city planning, and the infrastructure or urban systems (for example, Barth 1975; Galantay 1975; Reps 1981; Hamer 1990; and Cantwell and Wall 2001). The archaeology of modern European and North American cities for many years focused more on life in those cities than on the archaeology of the city as an evolving landscape and on its society despite a long tradition of archaeological study (Staski 1987:ix). However, Staski reports that historical archaeology in New England and in Seattle began to offer preliminary conclusions about "how the relative impacts of economic market forces . . . [shaped] the urban environment" and how "the physical and social configurations of a city—together representing the urban ecology—can mirror and influence one another" (x).

The work of Mrozowski (1987) in Boston and Newport and Ostrogorsky's study (1987) in Seattle began to point to the city as a macroartifact. Mrozowski examined whether or not "market forces were fuelling the urban development of these communities" (1987:4). Ostrogorsky concerned himself with economic and social forces and the ways in which they shaped the physical redevelopment of Seattle from 1851 to 1889 (1987:12). In this study, he found that "industrialization and urbanization, along with social stratification, are reflected in significant and co-ordinated terrain alteration" (12). This finding marked an important shift in the theoretical approach to urban archaeology, from archaeology in the city to the archaeology of the city.

Archaeologists have undertaken a variety of urban studies. The most relevant to my purpose, outside of Marsden's (1994, 1996) and Staniforth's (2003) maritime-oriented work, is Cantwell and Wall's examination of the urban archaeology of another port city, New York. They examined the entire city, in itself a daunting task because "viewing a modern city as an archaeological site and studying both its urban and pre-urban past constitute a radically new way of looking at an American city" (2001:4).

Cantwell and Wall note that Nieuw Amsterdam/New York was established in 1622 by Dutch traders intent on making this isolated island an entrepôt, with broad moorage ground for ships on a saltwater river that would not freeze in the winter, and "where the Dutch [would transfer] goods from riverboats to ocean-going ships for the long Atlantic crossing" (2001:154). This role continued well into the nineteenth century, as New Yorkers established international trade ties by sea, gradually assuming the role of the United States' principal port. The flow of raw and manufactured goods in and out of New York made the city "the country's foremost manufacturing center but its center of banking and finance as well" (161). The city's size and population boomed in response. Between 1790 and 1840, New York grew from 33,000 to 313,000 inhabitants.

The link that Cantwell and Wall describe between the growing maritime trade and the growth of the city's land base, particularly on the waterfront, is analogous to the processes of growth in San Francisco. "Making land" in New York commenced on its "most valuable real estate—along the shore adjacent to the east river port" (2001:224). Land-filling began in 1650, abetted by the English conquest of Nieuw Amsterdam and transformation of the city into New York. Of particular interest is the Dongan Charter of 1680, which allowed civic officials to sell water lots and build wharves, using them to "make land" between high and low water (225). This policy had two dramatic effects: it created much of the modern shoreline, but it also

> extended the city's shoreline beyond the shallow water near the natural shore so that eventually ships could tie up at landside wharves instead of having to anchor out in the river. Second, "made land" provided more

of the city's most valuable real estate—the low-lying area adjacent to the harbor—which merchants could develop to accommodate the warehouses, and stores they needed to handle the goods entering and leaving the port. By the end of the eighteenth century, these newly made waterfront parcels had become the bases of operations for some of the city's richest mercantile families (226).

This process, which began in the eighteenth century, continued through the early nineteenth century, and by 1840, lower Manhattan had achieved the shape that would characterize it for more than a century. Thus, we owe this concept of urban development and its effects on the emerging world system—especially in the realm of maritime commerce—to American merchants, some of whom immigrated to California during the Gold Rush.

The archaeology of urban New York, as illustrated by Cantwell and Wall, includes a range of sites that they describe in a chapter on the archaeology of landfill (2001:233). This landfill contains—in addition to discarded household goods, exotic materials suggestive of ships' ballast, clean fill, and garbage—bulkheads, wharves, and derelict ships "used to hold back the fill" (233). Cantwell and Wall's integrative approach—that is, their use of data from a variety of sites, including maritime ones (wharves, buried ships, ballast dumps, and "made land" reclaimed from the sea)—has direct relevance to the study of San Francisco's waterfront. Yet, while we are assessing an urban site borne of maritime trade as an entrepôt and developed as such, New York did so within a larger temporal space than San Francisco (the span of 1680–1840 in New York as opposed to 1849–55 in San Francisco). Cantwell and Wall's approach, like Marsden's, heretofore been unique in both urban and maritime archaeology.

URBAN ARCHAEOLOGY AND THE MINING FRONTIER

Donald Hardesty's work (1988, 1993) in the archaeology of mining settlements also has theoretical links with mine. While viewing inland hard-rock–mining sites, Hardesty drew on a maritime analogy in characterizing the "mining frontier . . . as a network of 'islands' colonized by miners. Island colonies participate in world systems, linking the frontier to the heartland of American and European civilization" (1988: ix). In his assessment of the Nevada mining frontier, Hardesty notes that "mining colonies were financed, manned, and supplied from the urban centers of America and Europe. Despite their geographical remoteness and small sizes, the colonies were linked to a vast transportation, communications, demographic, and economic network on a national and international" scale (1). He discusses the rich documentary record of mid- to late nineteenth-century world marketing systems and offers an innovative concept of interacting spheres materials, population, and information.

In my exploration of the frontier that was San Francisco, I follow Hardesty's suggestion of three interacting spheres. The materials sphere involves the transportation of materials between the frontier and the heartland. In the California Gold Rush, large oceangoing craft transported goods from various production centers and ports that were linked by the global maritime system to San Francisco. The goods were then transported in smaller scows, riverboats, and steamers up the bay and then up the Sacramento and San Joaquin rivers to Sacramento and Stockton. These two cities served as subordinate ports and as distribution centers, transferring commodities from the riverboats to wagons or loading them onto horses and mules for delivery to the mining camps. In this way, San Francisco, and by extension the California mining frontier, became tied to a global migration network.

Hardesty notes that the exchange of information, ideas, and symbols creates world systems structures. However, historians and technologists suggest that the rapid exchange of information and ideas was more the result of later nineteenth-century developments such as the telegraph in the 1860s (see Hardesty 1988:5). The relatively swift nature of maritime movement, and extensive correspondence between commission merchants, greatly aided integration of the San Francisco entrepôt into the world system, as Wallerstein might predict. This factor was particularly important in the early period, when many of the commission merchants relied on communication via sea to conduct business with the preexisting entrepôts of Valparaíso and Hong Kong, as well as the regularity of mail delivery by steamers via the Isthmus of Panama.

Though the historical record suggests that San Francisco's merchants engaged in wild speculation, suffered from a glut of certain commodities, and faced ruined fortunes (e.g., Rohrbaugh 1997; Holliday 1999; Brandes 2002), this picture is inaccurate. Commission merchants kept up a constant correspondence and followed the "prices current" feature of the San Francisco newspapers, with the latter also regularly dispatched by mail via sailing ship and steamer to distant ports and trading partners. Commission merchants also developed aspects of the infrastructure—particularly storeships for temporary storage of slow or nonselling merchandise—an idea borrowed from the British and American experience in the always-glutted opium market in China (Ho et al. 1991; Layton 1997). The material record of the *General Harrison* storeship is particularly illustrative of this practice. The locus of exchange in both mid-nineteenth-century Shanghai and San Francisco was the storeship.

Although I focus on *General Harrison*, Hoff's Store, and *Niantic,* like Hardesty (1988, 1993), I see value in assessing features separated by distance. This approach focuses "attention on the material remains of the total system, of human activity rather than an isolated part of the system" (Hardesty 1993:3). For example, I argue that the waterfront and the ships are more than a neighborhood: they are the loci of the system that made Gold Rush San Francisco succeed, not an isolated group of maritime sites. Ultimately, I come back to the approach argued by Staski and followed by Marsden and Cantwell and Wall to assess the buried waterfront's multiplicity of features and define the archaeology of early San Francisco.

THE MARITIME SYSTEM

The work of Staniforth and his study of the role of maritime trade in the development of the dependent colonies of Australia are also critical to this book. Staniforth notes that historical and maritime archaeologists often dismiss modern maritime trade, taking the view that the availability of extensive records of "shipping movements and detailed cargo lists" eliminates the need to excavate. "I suggest that while the available documentary sources are sometimes extensive, they are frequently not comprehensive. Furthermore, I suggest that taking a cultural perspective to examine economic activity can often illuminate different aspects of the past" (2003:17).

Staniforth enunciates a common criticism of maritime archaeology—particularly historical maritime archaeology of the past half-millennium—stating that it "incorporates a large amount of descriptive information derived from purely historical sources." He then discusses how his work places individual shipwreck sites and their associated artifacts into their cultural and historical context, "primarily in order to explore issues of cultural continuity and the transfer of cultural attitudes from Great Britain to the new Australian colonies" (2003:19). Taking this approach to San Francisco, I place individual buried ships, their surrounding infrastructure, and associated artifacts into a cultural and historical context to explore the nature of maritime trade and show how the maritime system created San Francisco.

Staniforth embraces Hodder's contextual archaeological approach, which acknowledges the complexity and variability of culture "in the form of societies and communities within their specific historical contexts" along with the "important part that individuals played within these societies" (2003:19). In adopting this perspective, he then examines the historical and social context of the ports of origin and destination for each of his sites (24). This approach is the one I champion in my assessment of Gold Rush San Francisco.

Staniforth adopts the *Annales* school's use of Braudel's three scales of history: *longue durée, conjunctures,* and *événements.* Though I consider the rise of San Francisco as part of the centuries-long rise of a world system (the *longue durée*) and look at *conjunctures* to assess fifty- to seventy-five-year cycles, I also focus on events. The nature of the sites, where massive development and change occurred in a short period, makes the Gold Rush waterfront of San Francisco a good model for assessing the archaeology of *événements,* or the events and individuals of a specific time. Heretofore this element has not attracted much archaeological or historical interest "because much of the archaeological record doesn't lend itself to event interpretations" (2003:27). The *General Harrison* site may be an especially good example of the archaeology of *événements,* but its true value lies in its association with the wider infrastructure of the waterfront, the conjunctures or social processes of the world system in the industrial nineteenth century, and the relationship of these elements to the Pacific's *longue durée.* The events and individuals of the Gold Rush period created San Francisco's waterfront and linked it and its individual merchants and storeships to Pacific and global maritime trade, showing how the application of an *Annales* framework can "illuminate wider issues from a specific case" (28).

In maritime archaeology, the event typically is the loss of the vessel—the shipwreck event—and this event has a place in the larger context of *conjunctures* and the *longue durée.* As I have suggested, much maritime archaeology has focused too heavily on largely meaningless (in the big picture) *événements* or on assessments of sites as unique time capsules (Staniforth 2003:30). Staniforth's approach, and my approach here, is to interpret the material culture "in terms of the societies for which they were bound . . . [linking] maritime archaeology much more neatly to historical archaeology since it treats the transport of cargo as a single step in a wider trajectory or system of use" (30–31). Staniforth synthesizes his historical and archaeological data to follow the full trajectory of his artifacts in colonial Australia.

Staniforth enunciates this theoretical adoption of world systems theory to maritime archaeology and the theory's relevance to historical archaeology as the archaeology of capitalism by reminding us that "it was the development and expansion of long-distance shipping that allowed the movement of people and goods across the world's oceans" (34). By adapting and incorporating world systems theory, maritime archaeology can move toward "a critique of modernity, addressing the origins, dynamics, and global spread of western industrial capitalism and its associated institutions" (34) and align itself more closely with historical archaeology in general.

More recently, Russell, Bradford, and Murphy also put forth a model of a maritime system that conceptualizes the "integrated maritime activities for a particular region (large or small) or time period, and their relationship to the larger capitalist world system" (2004:101). The assessment of maritime systems is as yet a growing theoretical area in maritime archaeology. It has potential in the study of maritime landscapes, and in the regional and thematic approaches I have discussed, although it might also provide a framework for assessing regional maritime systems, temporally distant systems, or event-based maritime systems, as well as conjunctures such as "the California Gold Rush, or the American Civil War or World War II" (101).

Another recent study, by Dellino-Musgrave (2006), examined shipwreck sites in Argentine Patagonia and in Australia to illuminate British material expansion in the eighteenth century. The seemingly isolated wrecks were local aspects of a global process. "Global processes such as capitalism, colonialism and consumption are influenced by local forces and manifested in events at a local level" (1). The wrecks, located in strategic waterways and ports, are material manifestations of Britain's eighteenth-century goal of dominating global maritime trade. Dellino-Musgrave did not base her research on Wallerstein's model but acknowledges the model's usefulness in understanding relevant systems within a worldwide perspective that "facilitates comparative analysis at global levels" (22). Dellino-Musgrave also echoes the Wallerstein model in analyzing shipwrecks and cargoes as social products and looking at the integration of wreck sites with land and maritime spaces. The "integral analysis between land and sea," argues Dellino-Musgrave, "is important to anyone who intends to understand maritime aspects of the past" (24). I agree.

The present shift in thinking in maritime archaeology coincides with ongoing debates and attempts to refine Wallerstein's original modern world systems model by incorporating a more direct maritime perspective (see, for example, Hugill 1993). A group of maritime historians gathered in Salem, Massachusetts, in 2000 for the World Marine Millennial Conference. The assembled scholars, whose papers are published in a postconference volume (Finamore 2004), discussed the role of maritime trade, commerce, naval warfare, exploration, and culture in a global context.

Critical to this discussion are the assertions of Fernández-Armesto (2004), who argued that a millennium of maritime endeavor resulted in a dramatic change in maritime technology and trade after 1490. A key change came with the rapid discovery of the fixed-wind systems that made long-distance transoceanic voyaging more practical over the next century. At that point, the modern era of global commerce began, made possible by maritime activity. Building on this idea, Janzen has characterized the oceans as highways between 1604 and 1815, noting that in this period, "European commerce flowed along oceanic highways that were truly global in extent. . . . It was an age characterized by what historians today refer to as 'mercantilism,' in which maritime trade was dominated by a rapidly expanding volume . . . and when European powers struggled increasingly . . . to control and use the wealth that traveled on these oceanic highways" (2004:102).

Mancke has echoed Janzen's view, suggesting that "early modern European expansion (1450–1800) was in fundamental ways an oceanic experience" (2004:149). Not coincidentally, the period that Mancke cites is the same time frame in which Wallerstein places the development of the "world-system." Mancke sees the emergence of a world system as a maritime-driven phenomenon, with "linkages of political power to transoceanic trade, colonization and piracy. . . . The expanding European powers defined the world's oceans, and not just territorial waters, as political space. . . . This development is a critical link between early modern state formation and empire building and the emerging definition of a global international system in the early modern era" (150). Mancke specifically pointed to "the profitability of overseas commerce that ultimately made these empires viable, thus undergirding the ability of mercantile wealth to jockey with landed wealth in defining the role of the state" (150).

Maritime historians have begun to embrace and perhaps appropriate the "world system," other scholars have critiqued it and sought to apply it in their fields. Arrighi offers the most specific critique, pointing out that "world capitalism did not originate within the economic activities and social relations that were predominant in the larger territorial organizations of the European world. Rather, it originated in the interstices that connected those larger territorial organizations to one another and their totality to other worlds" (1997:1).

Arrighi sees late thirteenth- and early fourteenth-century trade in the Eurasian world as an interstice in which the dominant organizations were not territorial states but "city-states, quasi-city-states, extra-territorial business networks, and other non-territorial organizations. It was within these organizations that the largest profits were made and various forms of capitalism thrived. As a rule, these profits originated in long-distance trade and high-finance, although they sometimes found their way into the reorganization of short-distance trade and production proper" (7).

Such was the case in the Pacific, before and during the Gold Rush, where the processes that were already in play created San Francisco. Integrating the Pacific Rim and its links to Asian trade addresses Frank's criticism of Wallerstein's "Eurocentrism" (Frank 1994). As we will see, the changes in Pacific patterns of trade that made the rise of San Francisco possible depended on the involvement of Hispanic and Asian capitalists as well as Euro-American business interests. Thus, San Francisco is more than an Anglo-American frontier. It is North America's first true Pacific entrepôt, a crucial outpost linked not only to the European and eastern United States markets but also to existing Central American, South American, and Asian markets.

THE GOLD RUSH SAN FRANCISCO WATERFRONT
AS AN EXAMPLE OF THE MARITIME SYSTEM

The Gold Rush of 1849–55 illustrates Frank's point that the "most important European contribution" after 1492 and for three centuries thereafter "was the injection of new supplies of American bullion—and thereby themselves [the Europeans]—into the already well established Eurasian economy" (1994:12). Though Frank was talking about Spanish-controlled silver and gold from Mexico and Peru, the analogy also fits California gold. The world economy, especially tied to the riches of the Far East, "remained firmly under Asian hegemony until the 1750–85 period, when Asian economic and political power waned" (13). During this time, Anglo-American entrepôts sprang up in the Pacific. These maritime-created frontier outposts provided the means for Europeans and Americans to rearrange the economic game in the Pacific to fit more neatly into the traditional Wallerstein model of a Eurocentric world system (which, after 1849, began to shift to a more American-centric one).

San Francisco was created by maritime capitalists already familiar with Pacific trade networks—with links to South America, Hawai'i, and China—who saw an opportunity and seized it (Gibson and Whitehead 1993:171–190). Purser (2003a) suggests that many of the capitalists, like football players, "ran out to catch the forward pass" of the Gold Rush. San Francisco's history, especially its instant history, "only makes sense if you plug it into the network it was already part of before 1849," albeit as a small player with great potential.

In my analysis of the data from San Francisco, I link the maritime-system model to Wallerstein's modern world system not merely to demonstrate that San Francisco was part of such a system but to gain insight into the continuing development and functioning of the modern world system in the Pacific at the midway point of the nineteenth century. This approach offers a more nuanced understanding of the regional aspects of the world system and may provide new insights into the historical archaeology of other Pacific Rim frontier cities and entrepôts.

By adopting the synergistic approach of modern historical archaeology—following the full trajectory of the Gold Rush storeships and their cargoes—I can determine how the commission merchants and their associates in San Francisco accelerated the arrival of the Anglo-American modern world system in the Pacific. In doing so, I can not only provide another test of the theoretical approach of a maritime system in world systems theory but also assess the role of the entrepôt in the development of a frontier. This assessment is relevant not just to ocean ports but to river ports, allowing us to determine the maritime factors that not only make new or instant cities work but also enable them to survive cycles of boom and bust.

Thus, I see the archaeology of the Gold Rush waterfront of San Francisco as maritime archaeology. Maritime archaeology has evolved to incorporate theoretical perspectives, and I follow others in treating it as a subset of world systems theory. San Francisco owes its rise to its participation in a maritime system that was part of the capitalist world system spreading globally in the nineteenth century. Though the city's growth was inspired by American desires to dominate Pacific trade, its development was a global effort, with ships laden with merchandise coming from ports throughout the world. The arrival of these ships was not haphazard or unplanned but the work of commission merchants, who controlled the flow of goods into and the flow of gold out of California. These goods and gold were funneled through the commission merchants' quickly built control point, the waterfront of San Francisco.

CHAPTER 3

Global Maritime Connections in the Pacific before the Gold Rush

In this chapter, I look at the *longue durée* to analyze the maritime system at work in the larger world system—in particular, through the integration of the peripheral zone of the Pacific. This new role for the Pacific region in turn led to the creation of San Francisco. To understand the role of San Francisco, we must first understand the larger picture, looking at the role of Asian trade in establishing interest in the Pacific. The subsequent development of maritime trade, commerce, and interest in the Pacific paved the way for the San Francisco Bay and San Francisco to play their key roles in the world system.

EUROPEANS ARRIVE IN THE PACIFIC

Before the arrival of European explorers in the late fifteenth and early sixteenth centuries, China and its Southeast Asian neighbors had developed an extensive trade network along the eastern shores of the Pacific. Maritime trade with Korea, Japan, Southeast Asia, and India dates back several hundred years, if not earlier. Through Indian and Arab intermediaries, Chinese and other Asian trade goods reached the Roman and later the Byzantine and European world for more than a millennium via both land (the "Silk Road") and sea. As Frank notes, a "world system" was at play in this period, in which "the core regions, especially of industrial production, were in China and India; and West Asia and Southeast Asia also remained economically more important than Europe"

(1994:12). To increase their access to the rich commodities of Asia, Europeans ultimately sought direct oceanic routes to the Pacific and thence to Asia starting in the late fifteenth century.

In the first European voyages, Portuguese navigators gradually worked down the west coast of Africa, around the Cape of Good Hope in 1498, and into the Indian Ocean to tap into the Indian market, before reaching Indonesia, the South China Sea, and Asia (Boxer 1969). Portugal established trade centers—not colonies in the traditional sense, but entrepôts—at Sumatra and Malacca in 1509, the Mollucas in 1512, Macau on the China coast in 1513, Timor around 1515, and at Nagasaki, Japan, in 1543 (Barreto and Garcia 1990:21). Spanish navigators, pushing west beginning with Columbus's voyages in 1492 were initially thwarted by the intervening landmass of the Americas. In 1520, the expedition of Ferdinand Magellan discovered the strait that bears his name, revealing a new oceanic passage into the Pacific via the tip of South America (Joyner 1994). In the next decades, English and Dutch competitors followed the Spanish explorers, with the Dutch pioneering the Cape Horn route in 1616 (Boxer 1965).

The Dutch gained a foothold in the area that is now Indonesia and a stake in the rich spice trade of the East Indies, establishing their own fortified trade centers such as Batavia and pursuing direct trade with the Japanese in competition with the Portuguese. The Spanish, however, ultimately prevailed achieving European "domination" of the Pacific and Pacific trade (Shaw 1988; Spate 1988), doing so by establishing an entrepôt at Manila in 1571. This move followed their conquest of Central and South American indigenous empires. Spanish maritime activities in the Pacific focused on trans-Pacific trade with Asia, using the Philippines as a base of operations from which "Manila galleons" annually carried spices, ceramics, silks, beeswax, and treasure across the Pacific to Mexico in exchange for Mexican silver (Schurz 1939; Díaz-Trechuelo 1988). This lucrative trade remained an important Spanish maritime activity through the early nineteenth century. It also inspired the development of a handful of Spanish Pacific ports to serve coastal trade, such as Acapulco, Mexico; Panama City, Panama; Callao, Peru; Guayaquil, Ecuador; and Valparaíso, Chile (Ward 1993; Early et al. 1998).

The richness of Spain's American empire and the ability to seize Asian goods by means of pirate attacks on Spanish ships in the Pacific inspired England to challenge the notion that the Pacific was a "Spanish lake" as early as the 1577 voyage of Francis Drake (Bawlf 2004). The English also engaged in direct competition and outright warfare with the Dutch

in the "East Indies," although they would not prevail in the Pacific until the eighteenth century (Boxer 1965; Cook 1973; Frost 1988; Fisher
and Johnston 1993). In fact, despite the presence of these various European powers in the Pacific, the true economic power was Asia, particularly China (Frank 1994:12). The dream of acquiring or controlling the
riches of China haunted European monarchs and later European entrepreneurs and capitalists for centuries.

The world system at play in the sixteenth to eighteenth centuries was
therefore still under "Asian hegemony, not European. Likewise, much of
the real dynamism of the world economy still lay in Asia throughout this
period, not in Europe" (Frank 1994:12). To access and then control the
Asian economy, European sea powers used their ships and maritime technology forcibly to create a series of entrepôts on the Asian coast. Regular voyages via the Cape of Good Hope tied these ports to Europe. To
gain a commodity for the Asian trade, Spain used silver bullion from its
American empire. The outward flow of silver was matched in the late
sixteenth century by a cross-trade in Asian goods in the Manila galleons
that sailed from the Philippine entrepôt of Manila to Spain's Mexican
port of Acapulco and to Panama City. These goods were then packed
across the Central American isthmus and shipped to Spain across the Atlantic (Schurz 1939). Asian goods also went south to Callao, the important southern port of the viceroyalty of Peru, which systematically
shipped out the silver and gold riches of the former Inca Empire via the
Strait of Magellan (Early et al. 1998; Ward 1993).

Asian trade injected new liquidity into the world economy. It made
important though limited changes in financial flows, trade, and production patterns in the world economy that allowed Europeans to expand
their participation in Asia (Frank 1994:12). Similar circumstances occurred between 1849 and 1855 as the shipborne outflow of California's
bullion from its newly established entrepôt of San Francisco injected new
liquidity into the world system. The gold-fueled changes in financial flows,
trade, and production patterns permitted mid-nineteenth-century Pacific
entrepreneurs and capitalists to participate more actively in the world
economic system, which had steadily been encroaching into the Pacific
Ocean since the late eighteenth and early nineteenth centuries.

THE "ANGLO-AMERICAN PACIFIC" IS BORN

Recognition of the Pacific region as a historical and geographical entity
did not occur until the late eighteenth century. The shipment of Amer-

ican silver bullion to the Philippines had initiated trans-Pacific commodity exchange in the sixteenth century "and thus brought the Pacific in a limited way into the world commodity market." However, the "economic integration of the entire Pacific Basin . . . relied on the developments of the ocean's eastern and northern portions," which would not come until the eighteenth century and the arrival of the Anglo-Americans (Igler 2004:695).

Driven by English ambitions for plunder, seafaring raids on Manila galleons and Pacific ports continued through the early eighteenth century, although by the last quarter of the century, the weakened power of Imperial Spain allowed Britain to establish a more pronounced presence (Cook 1973; MacKay 1985; Fisher and Johnston 1993). The British increased their presence both through naval expeditions, ostensibly to explore and survey the Pacific, and through the establishment of a colonial outpost in Australia at Port Jackson (Sydney) in 1788 (Staniforth 2003: 65–67). The new colony's founding ships proceeded from Port Jackson to Whampoa to load Chinese tea before returning home, a reminder that one of Britain's stakes in the Pacific was the maintenance and growth of its China trade. Gradually, the new colony began to trade with China in the nineteenth century.

Russia, also eager for a commodity to trade with the Chinese, already knew of the rich sea-otter furs off the Northwest Coast because of its exploration of the northern Pacific, most notably by Vitus Bering in 1742. To tap into the clearly valuable furs of the area, the tsar authorized settlement of the southern Alaskan coast at Sitka in 1784. Though Sitka was not an entrepôt, it was the base of operations for the Russian America Company, which continued to exploit the region's furs as a trade commodity through the mid-nineteenth century (Dmytrshyn, Crownhart-Vaughan, and Vaughan 1988).

The voyages of Britain's James Cook between 1768 and 1778 had the greatest impact on the emerging patterns of maritime trade in the Pacific (Frost 1988). Until then, the vastness of the Pacific and Europeans' ignorance of it, as well as Spain's closure of its American ports to foreign trade, "limited the impact of European challengers in this ocean basin" (Mancke 2004:159). Cook was the first to create an accurate map of the vast ocean. The British government then publicly unveiled Cook's discoveries to the western world by publishing his journals and charts. The combination of Cook's presence and Russia's ambitions spurred the last acts of Spanish colonial expansion on the Pacific, with the establishment of colonies in California and a short-lived outpost on the British Columbia coast at Nootka Sound between 1769 and 1792 (Cook 1973; Fisher and Johnston 1993). However, the Spanish Empire and its role in Pacific trade were coming to an end.

Britain and its newly independent colony on the eastern seaboard of the continent, the United States, were eager for increased commerce with Asia. As with the Russians, the opportunity came with Cook's fortuitous discovery of a valuable new commodity, the pelts of sea otters, during his 1778 voyage. The maritime fur trade attracted an influx of ships to the Northwest Coast of the Americas and then to California (Ogden 1941; Gibson and Whitehead 1993:103–130). With Cook's voyage and the expansion of British, Spanish, Russian, and U.S. trading ventures up and down the coast of North America, the Pacific world had a coherent reason to join the larger world system. And yet, as Igler states, "The relationship between Pacific ports, trading nations, and indigenous populations remained fluid during this period. The eastern Pacific cohered as a region so long as an open and inclusive waterscape provided the primary connection between the disparate borderlands" (2004:695).

Carlson argues that the Cook voyages and the resultant maritime fur trade show that an "external arena [like the unincorporated Northwest Coast and its furs, which were previously subject to limited and internal trade] can have a tremendous impact on the core and other incorporated areas within the system." It provides a preemptive desire for colonization and expansion. Because "luxury goods appear[ed] to offset the otherwise prohibitive costs of expanding the capitalist system," the new trade induced capitalists to expand and grow (2002:443). This commercial activity had profound consequences.

By the end of the eighteenth century, the maritime fur business dominated trade on the Pacific Coast of North America (Gibson 1992; Malloy 1998). It also created a triangular route of exchange that saw British and American ships trade on the Northwest Coast for furs; exchange the furs in China for tea, porcelain, and other goods; and then return either to Europe, the eastern seaboard of the United States, or Spain's remote and soon-to-be-independent Pacific colony of California. In California, they traded Chinese goods for bullion, minted coin, and California's hides and tallow. The hides and tallow, by-products of the vast herds of cattle on the huge ranchos, were shipped to the East to feed the growing industrial centers of leather production around Boston (Ogden 1941).

The maritime fur trade and the introduction of fleets of American and British whalers into the Pacific also opened up a new port—a way station and small entrepôt at Honolulu on the island of Oahu in the Kingdom of Hawai'i (Sahlins and Kirch 1992). Whereas Hawaiian sandalwood, another valuable trade commodity in China, was the impetus for trade and contact, Hawai'i's midocean position and its fresh water, firewood, and food built its stature as a port after 1825, and it became the "crossroads of the Pacific" (Beechert 1991; Gibson and Whitehead 1993:143–145).

The potential to acquire great riches through the maritime fur trade induced fierce commercial competition and the occasional diplomatic dispute between the Russians, British, Spaniards, and Americans (Gibson 1992). War between Britain and Spain over control of the Northwest Coast was averted in 1790 only through diplomatic exchanges. Spain also realized that it was overextended economically and militarily (Cook 1973; Fisher and Johnston 1993). A secret codicil of the Nootka Convention, signed in 1790 to stem the impending conflict, "allowed for freedom of navigation through the Strait of Magellan and the British right to trade and fish throughout the Pacific Basin" (Mancke 2004:161).

While British interests prevailed and Russian activities continued, including the establishment of a coastal settlement—Kolonie Rossiya (Fort Ross)—on the California coast in 1811, Russia's and Britain's domination of the Northwest Coast and the maritime fur trade faded with the Napoleonic Wars in favor of the Americans (Ogden 1941; Coughlin 1971; Gibson 1992; Malloy 1998). In one of its first independent acts, the United States established trade ties with China, and the fur trade was a means to gain a commodity for trade other than casks of silver (Smith 1984; Howard 1984; Hawes 1990).

THE ARRIVAL OF THE AMERICANS

In the early nineteenth century, American ships poured into the Pacific (Gibson 1992; Malloy 1998). In 1809, American entrepreneur John Jacob Astor established a fur-trading outpost, Astoria, on the coast at the mouth of the Columbia River (Irving 1870). Astor sold his outpost in 1813 because of the War of 1812, and control of the maritime fur trade passed to British interests (Hussey 1957:5). After 1825, the Hudson's Bay Company was the sole representative of British interests, and it established its presence by building a series of forts and maintaining a fleet of coastal trade vessels (Rich 1941, 1943, 1944; Hussey 1957). Largely thanks to these efforts, Britain retained a claim on some of its Pacific possessions, which would later become the Canadian province of British Columbia and the Yukon Territory.

American maritime traders continued to seek furs on the Northwest Coast, but much of the seagoing trade of the United States on the eastern Pacific coast centered on newly independent Mexico's northern province of California, whose hides and tallow continued to be traded to satisfy Californio tastes for Chinese trade goods from American traders (Ogden 1941). Others moved farther out into the Pacific, seeking natural resources such as *beché de mer* and sandalwood on the islands to exchange in the China trade (Hawes 1990; Gibson and Whitehead 1993: 155–162). The American presence grew dramatically, at first with larger numbers of merchant vessels, movement of the principal U.S. whaling fleet into Pacific waters, and the creation of the Pacific Squadron of the United States Navy (Johnson 1963). The goal was to make the Pacific "a vast American lake, the bridge to the wealth of the Far East from trading and whaling" (Dudden 1992:17). The primary American port to benefit from the entry into the Pacific was Boston, followed by surrounding New England ports engaged in whaling. New York maritime interests were also present on the Pacific but would not play a major role until the California Gold Rush.

Seeing opportunities for trade in the former Spanish colonies, particularly in Peru, Chile, and California, a number of Anglo-American settlers, some of them mariners, others merchants, established themselves on the coast. They acquired Mexican, Peruvian, or Chilean citizenship; adopted the Catholic faith; and married locally, all the while maintaining their economic and familial ties with the eastern United States and Europe (Hawgood 1958, 1970; Pitt 1966; Miller 1995). These settlers, as well as mariners, participated in the trade linking isolated Pacific communities to global commerce (Igler 2004:694). Thus, for the first time, interconnections linked ports like Callao, Valparaíso, San Blas and Acapulco, Yerba Buena, Sitka, Honolulu, and at the far western rim, Canton. The "future American Far West" occupied "a central position in the newly internationalized ocean basin" (694).

Igler has written extensively on the voyages that fueled the expansion of global commerce across the Pacific Basin but assigns equal importance to the ports, specifically the network that linked the future American Far West "long before the United States annexed its Pacific territories" (2004:705). One such port, arguably the eastern Pacific's first great entrepôt, was the former Spanish port of Valparaíso. It came to surpass Callao, the formerly dominant Spanish port of the sixteenth to eighteenth centuries, as a result of the variety of international shipping it handled and its connection to the maritime network in the early nineteenth century.

VALPARAÍSO: THE FIRST ENTREPÔT

The first place to attract expatriate merchants and mariners was Chile, whose port of Valparaíso, closest to the now-burgeoning Cape Horn and Strait of Magellan routes into the Pacific, had grown into the Pacific's premier entrepôt. Founded in 1543, Valparaíso languished until Chilean independence in 1824, when it took control of the region's trade away from Callao, the port of entry under Spanish rule (Monaghan 1973:13). Valparaíso was the base of Chile's merchant marine and naval forces. The port also served as a Pacific base for squadrons from the British, French, and U.S. navies as these nations sought military protection of their commercial interests. In 1810, the town's population was around 5,500. Thanks to the port's commercial and military activities, its population grew to 16,000 by 1822 then to 20,000 in 1987, not counting a floating population of some 3,000 Chilean and foreign mariners (Duarte and Requena 1970:10). Valparaíso maintained regular connections throughout South and Central America: "Chile's own national merchant fleet of 100 barks, brigantines, and schooners carried grain, flour, metal, lumber and coal to Peru, Ecuador, and New Granada [Colombia and Panama], bringing back fruits, cocoa, coffee, and sugar. These vessels, along with some 700 New England whaleships now sailing the Pacific, kept Valparaíso shipwrights busy and made the town very prosperous" (Monaghan 1973:17). The maritime connections also enabled trade with New Zealand, which exported lumber to Chile, and led to regular voyages to London and other European ports. Valparaíso was the first port of call for many foreign ships that entered the Pacific via Cape Horn.

The foreign connections led many foreigners, principally from Great Britain, to settle in Valparaíso. Enterprising Anglo-American and European merchants moved into the vacuum created by the collapse of Spain's American empire. They took advantage of the relative weakness and economic needs of the newly independent nations and came not so much on their own account but as representatives of American, British, or European houses, aiming to establish themselves as commission merchants (Mayo 1987:5, 17, 120–124). Thus, they were able to capture the rapidly growing maritime influx into the Pacific at the first decent port they encountered after rounding the storm-tossed tip of the continent.

In Valparaíso, foreigners constituted one-third of the city's popula-

tion (Monaghan 1973:8). Among this group were the commission merchant G. L. Hobson y Compañía and the American-born steam-navigation and railroad promoter William Wheelwright, a former shipping and
commission merchant (Fifer 1998). Other foreign-born commission
agents and shipowners were Cook, Wilson, Mickle, Hemenway, and Alsop, the last being of the New York and Connecticut banking and merchant family. A German firm, Schutte y Cía, began business in Valparaíso
in 1822, the year after independence (Monaghan 1973:9). They were not
the only merchants with connections to other foreign houses. By 1840,
Valparaíso had matured thanks to the trade connections the foreign merchants had opened to Australia, India, the Orient, California, Peru, England, and France (Duarte and Requena 1970:11). In 1842, the *Revista
Valparaíso* commented that Valparaíso was now "the main commercial
port of the Pacific, and has supplied to all the products of commerce that
have been required by the merchants of Bolivia, Peru, Ecuador and Central America and Mexico" (12).

Though Valparaíso was a great port, the town was cursed by a low-
lying waterfront that became a mudflat at low tide and was ringed by
high hills. The influx of foreign ships and capital allowed the merchants
to invest in the construction of a large central wharf for unloading goods
to overcome these disadvantages. By the end of the 1840s, the city had
become not only the busiest Pacific port but also one of the busiest ports
in the world (Monaghan 1973:13). In 1847, observer Max Radiguet described the waterfront: "The customs plaza, opening to the side of the
sea, was a center of bustling, agitated commercial activity which denoted
numerous and important commercial transactions; there were piles of
covered and tied lumps, barrels of all dimensions and forms, large boxes
painted brightly with mismatched letters, the laborious work of a Chinese painter. The workers, like ants, sorted the merchandise from that
pile, and with handcarts, distributed them into the depths of the warehouses" (quoted in Duarte and Requena 1970:13).

THE CALIFORNIA AND HAWAI'I CONNECTION

Though not as well established as their counterparts in Valparaíso, Anglo-
American entrepreneurs with northern Pacific interests shifted their focus from the Northwest Coast and its furs to trade with California and
Hawai'i. They were eager to transplant the success of Valparaíso to their
own areas of interest: Honolulu and California's Monterey and Yerba
Buena (the town that would become San Francisco). The pattern of mar

itime trade that had grown up on the Asian Pacific Coast beginning in the early nineteenth century had favored both regions. As Spain's strict trade restrictions waned and failed with the new Mexican regime, California as well as Hawai'i became the focus of numerous voyages (Judd and Lind 1974). Here merchants sought commodities for trade with China, including both natural resources like furs and goods they could gather directly or indirectly through commercial exchange (Igler 2004: 713). This free market coincided with the demise of older European monopolies in the Asian trade, especially the failure of Britain's East India Company to restrict American trade in the region. Starting in the 1820s, Chinese merchants eager for the benefits of competition sought to open their trade port of Canton, with the result that French, Portuguese, Spanish, non–East India Company British traders and a number of American firms became involved (713).

There followed a shift in the orientation of Canton's markets in the 1820s that expanded transpacific trade. Much of the new commerce focused on California, which served as a trade depot because of increased connections with Hawai'i, Alaska, and the Northwest Coast (Igler 2004:713–714), and on the coasts of Southern and Central America. "This new market environment found expression in open markets, burgeoning commercial ports, entrepreneurial shipping ventures designed to exploit specific commodities, and private traders who paid little attention to geopolitical boundaries" (709).

Igler has assembled a database for every known vessel that entered California between 1786 (when the area was a closed Spanish colony) to 1848. In all, 953 vessels arrived, "making it one of the most visited parts of the eastern Pacific" (2004:705). The majority of ships continued on to the Northwest Coast, Alaska, Hawai'i, Valparaíso, and China. Igler, using California as a point of reference, sees a broader picture that encompasses the eastern Pacific, "where independent traders competed for the goods and natural resources harvested from these commercial borderlands" (705).

American shipping in the Pacific grew rapidly after 1820 because of a surge in trade after the War of 1812, the rise of Pacific whaling, and market changes in Canton. Of the 953 ships that called at California, 44 percent were American, followed by British ships (13 percent), Mexican vessels (12 percent), Russian craft (7 percent), and the ships from seventeen other European nations. Igler consequently asserts that "U.S. *commercial* [emphasis in original] interests in the Pacific therefore long predated and ultimately influenced its geopolitical and military interests . . .

California's commercial activity was international prior to the worldwide convergence of the gold seekers, and, perhaps, more important, this internationalization of commerce mirrored developments throughout the Pacific Basin" (2004:707). This point is a critical element in my argument.

AMERICAN INTERESTS GROW

American interests focused particularly on California, not only because of official government interest in acquiring San Francisco Bay as a logical base for an American Pacific entrepôt, but because of the extensive nature of American maritime trade and the large number of Americans already established there (Cleland 1914, 1915). The first step in realizing American desires echoed the earlier European model of exploration.

From 1838 to 1842, the United States Exploring Expedition, under the command of Lieutenant Charles Wilkes of the United States Navy, surveyed the Pacific, touring the land, surveying the coast and some interior waters, and paying special attention to the British Northwest (and the activities of the Hudson's Bay Company there) and Mexican California (Stanton 1975; Viola and Margolis 1985; Philbrick 2003). One of Wilkes's officers, Cadwallader Ringgold, surveyed and mapped the Sacramento River, a Mexican internal waterway, as part of an exercise that some foreigners saw as a scientific exercise that concealed commercial interests and potential acquisition, at least as far as the expedition's interests in California and British America in the Northwest lay. Ringgold (1850) would later return during the Gold Rush to continue the task, this time for a private group of sponsors who paid for the first charts of San Francisco Bay and its approaches.

The Wilkes expedition, the activities of other Americans who were making key land acquisitions and encouraging prominent Californios to seek independence from Mexico, and closer economic and political ties with the United States (or efforts to become part of the United States) were parts of a plan to undermine Mexican authority in this important yet distant Mexican province (Hague and Langum 1990). How much of the plan was the brainchild of entrepreneurial capitalists and how much was the strategy of the government, or whether it was a combination of the two, remains both unclear and controversial, but the point is moot. American desires to pursue the nation's manifest destiny and establish a Pacific presence and port were paramount (Harlow 1982). These aspirations were finally rewarded in 1846, when war erupted between the

United States and Mexico over the United States' recognition of Texas's independence from Mexico and the subsequent admission of Texas to the Union (Singletary 1960; Price 1967).

It was no coincidence that the Americans had played a similar strategy of quiet and insidious integration from within in seizing Texas, formerly a Mexican province, by quietly establishing themselves as citizens and property holders (Singletary 1960). The Texan revolution alarmed Mexican officials, as did a quickly aborted attempt to conquer Monterey (California's capital) in 1842 by United States Marines and naval personnel (who were responding to a rumor of war) and the growing number of Americans in California. Mexico had limited means to deal with the threat, however (Harlow 1982; Eisenhower 1989).

The first American acts in the war on the Pacific Coast in 1846 were to create a band of irregular volunteer troops under the command of John Charles Frémont and to land marines and naval personnel to seize California's ports. Within a short time, the United States conquered California with naval forces, the marines, and an overland force of army troops. Despite outbreaks of localized resistance by a handful of Californio nationalists, the United States held California securely and quietly throughout the Mexican War, until its end in 1848 (Bauer 1969; Harlow 1982; Eisenhower 1989). The Treaty of Guadalupe Hidalgo, signed by both nations in February of that year, ceded California and the port of San Francisco along with nearly half of Mexico's national territory (Singletary 1960). The acquisition of California proved to be key to America's expansion into the Pacific. However, conquest alone did not achieve that goal. The discovery of gold in January 1848 provided the capital necessary to create the port of San Francisco, which in turn opened the door to the Pacific.

BRITISH ENDEAVORS IN AUSTRALIA AND A NEW ENTREPÔT ON THE PACIFIC

British interest in the Pacific, spurred by the explorations of James Cook, George Vancouver, William Broughton, and Matthew Flinders, slowed with the Napoleonic Wars and the subsequent War of 1812 with the United States (Gough 1980, 1992; MacKay 1985). British mercantile interests remained peripherally active in the eastern Pacific through the private trading and occasional exploring activities of the Hudson's Bay Company and the East India Company (Gough 2004). The wars with France,

the need to house a large number of prisoners of war, and Britain's social dilemma of jailing a growing population of the indigent poor who
had been reduced to thievery led to an interim solution in 1776: the beaching and housing of retired warships as prison "hulks" at dockyards and
along the Thames River. This action laid the basis for establishing overseas colonies for convicts in Australia. It also coincided with Britain's interest in strengthening its presence in the strategically important waterways and ports of the Southern Hemisphere—necessary to fulfill its
long-standing desire to establish domination of maritime trade (Dellino-
Musgrave 2006).

Britain established its first penal colony at Port Jackson (Sydney) in
1788, followed by new settlements at Swan River (Perth) in 1829 and
Port Phillip (Melbourne) in 1836 (Staniforth 2003:5). Though Port Jackson was established to relocate convicts as colonists, it was also a site for
free settlers, and by 1810, it had become an established mercantile port.
Tied politically to Britain, the colony was not reliant entirely on economic
linkages. Staniforth's archaeological investigations of the earliest days of
the colony suggest that trade networks extended beyond Britain to Indian ports, especially Calcutta (67).

The maritime system linked the new Australian port with the long-
standing patterns of Pacific and Asian trade that had first attracted European interest in the Southern Hemisphere. This pattern played out with
other settlements, and by 1803, a commercial infrastructure had developed in Port Jackson for the sale and "auction of goods directly from
ship, through wholesale warehouses and in commission warehouses"
(Staniforth 2003:71). Thus, a system was already in place when Australia
later established regular trade links with Valparaíso in the 1830s and with
San Francisco a decade later.

Swan River (Perth), established as a "free enterprise" settlement, had
a slow start until the introduction of convict settlers in 1850. Even then,
it grew slowly and was highly dependent on financial support from
Britain. Because of its proximity to Asian and Indian Ocean ports, the
colony traded directly with some of them, although its level of imports
from Britain never fell below 70 percent. Small and isolated, it did not
realize the economic benefit that eastern Australia enjoyed as the California Gold Rush and trade with California and South America led to
Australia's own gold rushes (Staniforth 2003:126).

By contrast, Port Phillip (Melbourne), settled in 1836, followed Sydney's example and grew rapidly, thanks to a wave of immigration that
introduced a "period of intense speculation" as merchants imported car-

goes to meet the needs of the burgeoning town. The arrivals included ships from ports throughout Britain, other Australian settlements, South Africa, India (Calcutta), and Canada (Montreal) (Staniforth 2003:102–103). In 1841, at least two hundred vessels arrived at Port Phillip, which was well situated to play a role in the expanding Pacific trade as the world system adapted to the maritime demands of the California and Australian gold rushes.

The final British entrepôt on the Pacific was Hong Kong. Britain established its new port through a forced treaty with China after decades of operating tenuous and often unsatisfactory trading centers in China. British interests were particularly unhappy after Canton opened its gates to all variety of foreigners, effectively ending the English East India Company monopoly in the 1820s (Keay 1991; Farrington 2002). The prime focus of trade into China now was opium (Layton 1997), shipped by British and American traders from British-controlled India. Opium-fueled trade shifted the patterns of Pacific and China trade, largely in favor of the British businessmen in Hong Kong and Canton who had direct access to the drugs through India. To remain competitive, traders in American Northwest Coast fur and California hides and tallow also turned to drug running, using the profits to buy the Chinese merchandise they sold to California and other markets (Layton 1997).

The opium could not be landed on the Chinese-controlled shore. Instead, on the Anglo-American–dominated water, merchants stored the drug in hulks that were floating warehouses, dismasted and housed over to meet the need for easily movable real estate in a volatile environment. The hulks remained a safe haven even after Chinese efforts to interdict the drug trade led to war in 1839 (Waley 1958). When the Opium Wars ended in victory for Britain and its American allies, Britain gained Hong Kong as a treaty concession.

When established in 1845, Hong Kong served as both a military base and a China trade entrepôt, giving British entrepreneurs yet another advantage over their foreign rivals in Canton. The British also used storeships or hulks, like those at Canton. The hulks of Hong Kong and Canton played an important role in the European expansion of both ports, and like the British prison hulks and the Royal Navy's hulks, they provided a template for their use in the development of the new port of San Francisco four years later. Englishmen and Australians were familiar with them. By 1849, England had used fifty-three hulks as floating prisons or receiving ships in the United Kingdom and sixty-seven hulks abroad in diverse ports like Gibraltar, Malta, Sierra Leone, Ascension Island, Saint

Helena, the Cape of Good Hope, Bombay, Trincomalee, Hong Kong, Hobart, Halifax, Bermuda, Barbados, Havana, Martinique, Tortola, Jamaica, Antigua, Rio de Janeiro, Callao, and Valparaíso (Johnson 1970; Campbell 2001). In 1849, twenty-seven British hulks were in service overseas, and eight remained afloat and in use in the United Kingdom (Watson 2001). Americans knew of hulks—the British had floating prisons during the American Revolution—and after the war, American mariners, like those of other countries, encountered them whenever they docked at a port with a British naval presence.

Transpacific trade with China had languished as the maritime fur trade faltered after 1820. The subsequent, almost desperate introduction of other Pacific commodities for trade with the Chinese—sandalwood and *beché de mer*—had kept the lines of trade open, albeit at a low volume, until the British introduced opium into the equation. The introduction of California gold once again injected bullion into the trade and spurred a regular transpacific exchange. This time, the exchange was directly with a new American port on the Pacific Coast. A number of the China-based merchants who traded in and out of Hong Kong and Canton, American firms who did business in China, and merchants readily familiar with the California market because of pre–Gold Rush trade either sent cargoes or relocated themselves to San Francisco from Canton and Hong Kong after the gold discovery (Layton 1997).

THE FORTUITOUS CALIFORNIA GOLD RUSH

By 1845–46, the Pacific market, now with its own regionalized world system, had been developing for decades in response to the influx of the British and the Americans. Two other factors in its growth were the rise of Valparaíso in response to the growing importance of the shipping routes at the tip of South America and the growing coastal trade of newly independent Latin American nations, which, now freed from Spanish trade restrictions, could welcome foreign trade. More importantly, however, the stage for even greater change was set as these ports now linked not only to each other but also to global maritime trade. Regular voyages from Honolulu to Canton; Sydney to Melbourne; Valparaíso to Callao, Guayaquil, or Panama; and Mazatlán or San Blas to Monterey and Yerba Buena were now the norm. Many maritime mercantile capitalists with Pacific interests had gained precious business knowledge. Several were in key locales from which they could quickly maneuver if new opportunities arose. Asia's, particularly China's, centuries-old dominance of Pacific trade shifted in favor of the growing power of the European world's economic system.

The only element needed for the final absorption of the Pacific into the world economic system was a new commodity that would provide the liquidity necessary to introduce more ships and shipping to the Pacific. That catalyst came when the United States forestalled both French and British interests and seized California from Mexico in actions between 1846 and 1848 and then when gold was discovered in the newly conquered territory. This discovery prompted a "rush" of thousands of ships, the global shift of maritime trade, and the creation of a major new entrepôt, San Francisco, which quickly bypassed its frontier period of development in less than two years to become the principal port (in volume of shipping and value of trade) on the Pacific Ocean and a major player in global maritime commerce. Particularly significant was San Francisco's post-1849 dominance of coastal trade, from Valparaíso to Vancouver Island. Steamers connected the Isthmus of Panama to shipping lanes on the Caribbean and Atlantic after 1849, and transoceanic trade via clippers around Cape Horn began after 1850. Most significantly, San Francisco was the United States' new gateway to Asian trade (Wright 1911; Perry 1994).

These changes, especially the shift of China trade's from its formerly westward movement (Southeast Asia, India, and Europe) to an eastern flow toward San Francisco, allowed the new city to prosper without relying solely on its links to the gold mines. San Francisco prospered as an international port with its own ties to Asia and Europe, becoming the entrepôt by which Europeans could seek California commodities like gold and later wheat and lumber. San Francisco provided a new focal point for the China trade, particularly after the American introduction of regular transpacific steamship service to the Orient in 1867 (Kemble 1943). The ocean between China and California was no longer a barrier but a highway (Igler 2004:713).

In addition, by 1850, California, Oregon, and Washington had stronger commercial and political ties to the transcontinental nation (Igler 2004:695). They were able to forge these ties by assuming risk, using tremendous amounts of capital (California gold), and rapidly building San Francisco as an entrepreneurial hub. This construction of San Francisco as a key maritime player was not an isolated accident of the Gold Rush. It was the culmination of decades of work by a group of mercantile capitalists, who seized the moment, between 1848 and 1851, to alter forever the patterns of global maritime trade. The new entrepôt would

outlast the mining boom. It survived destructive fires and political challenges to its status as America's major port on the coast because these
merchants and their backers constantly overcapitalized and rebuilt to pursue greater gains in the world economy, ultimately hoping to fulfill the
age-old dream of tapping the riches of the Orient.

CHAPTER 4

Development of the Gold Rush San Francisco Waterfront

European interests in the Pacific, growing out of the desires for Asian trade, culminated in the dominance of American traders in the early nineteenth century and the conquest of California as a base for Pacific expansion. The discovery of gold was a fortuitous spur to achieving American dreams of Pacific trade dominance and a direct ocean link to the China trade. San Francisco became the locus of that effort, becoming the destination for the many ships and gold seekers that made up the Gold Rush. However, the rise of San Francisco was possible only because of intensive overcapitalization and rapid development.

San Francisco owed its rapid rise to political domination by commercial interests, the appropriation of government land for unregulated waterfront development, and the hasty construction of waterfront infrastructure through piers, piling-elevated buildings, and ships converted into floating warehouses. I have examined the histories of three ships— *Niantic, Apollo,* and *General Harrison*—as examples of this type of development. These waterfront improvements laid the foundations for San Francisco's ultimate survival and success as America's entrepôt for Pacific and Asian trade.

GOLD DISCOVERY: IMPETUS FOR DEVELOPMENT

Throughout the last months of 1848, reports of a tremendous gold discovery in far-off California reached the eastern seaboard of the United

States and foreign capitals. By December, California dominated the news. The president of the United States, James Knox Polk, reported to Congress on December 5 that the news of gold was true and that the gold mines were "extensive." As proof, the U.S. government displayed 230 ounces of near-pure gold that military officers had brought back from California (Holliday 1981:42).

By the end of the year, the rush was on for California. The primary destination, nearly to a ship, was San Francisco, which in most mariners' minds was the bay, not the tiny village that had presumptuously taken the name in 1847. John B. Goodman III, an amateur historian with a keen interest in the vessels that cleared ports on the East Coast of the United States and Canada to head for California between December 1848 and the end of 1849, spent decades assembling a comprehensive "encyclopedia" of the vessels in the "Gold Rush fleet." Goodman's final count of 762 vessels did not include ships from South or Central America, Europe, Australia and New Zealand, or the Orient (Goodman 1987).

Presumptuously or not, San Francisco capitalized on several fortuitous factors to become the great entrepôt of the Gold Rush. The founding of the town as a commercial center in 1835 and its subsequent growth during the Mexican War made it the largest settlement on San Francisco Bay. Within close proximity to the Golden Gate, it was a logical first stop for sea-weary passengers and crews after a prolonged voyage to California. The settlement, small as it was in 1847 and 1848, offered a sheltered anchorage, saloons, restaurants, and access to goods and services. Bolstered in 1848 by the first influx of wealth from the gold discovery, this bayside settlement became the point of entry for every vessel sailing for California's gold fields, as well as a transfer point for smaller vessels to enter the rivers that drained from the Sierra Nevada into the bay.

DEVELOPMENT OF THE WATERFRONT, 1849–1850

San Francisco rapidly developed to meet the needs of arriving ships that discharged passengers and cargo, first on its beach and later on its wharves and piers. Between 1849 and 1851, more than a thousand ships called at San Francisco and went no further, because they were too large to navigate the rivers. Instead, would-be gold miners and their supplies made their way to the upper reaches of the bay and entered the river systems. Running up the Sacramento or the San Joaquin, they sailed and steamed in smaller craft to the river ports of Sacramento, Marysville, and Stockton, the jumping-off points for the mines (Lotchin 1974; Delgado 1990a; Benemann 1999).

San Francisco boomed because of this transshipment of people and goods as tens of thousands regularly passed through the city. Businesses flourished as they served the needs of recently disembarked passengers. Miners weary of more primitive conditions in the interior returned to San Francisco. The maritime traffic calling at the waterfront also bolstered the economy, as San Francisco's merchants sent vessels to ports up and down the coast to obtain merchandise to feed the needs of the city and its inhabitants. Foodstuffs came from Hawai'i and other Pacific islands; fruit and beef came from Mexico; and grain and manufactured goods came from Chile, Peru, and China. Lumber and wool came from New Zealand, and lumber and wheat came from Oregon. Within two years, lumber was arriving from Puget Sound and the forests of British Columbia. This regular trade not only fed the burgeoning population but also provided the materials to expand the city, especially raw lumber from the Northwest Coast, now linked again to California with a new natural commodity.

As early as July 1849, observers were describing the pace of growth and expansion as "animated" and "propelled by the indomitable perseverance" (Letts 1853:47). The population, estimated at 2,000 in February 1849, grew to 3,000 by March, 5,000 by July, and somewhere between 12,000 and 15,000 by October. The population fluctuated between 20,000 and 40,000 during the spring of 1850 (Berry 1984:21). The city's "nucleus of tradesmen, craftsmen, and others working in service industries supported a comparatively high floating population," as miners arrived in the city in the fall and winter months "either heading home or seeking a more comfortable winter abode" (21).

However, this rapid growth created problems too, such as where to house the people and the goods. In May 1849, French Consul J. A. Moerenhout described the situation to his superiors in Paris:

The fact is that the shipments from all parts of the globe exceed all estimates and all expectations. To this I will add what I have had the honor to point out in my earlier dispatches, that in this country there are no government stores or warehouses, that the private warehouses of the business men are insufficient, that the costs of unloading and storage are from 10 to 20 per cent per month for bulky articles, that customs duties are high and payable in cash, that commissions are high and interest on money from two to five per cent per month, and that if a cargo cannot be sold on board and is stored, it will be eaten up within three or four months by the enormous charges and expenses of all kinds (quoted in Nasitir 1935:58–59).

The problems were soon to be resolved. Moerenhout wrote again to his superiors in Paris in October 1849:

> Business continues to show an activity that more and more surpasses all probabilities and exceeds the most foresighted estimates. Entire cargoes are still readily disposed of and with the exception of a few articles, among which unfortunately are brandies, merchandise continues to sell well, some articles with large profit, such as flour and wines, which have gone up, the former from $ 12 to $20 a sack or barrel, the latter from $20 and $25 to $75 and $80 a cask. Everything seems to indicate that if the arrivals, especially from the United States, let up a bit, this country will continue to be not only the largest but also the most profitable market for foreign commerce in these seas (quoted in Nasitir 1935:70–71).

The key to success was an extralegal seizure by the city's politicians of government land, namely the tidal flats in front of the town. The majority of the city's early politicians were merchants or speculators who directly benefited from taking over the government's submerged lands (Davis 1967). Once appropriated, these lands were sold and developed as water lots.

San Francisco was ill equipped for its new status as the principal American port on the Pacific (Lotchin 1974:9). Crowded beyond its capacity, the small settlement was hemmed in on three sides by huge, shifting sand dunes and by a shallow 6- to 18-foot-deep, 336-acre cove (National Oceanic and Atmospheric Administration 1841). The cove was a stagnant pond of thick, foul mud at low tide. The city met the demands of growth by moving out across the mud flats and then into deeper water. Starting in 1847, the city fathers subdivided and sold the flats in front of the town as "water lots" (Soulé, Gihon, and Nisbet 1855:182). The initial subdivision created 450 lots, "all contained between the limits of low and high-water mark; and four-fifths of them were entirely covered with water at flood tide" (182).

In July 1847, the alcalde (mayor) of San Francisco sold two hundred lots in a public sale. The ads promoting the auction proclaimed, "The site of the town of San Francisco is known by all navigators and mercantile men . . . to be the most COMMANDING COMMERCIAL POSITION on the entire western coast of the Pacific Ocean, and the Town itself is no doubt destined to become the COMMERCIAL EMPORIUM of the western side of the North American continent" (*Monterey Californian,* April 17, 1847).

On January 3, 1850, upon completion of a new survey, a second public sale by the city sold an additional 343 lots (Dwinelle 1867:211–213).

These lots provided the city's most dramatic expansion. The area around Portsmouth Square, the commercial heart of the city since 1835, began to lose importance by the end of 1849 when water lots became the most desirable real estate in town. Frontage along the bay allowed easy access to off-loading ships, and the water lots provided space to expand the infrastructure to accommodate the booming business of maritime mercantile activity as more and more ships arrived.

CREATING THE WATERFRONT INFRASTRUCTURE

Before 1848 and continuing into 1849, boats landed goods on the beach at the foot of Clay Street, which ran up a slight incline to the southeast corner of Portsmouth Square. By 1849, stores and offices bounded the square, marking it as the commercial heart of the city. Another landing near the foot of Sacramento Street at its intersection with Montgomery Street provided additional space for boats to land, but both this and the Clay Street landings were inadequate. The sites had no facilities for landing or stowing goods. English forty-niner William Shaw described the scene: "The streets were piled with merchandise of every description; high tiers of goods formed barricades before many houses, as warehouse room for stowage adequate to the shipping discharge could not be had . . . Fronting the harbor . . . cases, casks and bales, to the amount of thousands of pounds, lay . . . exposed to the weather" (1851:46).

Some merchants recognized the inadequacy of these landings as early as 1847, when they built an additional landing at the foot of Broadway Street at Clark's Point, a promontory at the base of Telegraph Hill at the northern end of Yerba Buena Cove that fronted deeper water (Davis 1967:177). However, not until 1849 did other wharves follow, thanks to financing by private entrepreneurs who obtained long-term leases of the submerged rights-of-way of the city's streets between the water lots.

In the summer of 1849, after several false starts, entrepreneurs built the first wharf bridging the shallows of the cove. Funding came from private interests with assistance from the city and two merchants with long-standing ties to shipping: Henry Mellus, a former Bryant & Sturgis agent, and William D. M. Howard, who, like Mellus, was another veteran of the Pacific maritime trade (Davis 1967:187–189). Mellus and Howard had settled in California in the early 1840s. Active in maritime trade, with their own ships running to Hawai'i and South America, they branched out as ship's agents and were early investors in Yerba Buena (161–164). In 1845, they formed a partnership, and in 1848, they built a store at the southwest corner of Clay and Montgomery streets, adjacent to the principal landing spot on the beach and hence one of the best mercantile locations in the town.

Mellus and Howard were among the first merchants to recognize the need for and benefits of a wharf, and they became the principal promoters of the Central Wharf project. The city granted a right-of-way across public lands, as did Mellus and Howard, who owned the block bounded by Clay, Sacramento, Sansome, and Battery streets so that the access street for the wharf could pass through. Their motives were altruistic and profitable. The wharf "enhanced the value of the remainder of the block and increased the wealth of the firm (Davis 1967:177). The Central Wharf Joint Stock Company, formed in April 1849, raised $100,000 in a matter of days. By the first week of May, the company advertised for proposals to build a 36-foot-wide, 700-foot-long wharf. The principal shareholders were other merchants, including Cross, Hobson & Co. (a Chilean firm that had relocated to San Francisco); James C. Ward; Joseph L. Folsom; DeWitt & Harrison (commission merchants like Cross, Hobson & Co.); and Samuel Brannan (Eldredge 1912:574).

By August 31, 1849, the *San Francisco Daily Alta California* (hereafter the *Alta*) could report, "Piles for its support have been driven for a distance of three hundred feet, and about half that distance is already completed and planked." On September 20, the paper announced, "Work has so far progressed as to admit small vessels and scows coming alongside." The new wharf was immediately profitable. At the end of 1849, after four months of operation, the Central Wharf Joint Stock Company paid a 10 percent dividend to the shareholders (*Alta,* December 29, 1849). Central Wharf also solicited praise and imitation. As visitor William Kelly remarked in 1850, "There is one great drawback to the harbor in the shallowness of the water around its shore, which prevents vessels from discharging within a mile of a landing; while the expense of discharging by means of scows or flat-bottomed boats, from the enormous rate of labor, involves an outlay almost equal to the freight. To obviate this, some very long and substantial piers have been lately constructed, extending out a great distance, but still far short of the deep water, and only affording accommodation for small craft, but their continuation to that point is contemplated" (Kelly1950:148–149). The success of Central Wharf compelled the city government to order contracts for wharves at the foot of every street, commencing with Market, Broadway, and Pacific streets.

The city tried and failed to finance the wharves. Private enterprise stepped in, and the city granted five-year private contracts to build the wharves, stipulating that contractors would pay a percentage of the profits as rent. Meanwhile, several entrepreneurs built private wharves, particularly to connect to their own water lots and the piling-supported structures on them. Between April 1849 and December 1850, nine wharves arose on the cove, ranging from 250 to 975 feet long and representing 6,000 feet of total wharfage. More than $1 million dollars (the equivalent of $22.73 million, in 2008 dollars) had been expended to build them (Hittell 1878:164–165).

The number of piles on the wharves was substantial. Excavation at the Hoff's Store and other Gold Rush sites has yielded a number of wharf piles as well as those that supported waterfront buildings. Mostly redwood *(Sequoia sempervirens)*, these pilings range from 12 to 18 inches in diameter and have surviving lengths of 50 to 65 feet. These findings fit with an advertisement by J. B. Bidleman in the *Alta* on June 14, 1850, in which he promotes a "new and very powerful pile driver capable of driving piles 12-inches across the head and 50 feet hoist." Given the tidal range of San Francisco, most would have risen an additional 10 feet on average above the level they burned down to in the May 4, 1851, fire. If the wharfage around the Hoff's Store Site is an indicator, they were spaced every 10 feet, on average (Walsh 1990:23). Given Central Wharf's 6,000 feet of wharfage and its two rows of piles, the total works out to 1,200 piles.

This calculation allows us to determine costs through another source. A March 28, 1850, contract between water-lot owner Elbert P. Jones and pile driver Erasmus D. Keyes provides terms and costs that were likely standard at the time: "piles to be driven to hard bottom & sawed off" to provide the base for a cap or sill, at a "rate of one dollar for each and every running foot" for the pile and a cost for driving them of "twenty five dollars for each and every pile" (Elbert P. Jones Papers 1846–52). For a 75-foot-long pile, the cost would have been $100. Thus, the 1,200 piles of Central Wharf likely cost $120,000 ($2.72 million in 2008 dollars). The remaining $880,000 reportedly spent on wharf construction went to lumber, hardware, and labor, an amount that is in accord with building prices of the time.

One wharf, built at the foot of Sacramento Street, was Howison's Pier, erected in early 1850 and remaining in place until the Sacramento Street wharf replaced it in 1851. The foot of Sacramento Street, like the foot of Clay Street, had already "stood prominent as a reception point for merchandise in 1849 and early 1850" (Bancroft 1888:178). With the construction of Howison's and later of the Sacramento Street wharf and the private Clay Street wharf, the area between and surrounding these two piers, especially Central Wharf, became the new commercial heart of San Francisco. William Heath Davis, a long-standing resident and an early maritime participant in the Pacific trade and investor in Yerba Buena/San Francisco, claimed that by 1850, Central Wharf had become the most significant site in the city. "The Central Wharf . . . was the thoroughfare for communication with vessels, and was crowded from morning 'til night with drays and wagons coming and going, Sailors, miners, and others of all nationalities; speaking with a great variety of tongues, moved busily about; steamers arriving and departing, schooners were taking merchandise for the mines, boats were crowding in here and there—the whole resembling a great beehive, where at first glance everything appeared to be noise, confusion, and disorder" (1967:178).

The scene was anything but disorder and confusion. The wharves and the intervening buildings alongside them had shifted the commercial heart of San Francisco to the waterfront. The water was home to the exchange of goods to and from ships, overseen by merchants and agents who lived and worked in the heart of this new business district, and this hub of activity created an entrepôt. Of twenty-one shipping and commission merchants listed in the San Francisco city directory, the majority (fifteen) were listed within the nine-square-block area bounded by Montgomery, Jackson, Front, and California streets. Four were located on Sacramento, five on Montgomery, and four clustered around the intersection of Jackson and Sansome (Kimball 1850).

Alongside the wharves, water-lot owners began to line the water lots with piling-supported warehouses. On August 31, 1849, the *Alta* noted that on a private wharf at the foot of Pacific Street, the firm of Cross, Hobson & Co. was "erecting a large building . . . which is to answer as both a storehouse and wharf," whereas "Messrs. Northam and Gladwin have also erected a large warehouse at the foot of Pacific Street, which will answer the purposes of a wharf also."

After a brief hiatus during the winter of 1849–50, building resumed at a frantic pace, as new wharves and buildings filled in the water lots. Among the other wharves built on city-street alignments starting in 1850 were the Jackson, Vallejo, Market, Pacific, and Washington Street wharves (Hittell 1878:164–165). The wharves were key to commanding the maritime trade. An advertisement in the *Alta* on October 10, 1850, described Cunningham's Wharf, a private venture: "Having twenty-six feet of water at its end, and sufficient at the sides for the largest class vessels, [it] offers great inducements to them [ships] to land there, as by doing so they would be able to discharge in one-half the time and at much less expense than they would be put to by lying in the stream."

On October 23, 1850, the *San Francisco Evening Picayune* reported, "[The] click of the hammer, and the whir of the saw are continually heard. Large substantial warehouses, with numerous floating depots for the storage of merchandise, line our wharves and waterfront." In the end, San Francisco had an entire commercial district standing on piles. As one account noted, by late 1850, the "corners of Sansome, Battery, and Sacramento streets were originally on piles—little piers just large enough to accommodate the stores and premises forming the junction of the streets. At high tide goods could be lightered from the shipping to the stores, and from the stores to the Sacramento and Stockton steamers" (Barry and Patten 1873:107).

By early 1851, the result was a unique and extensive, rapidly and expensively built commercial district, aptly described by Gold Rush visitor Vicente Perez Rosales:

> Long piers, supported on redwood piles, were being constructed or were being further extended at the end of every street that ran down to the beach. These carried the street out over the tidal flat, and provided railways and foundations for additional buildings. At one place a lack of ready materials for piers had been solved by piling boxes and sacks of earth across the muddy beach; at other locations, so as to not lose time, piers had been improvised by grounding ships at the ends of streets and laying beams up to them; and there, too, shops and offices were built (quoted in Beilharz and López 1976:65).

While extensive, this form of development was not expensive. On January 25, 1849, for example, Elbert P. Jones contracted with carpenter Daniel Stark to build a twenty-five-foot by fifty-foot "substantial frame house, or warehouse," "one story or (10 ft.) ten feet high in the walls" for $1,300 ($29,458 in 2005 dollars), exclusive of the pilings it stood upon (Elbert P. Jones Papers 1846–52). Given these and assuming a spacing of 10 feet between piles, but with a middle row of piles for better support along the 25-foot ends of the structure, I estimate that 15 piles were adequate to support the building. Thus, the pilings—at $100 each, for a total of $1,500 ($33,990 in 2008 dollars)—essentially doubled the total to some $2,800 ($63,448 in 2008 dollars) or $2.24 per square foot ($50 per square foot in 2005 dollars). This 1,250-square-foot building provides a scale by which to estimate a larger warehouse or store, at $50 per square foot. The Hoff Store site, which probably represents two three-story buildings built in the spring of 1849, was 80 by 30 feet (Walsh

1990:23, figure 3–2). At three full stories, the 7,200-square-foot building(s) would have cost $16,128 in 1849, or approximately $360,000 in twenty-first-century dollars.

A "VENICE BUILT OF PINE" AND ITS STORESHIPS

A shortage of buildings and the need to protect millions of dollars of cargo landed on the beach or stacked on the wharf also led to a boom in building construction. However, the need for storage space and the high cost of lumber, bricks, and hardware, all of which had to be imported, led entrepreneurs to seek another alternative. They turned to the growing number of idled ships that clogged the waterfront for a solution to the Gold Rush building shortage. Britain's use of dismasted or housed-over hulks as prisons and Canton's and Hong Kong's use of vessels as opium warehouses, probably provided the template, particularly considering that many of the capitalist merchants developing San Francisco were familiar with Canton and Hong Kong. Merchants and speculators converted more than two hundred ships into floating buildings between 1849 and 1851, turning most into warehouses, or storeships, and others into hotels, offices, prisons, and a church.

The use of these ships as buildings was one of the decisive factors in rapidly transforming San Francisco from a village into a working port and major city. The idling of so many vessels was a fortuitous circumstance that provided much-needed warehouses and other protected spaces and enclaves. Not only was there a floating population; but so too was much of the town's infrastructure and real estate floating. This fact made San Francisco unique among frontier settlements, not only in the United States but also along the entire Pacific Rim.

No other frontier port was ever so water oriented in its structure and role, a fact recognized by one Chilean visitor from Valparaíso, and hence well versed in the role of an entrepôt, who sagaciously commented that the city was a "Venice." Others commented on San Francisco's unique nature as well. French argonaut Etienne Derbec, in a letter home on December 1, 1850, wrote that though San Francisco was growing on all sides, "it is especially in the neighborhood of the port that the city's developments have been the most extensive . . . the city has expanded over the water in regular sections, and one day San Francisco, like Venice, will see its streets plowed by innumerable boats, and ships of all sizes will be able to unload their cargoes at its stores" (cited in Nasatir 1964:164).

As merchants and consortia hastily erected wharves along the waterfront, some merchants quickly acquired storeships to moor alongside the wharf to serve as instant buildings. On August 31, 1849, for example, the *Alta* reported that the owners of the wharf at Clark's Point (at the base of Telegraph Hill) had laid the bark *Janet* alongside the wharf and invited incoming vessels to lay alongside the storeship and discharge their cargo "as well as at any pier in New York." Not to be outdone, the developers of nearby J. H. Merrill's pier advertised on the same day that they had chartered a vessel to serve as a dockside storeship and to "greatly increase the facilities for discharging cargo."

Historical accounts are few, but photographs of the waterfront and a few drawings suggest that the conversion of a ship to storeship was often a temporary affair that required little modification to the vessel. The owners would down-rig a vessel, removing the sails, much of the running rigging, and occasionally the topmasts and other spars. On other ships, the yards were simply cockbilled (rigged at a steep angle so that they did not protrude beyond the decks to snag other ships' rigging) to provide clearance for passing vessels and to serve as booms for shifting cargo into and out of holds. Moored in deep water off the city front, these storeships were accessible to small boats and lighters (barges), but more significantly, to other vessels, which could moor alongside a storeship and discharge directly into its hold.

Of the hundreds of vessels converted to storeships during the Gold Rush, the majority were largely left unaltered and simply swung at anchor for a couple years. After 1851, as the pace of Gold Rush arrivals by sea abated to a steadier pace, a number of storeships returned to sea duty. On May 4, 1851, the *Alta* reflected this change in an advertisement for the sale of two storeships, the bark *Damariscotta* and the brig *Sussex*. The *Damariscotta*, "4500 barrels capacity . . . is well found and can be sent to sea without expense"; the *Sussex* "180 tons burthen, 4 years old, is a good sailer and a large carrier . . . and is in good order for sea."

However, other ships never cleared for sea. The practice of converting ships to buildings continued to expand at an unparalleled scale in Gold Rush San Francisco. A speculator could buy a ship, anchor it in the shallows or the mud, take down the masts, house over the decks, and quickly link the ship to shore by a small pier without having to spend large sums on landfill. The result of this work to create "ship-buildings" and rapidly erect wharves and piers was a commercial district that Chilean visitor Benjamín Vicuña Mackenna described as "a Venice built of pine instead of marble. It is a city of ships, piers, and tides. Large ships with railings, a good distance from the shore, served as residences, stores, and restaurants. I saw places where the tide had flowed down the street, turning the interior of houses into lakes. The whole central part of the city swayed noticeably because it was built on piles the size of ships' masts driven down into the mud" (as quoted in Beilharz and López 1976:194). Other ships, hemmed in by the rapid pace of wharf construction and landfill but not built upon or housed over, were nonetheless trapped on a changing cityscape. These ships remained part of the waterfront scene in San Francisco through the mid-1850s.

No consensus exists on the date of the first "conversion" of a ship to a storeship. Chilean argonaut Vincente Perez Rosales claimed that a countryman was "one of the first to transform his ship into a home ashore" by beaching an "old and useless" bark on the mudflats at high tide and then laying "his masts and spars to form a bridge across the mud" (quoted in Beilharz and Lopez 1976:66). He may have been referring to the Hamburg bark *George Nicolas,* advertised on June 28, 1849, in the *Alta* as a "STORE SHIP. The Hamburg Bark *GEORGE NICOLAS*, 230 tons burthen, is ready to receive goods for storage, &c. Apply to her consignors, CROSS, HOBSON & CO." Given that Cross, Hobson & Co. was a Chilean firm, Rosales' reminiscence may be correct.

An 1882 account of the Gold Rush waterfront states that two San Francisco merchants "inaugurated the storage of good afloat" in the British bark *Lindsays* (*Alta,* May 29, 1882). *Lindsays* arrived from Sydney, Australia, on June 18, 1849, with cargo to order and twenty-eight passengers (*Alta,* June 21, 1849). An advertisement in the *Alta* for the storeship confirms that the owners of *Lindsays* were Francis Gray and Anthony Easterby, the latter an English merchant who had sailed to San Francisco to take advantage of the trade. On November 8, 1849, they advertised their "BONDED STORE SHIP . . . having obtained a Bonded License, they are prepared to store goods on board the bark *Lindsays* on reasonable terms, and having a great number of lighters, they can discharge vessels with great dispatch."

The storeship was a success. On January 14, 1850, Easterby wrote to his brother in London, "We are still storing in the *Lindsays,* but our business has increased so much that we are in truly for a larger vessel if we can raise funds to purchase. We shall then place her hard & fast aground and build a wharf round her. . . . We have this day bought a water lot for the ship" (Easterby 1850).

Although *Lindsays* was not the first storeship, it was probably the first to be "bonded" and insured, an important distinction and key to business success. Buoyed by their good fortune with their first storeship, Easterby and Gray ultimately purchased six additional vessels: the storeships *Edwin* (purchased by Cross, Hobson & Co.) and *Henry Ewbank; Mentor,* used to store mercury; and the ships *York, John Brewer,* and *Eleanor,* "used for several years to store Chile flour for the importing houses of W. Meyer & Co., Cramer, Rambach & Co. and Isaac Friedlander" (*Alta,* May 29, 1882). Their success also inspired others. Before Gray and Easterby beached their first storeship, another vessel was already up on the mudflats in search of additional profits.

NIANTIC

The July 1849 arrival of *Niantic* was the first recorded instance of a ship's being hauled ashore and housed over to become a storeship. The ship's crew quickly deserted her, and on August 2, shipmaster Henry Cleaveland advertised that the ship and outfit were for sale. An advertisement in the *Alta* on August 9 reported, "She is a fast sailer and ready for any voyage; she will be sold at a bargain if applied immediately, together with a large quantity of merchandise suitable for this market." Instead of returning to sea, however, *Niantic* became a storeship. Entrepreneurs had already turned a few other ships into floating warehouses, but businessmen Sam Ward, Charles Mersch, and Adolphe Maillard, along with James Whitehead, Elbert P. Jones, Alfred Godeffroy and William Sillem (the latter three all silent partners) decided to try something different. Godeffroy was the California representative of J. C. Godeffroy and Co. of Hamburg, Ward's personal bankers.

The men purchased *Niantic* and hired Captain Noyes to beach her on the mudflats directly off the center of the town. Waiting until high tide, Noyes towed *Niantic* into position on lot 129 at the foot of Clay Street. Pulling out the masts and removing the ballast, Noyes and the laborers he hired beached the ship in the shallows, as close to shore as possible, so that the water surrounding the ship would lay only a few feet deep at high tide. The wharf that surrounded the ship was only 2.5 feet above sea level, close to the turn of the bilge (where the hull curved up from the bottom to form the sides) of *Niantic.* Thus, at low tide, the ship was essentially high and dry in the wet mud (Delgado and Frank 1983:326). Colonel James J. Ayers, encountering the sailors hired to do the job, reported,

> [They] told me they were working for Captain Noyes, who had taken the contract to work float the old whaling bark *Niantic* over the mud flat and place her on a corner water lot . . . A temporary foot-bridge had been laid from Montgomery street to the vessel, and passing over it, we climbed on

board the *Niantic*. The hulk was snugly in place, at the northeast corner of Clay and Sansome streets. My friends told me all about how they had floated the *Niantic* over the shallow flat. They lashed the empty oil casks, with which she was abundantly supplied, to her bottom and thus floated her by slow stages when the tide was high into the berth she was destined to occupy (Ayers 1922:32–33).

Niantic was farthest ashore of all the hulks on the waterfront and was soon surrounded by construction.

Workers hemmed in and supported the ship by driving pilings alongside it, some of them reportedly the ship's masts, and built a stage to surround the ship on the port side and at the stern. They also built a large wooden "barn" to cover the weather deck, with a low-pitched plank roof leading to the elevated offices they erected on the poop deck. Two large doors cut into the sides provided access to pedestrians and carts on the wharf and to lighters and boats on the open-water (starboard) side. On January 28, 1850, the *Alta* advertised "STORAGE—in the *Niantic* Warehouses, foot of Clay Street. . . . The owners of the ship *Niantic* announce to the public . . . that said vessel is now ready to receive storage upon the most favorable terms. From the facilities offered of receiving and delivering goods, both afloat and on shore, with security against rain and fire, they confidently recommend these warehouses to the mercantile community." The rates for storage were $1 per month for a 196-pound barrel, and $10 per month per ton of 40 cubic feet.

The partners offered "For Rent—on the *Niantic* Wharf—one store, 40x40 feet," as they expanded their business (*Alta*, May 4, 1850). On July 16, 1850, Charles Mersch wrote to Sam Ward, who had just sold his interest in *Niantic,* "The city is advancing rapidly on the mud flats and will continue to advance until she arrives in deep water . . . the value of the *Niantic* property must increase considerably as a result. It is true that before this day comes the vessel and all the improvements could fall prey to flames and make us all suffer a considerable loss" (Mersch 1850).

Mersch reported that an artesian well next to the ship provided water for the storeship and for sale. "We have sold 10,000 gallons on two consecutive days." The water flowed out of *Niantic*'s pump log, which when hammered into the mud as a piling, had struck the well in the "midst of the sea," as Mersch reported.

Mersch ended the letter by telling Ward that the upper deck rented at $1,100 per month and that a small warehouse (probably the 40- by 40-foot store) he had built on the wharf next to the ship was bringing in $600. If he could make another $300 a month in water sales, the additional

$2,000, when joined by the approximate $1,500 in lower-deck rentals, would provide $3,600 a month, or $43,200 a year. A receipt in the Gibb papers at the California Historical Society records a payment to Whitehead, Ward & Co. by Daniel Gibb "for rent of two rooms under the poop deck of the *Niantic* Storeship from 17 June until 17th of July 1850" (Gibb 1850). On June 18, Gibb advertised in the *Alta* that he had taken "temporarily, an office in the *Niantic* store ship . . . where he [Gibb] offers for sale" a variety of cargo from the Dutch schooner *Trekvogel*, "just arrived from Valparaíso." Gibb was the San Francisco representative of his family's Valparaíso commission-merchant firm and a friend of one of the *Niantic* partners, James Whitehead, another Chilean.

The commission-merchant business Whitehead, Ward & Co. was the San Francisco branch of a Valparaíso firm, Waddington, Templeman y Cía, founded in Valparaíso in 1817 by Josué Waddington, an English expatriate. According to a January 31, 1850, advertisement in the *Alta* for the *Niantic*, the firm's members were investors in the storeship along with Ward, Mersch, Maillard, Godeffroy, and Sillem; the advertisement was signed by "the owners of the ship," Whitehead, Ward & Co.

The partners used *Niantic* for their various enterprises. In September 1849, according to the September 6 edition of the *Alta*, Godeffroy & Sillem moved from the offices it had occupied on Sacramento Street to new quarters on *Niantic*'s poop deck, either to join Ward, Mersch and Maillard as partners in the storeship or perhaps to manage it for them. On July 4, 1850, they advertised that their parent firm in Hamburg was about to dispatch packet ships to San Francisco, presumably full of cargo, and that "persons residing in California, who wish their friends to come to San Francisco, can secure their passage by applying on board" *Niantic*. A month later, on August 6, 1850, they advertised the sale of a large stock of lumber. A few weeks later, on August 28, Moorhead, Whitehead & Waddington, from their offices in the "Yellow House, *Niantic* wharf," advertised the impending sailing of the packet ship *Virginia* to Valparaíso. They also advertised the "Chile and California Flour Co . . . for a regular supply of Chile Flour for this market." In an *Alta* ad on September 28, 1850, Godeffroy, Sillem & Co. announced the sale of a lot of cargo "received by late arrivals" that the firm was storing in *Niantic*: "30 tons square and flat bar iron; white, blue, and red Mackinaw blankets; silk handkerchiefs, tin plates refined loaf sugar, champagne, assorted liquors, best Irish whiskey, Madeira and sherry wine in cases, fruit, syrups, biscuits and crackers in tins, preserved fruits and vegetables, pickles, superior furniture, one piano, printing and writing paper, ravens duck, iron and brass bedsteads, For sale by GODEFFROY, SILLEM & Co. *Niantic* wharf."

In addition to goods on storage, and their own merchandise, the partners rented offices (such as Gibb's) to other merchants. On July 30, 1850, the merchant firm Plummer & Brewster announced in the *Alta* that it had "removed to the Niantic Warehouse, foot of Clay street, up stairs, where they will continue their business." Another firm in the hulk, Hussey, Bond & Hale, "sole Agents of the Patentee, *Niantic* warehouses," advertised on August 13, 1850 that it had "fire proof paint" for sale. The *Niantic* partners may have also rented rooms in the storeship to lodgers. According to one apocryphal San Francisco tale, the legend "Rest for the Weary and Storage for Trunks" greeted visitors as they approached *Niantic*'s doors (Scherer 1925:84).

Other business names and advertisements also covered the hull, according to one contemporary account. William Kelly, writing about a March 1850 visit to *Niantic,* recounted a visit to William Sillem. Kelly's is the most detailed written description of *Niantic*'s appearance yet found, other than the Mersch letter, and it corroborates Mersch's comments about the financial success of the venture to beach and convert the ship:

> On inquiring where my friend, Mr. S[illem], was located, I was told that I could be landed at a stair-foot leading right to it; and was not a little surprised when we pulled alongside a huge dismantled hulk, surrounded by a strong and spacious stage, connected to the street by a substantial wharf, to find the counting house on the deck of the *Niantic,* a fine vessel of a thousand tons, no longer a buoyant ship, surmounted by lofty spars and streamers waving in the wind, but a tenement anchored in the mud, covered with a shingle roof, subdivided into stores and offices and painted over with signs and showboards of the various occupants. To this base use was my friend obliged to convert her rather than let her rot at anchor, there being no possibility of getting a crew to send her to sea. Her hull was divided into warehouses, entered by spacious doorways on the sides, and her bulwarks were raised about eight feet, affording a range of excellent offices on the deck, at the level of which a wide balcony was carried around, surmounted by a veranda, approached by a broad, handsome stairway. Both stores and offices found tenants at higher rates than tenements of similar dimensions on shore would, and returned a larger and steadier income, than the ship would have earned if afloat. The office of my friend stood abaft, over where the cabin used to be, with windows of three sides, and, as I remarked to him, only suited a person of essentially mercantile mind, unleavened by the slightest tinge of poetry or romance, as no one else could sit down poring over ponderous account-books, while his desk commanded a series of most splendid views (Kelly 1950:147).

In addition to creating the storeship, the partners constructed a series of smaller structures on pilings around *Niantic*. One of these structures was the "Sullivan House," occupied by the commission-merchant firm of Danforth B. Besse, Kingsbury Root and George T. Sullivan, which advertised in the *Alta* on February 2, 1850, that from its warehouse "at the foot of Clay Street, on the *Niantic* Wharf," it would devote its attention "to the selling of vessels and cargoes, merchandise of all descriptions, real estate, etc." A week later, Besse sold out to Sullivan and Root, who advertised their services as "auction and commission merchants" on February 21, noting that they paid "particular attention" to selling cargoes. The Sullivan House was probably the 40- by 40-foot structure Mersch mentioned in his letter.

The *Niantic* partners also owned a "30 × 40 lot on Clay Street . . . between the ship and Roach-Woodworth" (Delgado and Frank 1983:326). Roach and Woodworth were prominent San Francisco commission merchants. In 1849, they built a large warehouse on pilings some 50 feet offshore of the Clay Street Wharf between Clay and Washington streets near *Niantic*. Roach and Woodworth advertised that they were connected to the Clay Street wharf by a private wharf, "and the two together offer greatly increased facilities for landing merchandise" (*Alta*, August 31, 1849). Others followed Roach and Woodworth's example to be close to the storeship; commission merchants Simmons, Hutchinson & Co. announced in an *Alta* advertisement on February 9, 1850, "They have removed to their new Iron Store, foot of Clay street, near the *Niantic* warehouses." Several months later, on October 9, merchant Fred Leppien advertised that he had "removed to foot of Clay street wharf, next to the *Niantic*, and offers for sale woolen and cotton hosiery, blankets, woolen and cotton undershirts, drawers, and other clothings [*sic*], also Philadelphia bottled ale and porter, claret in boxes, Havana cigars, assorted pickles, &c."

OTHER STORESHIPS ON A CHANGING WATERFRONT

As Sillem explained to Kelly during his visit to *Niantic*, "Others were not slow in following his [Sillem's] example, while those who could not get waterlots to purchase let out their ships, as they swung at anchor as marine stores and boarding-houses" (Kelly 1950:147). Perhaps after watching *Niantic*'s conversion, commission merchants Starkey, Janion & Co. advertised in the *Alta* on August 24, 1849, for "a vessel of about

500 tons, for a storeship." An entrepreneurial ship owner (or captain) advertised in the paper on November 7, 1849, that he was "in possession of a vessel, perfectly tight and holding 200 tons, which he will let, to be used as a store ship, together with his services as a storekeeper, if required, at a very moderate rate . . . the vessel may be moored to suit the convenience of the persons hiring her." On December 10, Finley, Johnson & Co. on Clay Street advertised that the firm was taking goods on storage "at equitable terms, on board the ship *Salem*" and selling the ship's equipment and caboose [deckhouse]. On December 21, John Redmond advertised that he was taking goods for storage on board the brig *Talca,* "lying about a cable's length off the foot of Washington Street. This vessel is in excellent condition for storing goods of all sorts."

By early 1850, with a large number of laid-up vessels crowding the waterfront, incapable of a quick return to sea, their owners or agents advertised them for sale in the *Alta* as storeships. The advertisements emphasized storage capacity, not their sailing qualities. On August 24, 1850, the owner of the ship *Ganges,* Leonidas Haskell, offered her for sale in an *Alta* advertisement: "Will make an excellent storeship, or can be sent to sea with small expense." Other advertisements in the paper also claimed that storeships, moored away from the downtown core's frequent fires, provided security from fire and theft, as well as ready access by water, particularly for active vessels. Others advertised inexpensive rates occasioned by the relatively minor cost of storeship conversion as opposed to warehouse construction. On November 4, 1850, Markwald Caspari & Co., for example, advertised "STORAGE AT REDUCED PRICES . . . on the well known storeship *Thomas Bennett* . . . Goods, received or delivered, either ashore or afloat, free of expense."

A variety of storeships appear in the newspapers with increasing frequency throughout 1850 (the following examples being from the *Alta*). On January 11, 1850, William Greene and A. Lothrop advertised that they had leased the bark *Janet* and moored her next to Clark's wharf, where they were "prepared to receive storage . . . on the most favorable terms." Ten days later, on January 21, Macondray & Co. advertised they were ready to receive and insure goods aboard the storeship *Panama.*

On January 30, the newly fitted storeship *Georgian,* "at the foot of Jackson street . . . ready to receive cargo . . . [with] excellent accommodations for a large number of persons" was offered for sale. On March 9, the owners of the "large and substantial ship *Ganges,* lying off Central Wharf," noted she "will be kept hereafter as a storeship, for all kinds of merchandise free of custom house duties." Two days later, Captain Ayshford of the "Iron Ship *Antelope,* 1200 tons burthen, in 5 compartments" lying near the Fremont Hotel, announced the vessel would take in storage "at $4 per ton of 490 cubic feet per month." On May 9, the "bonded storeship *Zuid Pool,* lying off Clark's Point," offered storage "as low as any warehouse or any storeship in the harbor."

Not to be outdone, Peter Le Guevel opened a hotel on board an unnamed vessel, known only by his July 30, 1850, advertisement for carpenters to build "a house on" the "hulk known as 'Bay Hotel,' below Clark's Point." On August 20, 1850, commission and mercantile agents Wildes T. Thompson, Edward W. Griffin, and J. Davis Hawks advertised that their new firm of Thompson, Griffin & Co., at the "corner of Jackson and Front streets, are prepared to take charge of cargoes and consignments, and will keep constantly on hand a general assortment of goods as are wanted in the country trade. Storage taken on board the storeship *Globe,* lying at the wharf, where vessels of large class can discharge and load at all times." On October 1, C. E. Hunter & Co. advertised its storeship, *Morrison,* "built entirely of live oak, and . . . one of the strongest vessels in port."

An advertisement in the *Alta* on October 4, 1850, offered storage for "Merchandise of all kinds, and Baggage, will be stored in the ship *Tahmaroo,* at the lowest rates, Apply on board, near Agnew's point." However, not all entrepreneurs wanting to cash in on the need for storage space could duplicate *Niantic*'s success. The next step was to acquire larger numbers of storeships for a cheap price and make profits through large volumes of storage.

By late 1850, dozens of storeships lay off San Francisco's waterfront, with others hauled in close and housed over. On October 23, 1850, the *Evening Picayune,* noting "City Improvements," commented on the "numerous floating depots for the storage of merchandise." The large number of available vessels, often at fire-sale prices, and the potential for profits inspired some merchants to acquire as many vessels as they could for storeship use. On January 9, 1851, Moorhead, Whitehead & Waddington, still aboard the *Niantic* storeship, advertised in the *Alta* that they wished "to purchase a number of good strong vessels for storeships."

However, as Sillem told Kelly, finding a suitable water lot with sufficient access, paying for beaching and conversion, and then filling the ship's hold with goods from paying customers required a significant outlay of cash in a speculative market. Some of those who bought into the storeship business quickly backed out. On November 7, 1850, S. A. and J. G. Thayer offered their storeship *Calumet* for sale in the *Alta,* with her "full inventory, besides considerable storage, which will be transferred along with the ship." On November 5, a partner in another, unnamed storeship offered his "one-third interest in a store-ship, scow, boats &c. together with a like interest in a water lot on Front street . . . The storage and lighterage business will be continued by the other owners." This game was not for the meek or for those who did not already possess the means to convert vessels to storeships. For those who were not commission merchants, such an endeavor was difficult, as the owners of the ship *Apollo* discovered.

APOLLO

The conversion of *Niantic* into a storeship inspired the beaching of another vessel: the next one to be pulled ashore was *Apollo,* a September 18, 1849, arrival. *Apollo*'s voyage to San Francisco was a speculative venture financed by the *New York Sun* publisher Moses Yale Beach and his sons Moses Sperry, Alfred, and Henry Day Beach. *Apollo* had sailed with passengers and cargo under the supervision of another brother, Joseph Perkins Beach. Joseph Beach, joined by brother Henry, who arrived on September 26, offered the goods aboard *Apollo* for sale, although access to the ship was difficult. An advertisement in the *Alta* nine days after the ship's arrival, on September 27, noted, "The Ship *Apollo* from New York, having on board a well assorted cargo, now lies in the harbor off the foot of Sacramento Street." On October 11, an *Alta* advertisement presented the cargo for sale, but the goods moved slowly, and plans to take the ship to Sacramento or to return to New York to pick up other passengers and cargo slowly died over the next few months.

On November 8, *Apollo,* abandoned by most of her crew, an *Alta* advertisement offered the ship "for sale, freight or charter, ready for sea, or any other service." The Beach brothers paid $200 to have *Apollo* hauled ashore close to *Niantic.* Through December 1849, workers stripped the ship's ballast, masts, and rigging. Beached in the mud off the foot of Sacramento Street on lot 171, *Apollo* faced west, her bow facing Sansome Street, with her stern close up against the road that would become Battery Street. Piles driven alongside the ship kept her in place but left her free to move up and down with the tide (Delgado 1986).

An *Alta* advertisement for "wharfing and carpenter work" for the newly beached storeship on January 2, 1850, was followed by another advertisement just sixteen days later that announced that the storeship's proprietors were "prepared to receive good upon moderate rates of storage" aboard *Apollo*. The advertisement described the ship as "adjoining Central Wharf . . . and approachable from nearly all tides; it is believed that contemplated improvements will render this ship the most commodious, spacious, and safe storage warehouse in this port." The same ad offered for sale the rigging and gear stripped off the ship during her conversion: "standing and running rigging, blocks, refuse iron, etc." These items did not sell immediately.

An advertisement in the *Alta* on February 7 offered *Apollo*'s "water casks, three lower masts, bower, stream and kedge anchors, chains, cordage, etc. for sale at the *Apollo* warehouses." A lithographed broadsheet advertised the *Apollo* warehouses and the services provided aboard:

> Advantageously located at the foot of Sacramento Street, and connected by strong bridges to the well-known Central Wharf. *The Apollo Warehouses* offer uncommon advantages for storage of all descriptions. They are approachable for lighters at nearly all tides, while for commodiousness, business convenience and safety from fire and all other risks, they are truly unsurpassed. Storage of nearly every description taken upon the most moderate terms. Trunks and Chests safely stored; Lumber stored; Goods received and delivered on Central Wharf, when desired. Liberal advances made on all kinds of saleable merchandise. Goods received on consignment. Ships discharged, and prompt attention to orders for lighterage. Open Policies for the Insurance of Merchandise, when desired (*Apollo Warehouses*, 1850).

An advertisement in the *Alta* on February 21, 1850, reminded prospective clients that *Apollo* was "fitted expressly for storage purposes, and possessing the most spacious accommodations." Thanks to its wharf connection and easy access to shore, it lay in a location that is "unsurpassed in this port."

In March 1850, desperation was apparent in an ad that threatened to sell cases and a barrel left in the ship at auction "unless the charges of freight, lighterage and storage upon them are paid" (*Alta*, March 15, 1850). By summer's end 1850, Henry Day Beach relinquished day-to-day operation of the storeship, leasing it to the firm of Reese & Blakeley, which announced in the *Evening Picayune* of August 29, 1850, that it had control of the ship and was ready to receive items for storage.

The ship did not prosper as a storage depot, perhaps because it was hemmed in and could not compete with the dozens of other storeships that could still offer customers open-water access. Henry Day Beach, busy establishing a banking and exchange business in Sacramento, visited San Francisco every month to collect rent from the "*Apollo* property" from

his tenants. His letters to his brothers (who were also his business partners) record his frustration with the costs of converting *Apollo,* the subsequent expenses, and the decline in income as his tenants were unable
to meet their rent. As early as January 1850, he wrote,

> I think the way I worked and toiled on the *Apollo* property (I know it has
> shortened my life 5 years) has effectively cured me of speculation in this
> country—now it is my turn, and someone else may speculate to his heart's
> content, if he will only give me the tangible securities and 10 percent per
> month. And now after all has been gone through, my mind refers back
> to Father's explicit directions to me before starting from home about the
> *Apollo* as a store ship, of his subsequent requests to have her hauled up
> as a store ship, of my belief that it would be very profitable, that it could
> not exceed $25,000 in whole cost, but that the enterprise was too much
> for my means—from the first I considered it a speculation and enterprise
> undertaken by me for father's account—I worked and toiled and used my
> name and credit individually in order to save him from any liability therein,
> and finding it to cost so very much more than my estimate, on money at
> such enormous rates of interest, I laid awake nights and worried and fretted
> myself nearly crazy, lest the whole concern should fall through, and be
> sold at forced sale, and father be a heavy loser by my business transac-
> tions, even when carried forward at his request. It did work through, but
> the experience of that time, will never work out of my recollection (Beach
> 1850).

In December 1850, Beach reported that he was collecting $1,700 a
month in rent from five tenants: Reese & Blakeley, who rented the "storage portion" of the ship for $500; Messrs. Arrigoni, Shroder, and Attar,
who operated a sailor boardinghouse "between decks from stern to main
hatchway" for $500; Messrs. Kashew & Bigley, who operated a grocery
and a restaurant in a small shed on the wharf running along the ship's
port side, next to *Apollo*'s stern, who paid $550; and C. J. Mitchell, who
ran a liquor shop in a shed near the bow and paid $150 a month (Beach
1850). The annual rents, at $20,400 a year, were $18,000 a year less
than the amount *Niantic*'s owners were collecting in rent. Even that
amount was not secure. Beach noted, "The dull months of the season
having fairly commenced I have been obliged to make a reduction on
some of the rents. It will be very fortunate if I am not obliged to reduce
still more during the winter."

Beach also wrote his brothers that two-thirds of the adjacent property
owners had petitioned the city to plank Sacramento Street, and the city
was passing an ordinance to do so, with the owners of private property
paying for the improvement. Beach was assessed $14 a foot, or $1,914.

Under instructions from his brothers not to incur any additional expenses, pressed by creditors, and facing declining revenues, Beach was balking, although he admitted he would ultimately have to pay: "This being done will probably injure the storage business, yet as the lease of the storage portion of the ship is *secured* it will make little difference there, while otherwise it will tend to the improvement of the property" (1850).

In answer to his brothers' questions about selling *Apollo*, however, Henry also balked, explaining how the development of the waterfront had ultimately trapped the ship and reduced its value:

> When I first brought up the ship it was placed in such position, that it would have necessarily increased in value, as the city was built around it, and this I firmly calculated upon. A city ordinance was passed, and every one considered it effective, that Battery Street, one block each side of Central Wharf, to Sacramento Street on one side, and Clay Street on the other, should for ever remain open, and from a *slip* out to deep water. In this event I well know that the value of the property at the head of the slip would be greatly enhanced. For a long time this ordinance was very effective, and everything looked favorable for its being carried out to the letter. Something different however has turned up, and I now find on my return here the head of the slip located two streets farther out, and the *Apollo* shut in and likely to be densely built around. I think this makes a difference of at least $20,000 in the value of the property. At $25,000 I should advise to sell, as rents will doubtless be so much reduced before long that a better income could arise from the use of the money than can be obtained from the property. (Beach 1850)

The decline of Reese & Blakeley's business is evident in an advertisement in the *San Francisco Daily Herald* on December 12, 1850, in which the firm advertised "STORAGE! STORAGE! At $2 per ton" and a subsequent ad in the paper just three months later, on March 31, offering "Light goods stored at $1.50 per month."

By February 1851, Beach was still tussling with tenants to collect rents. However, he wrote, "There is no opportunity to sell on fair terms—all the neighbors are reducing rents and I expect I shall have to follow suit. Nothing further about planking Sacramento street. I would not think advisable to sell (with present income from rents) without getting a much better price than is now possible to obtain. In the companying statement I forgot to say the Union Saloon, heretofore paying $150 per month quite punctually, has been suddenly closed and proprietor 'vamoosed.' Of course I have again 'ticketed' it to let" (Beach 1851). The saloon, in one of the sheds built next to *Apollo*'s stern, was a victim of the trapped storeship's poor location.

A month later, in March 1851, Beach was cautiously optimistic. "The rise in the value of the property from neighboring improvements I think sufficient to ensure its sale at $25,000 were even the buildings on the lot destroyed by fire. The street is about being planked from Montgomery to Davis St., it will eventually assist in value of the property, and also its rents—don't know whether I will be required to contribute or not, or if so how much. It is my impression that immediately upon being filled or planked to Davis St., a company will add a T wharf to the end of the street, making it the same crowded thoroughfare as is the Central Wharf at present." He had rented the saloon to shipping agent Charles K. Wise and his business partner "Mr. Leonard," who ran it as the Apollo Saloon, a coffeehouse and eatery.

> Since my last advices the rents of the "Apollo Saloon" have been regularly paid but reduced about $75 per month. The little known saloon is occupied, but no rent paid as yet. The rent of the ship portion became due on the 12th and is usually paid with promptitude. This month they promised to make a payment on account of storage, as also the rent. Thus far I am not advised of its payment. The city authorities are about filling in all the streets out to Sansome street, which is within one block of the ship. It is contemplated also, and an ordinance passed, to plank Sacramento st clear out to Davis. I have heard of no movement in regard to this. Very soon such improvement must take place, and will add to the value of the property, and increase the rents very materially (Beach 1851).

Beach wrote that he expected the property would become "still more valuable, as it inevitably must, when the streets are filled and solid all around, (the *Niantic* is now solidly enclosed with earth all around) and the wharf extends from the foot of Sacramento street, same as Central Wharf, it is quite probable that the rents of the property may again become $2500 per month" (1851)

Unfortunately for Beach and his family, the *Apollo* property burned during the May 4, 1851, fire, destroying their investment. Several months later, in August 1851, Beach reported that the water lot on which the ship had sat had been filled in, but nothing else had happened and he was awaiting instructions on whether to lease or sell the lot. By year's end, he had yet to hear from his brothers. *Apollo* had been a difficult and costly venture and had not been the success the Beaches had anticipated. However, the beaching of *Apollo* provided an anchor for additional development of the waterfront, and it also inspired another, more successful storeship two blocks to the north.

GENERAL HARRISON

The ship *General Harrison,* a February 3, 1850, arrival, was the third vessel to be hauled close to shore and converted into a storeship. The vessel was consigned to E. Mickle & Co., owned by Chilean-American commission merchants who had been in business in San Francisco since January 1849. Etting Mickle and his business partner, William Tilling-hast, operated their store just below the northeast corner of Montgomery and Clay streets. From this vantage point, the partners must have watched with interest as *Niantic* and *Apollo* were converted into beached storeships in late 1849. *Niantic* in particular was directly in front of them, and *Apollo* loomed up from the shallows just two blocks to the southeast.

Work on the two beached storeships ended in January 1850; with an advertisement pronouncing *Apollo* ready to receive goods on Friday, January 18, and another deeming *Niantic* ready ten days later, on Monday, January 28. Perhaps realizing that *General Harrison* would have difficulty clearing San Francisco because of its size and probably be delayed in off-loading the cargo, or perhaps acting on previously issued instructions from the ship's owners, Mickle & Co. advertised the ship for sale on February 23, just twenty days later. The firm ended up purchasing *General Harrison* itself on March 7 and prepared to beach her on a water lot it owned just beyond *Niantic.*

Mickle & Co.'s decision to purchase *General Harrison* and convert it to a storeship may have stemmed from the partners' awareness that the *Niantic* storeship was a going concern, earning $3,200 a month in rent. Mickle and Tillinghast may have picked up this information from their friends from Valparaíso who owned and managed the ship; or they may simply have observed *Niantic* at work directly in front of their office. They might also initially have intended to return the ship to sea, given the wording on the ship's new registry, granted on March 7, 1850, in San Francisco (Registry 1850).

Instead, Mickle & Co. converted *General Harrison* into a storeship and moored her on the alignment of the Clay Street wharf on lot 141 in the spring of 1850. The lot had been auctioned off on January 18, 1850, which presumably was when Mickle purchased it. (The *Alta* announced the impending sale on December 14, 1849.) Workers lightened, dismasted, and housed over the ship to convert it into a storeship and then hemmed her in with pilings at her final moorage. On May 30, 1850, the company advertised *General Harrison*'s new career in the *Alta:* "This fine and commodious vessel being now permanently stationed at the corner of Clay and Battery streets, and in readiness to receive stores of any description, offers a rare inducement to holders of goods. Terms exceedingly moderate and the proprietors are determined to afford every satisfaction to those friends who may avail of the facilities presented. Apply to E. Mickle & Company, Clay Street Wharf."

The conversion of the ship to storeship coincided with a burst of construction in the spring of 1850 that pushed the city's waterfront out onto the water lots. Even a major fire that burned out three square blocks and destroyed some three hundred buildings on May 4, 1850, barely interrupted the pace. On May 11, the *Alta*'s editors remarked, "It is really surprising to see the rapidity with which the burnt district is being built over again. In a few days more it will be entirely closed in."

On July 23, Mickle advertised "to let—the basement of our warehouse on Clay street wharf, suitable for offices or a general merchandise store." A few days later, the partners placed a prominent advertisement for the firm, and on July 26, offered "for rent their warehouse, the *General Harrison,* foot of Clay street wharf, or they will receive therein goods for storage." Some takers stepped forward for the ship's rentable spaces. J. McElwain, advertising that he was renting a house on Prospect Street, invited people to apply to him in the "basement of E. Mickle & Co., foot of Clay Street."

Mickle & Co. did very well with its new storeship. In early August 1850, the newly founded San Francisco Chamber of Commerce set rates and commissions, thus providing a detailed look at the amount Mickle & Co. could expect to earn. The rates allowed them to assess a 10 percent commission on the sale of merchandise, a 10 percent commission on goods received on consignment, 5 percent for the purchase or sale of vessels as well as for the procurement and collection of freight, flat fees of $200 for receiving and clearing vessels from foreign ports, and $100 for the same service for vessels from U.S. ports. The rates for storage were $4 per ton of 40 cubic feet, and $3 per ton of 2,240 pounds per month, "consignee to have the option of charging by weight or measurement" (*Alta,* August 14, 1850). The firm also assessed fees for freight and delivery of merchandise. By the time a vessel arrived and Mickle's firm had cleared it with the government officials, landed the goods, stowed them in *General Harrison* for a month or two, sold the goods, and delivered the goods to the buyer, a single crate or barrel would earn them more than a few dollars.

At this stage, the firm was well established in town, and Mickle and

Tillinghast were prominent members of the community. For example, Tillinghast served as treasurer for the First California Guards, a privately organized paramilitary group established to promote law and order in the town (*Alta*, January 28, 1850). The organization was a precursor to the later, more famous Committee of Vigilance, and as with them, membership was an indication of social and business stature in town. In 1851, both Mickle and Tillinghast were members of the first Committee of Vigilance, which was headed by fellow commission merchant William Tell Coleman. Tillinghast later served with the second Committee of Vigilance in 1856 (Scherer 1939).

No detailed records exist of the day-to-day business of the storeship. However, Mickle & Co.'s advertisements in the *Alta* give an idea of the quantity of goods moving in and out of *General Harrison* after her conversion. The advertisements show that auction sales generally occurred monthly. In this fashion, the ship continued in business through the spring of 1851. However, continued construction on the waterfront gradually hemmed in the storeships closest to the shore, including *General Harrison*. In January 1851, crowded shipping boxed in the ship, and the Battery Street wharf and its fill were approaching from the south. On April 12, 1851, a story in the *Alta* commented on *General Harrison* and her neighbors *Niantic* and *Apollo*:

> It looks very curious in passing along some of the streets bordering on the water to see the stern of a ship with her name and the place from which she hails painted upon it, and her stern posts staring at you directly on the street. These ships, now high and dry, were hauled in about a year since as storeships, before the building was carried on in that section of the city in so rapid a manner, and now find themselves out of their natural element and a part of the streets of a great city.

THE WATERFRONT, 1850–1851

Apollo, Niantic, and *General Harrison,* with their varied individual successes (or lack thereof), formed the core of the rapidly redeveloped commercial center of the city on its expanding waterfront. This area was the heart of the entrepôt, transformed from a mudflat to a series of wharves, storeships, and piling-supported structures in the space of a year. The storeships and their neighborhood elicited much comment. In late 1850, one visitor, English author and artist Francis Marryat, commented, "The front of the city is expanding rapidly into the sea . . . this has left many of the old ships, which were a year ago beached as storehouses, in a curious position; for the filled in space that surrounds them has been built upon for some distance, and new streets run between them and sea, so that a stranger puzzles himself for some time to ascertain how the *Apollo* and *Niantic* became perched in the middle of the street" (Marryat 1855:48).

The hemming in of the ships was the result of the waterfront neighborhood's high desirability and potential to generate profits, as the earlier advertisements had stated. For example, on May 15, 1850, merchant William Reynolds placed an advertisement in the *Alta* requesting any "ground floor, capable of being used as an auction store, to be situated on Montgomery street, as near Clay and Washington streets as possible."

The storeships and the wharves had shifted the mercantile district to the exact location that Reynolds wanted. However, the commercial center was about to move farther east from Montgomery Street and the beach. On June 28, Gillespie & Co., real estate magnates and developers, advertised "Warehouse Lots on California street, between Sansome and Battery streets. Also, for Sansome street, between California and Pine." On July 9, the editors of the *Alta* commented, "The proprietors of the water lots are piling their property with the view of building upon it, and wharves are constructed in every direction."

Just a month later, on August 10, the editors noted that these "desirable water lots" were in "sections of the city that are rapidly improving, being at the foot of Pacific street and Sacramento street, and at the end of Howison's Railroad wharf, upon the latter we observe that there rests a large storeship, already placed, which greatly enhances the value of the lot." The "railroad wharf" was an ingenious "hand-car tramway" that stretched along Howison's Pier, itself a "narrow, little strip" just wide enough for the tramway and "room each side for one person to walk" (Barry and Patten 1873:107). The storeship in question was the ship *Thomas Bennett,* which lay at the south side of the pier "at the corner of Sansome street." Philip Caduc, a pioneer stevedore on the waterfront, had built the pier and brought in *Thomas Bennett.* Later he added the brigs *Casilda* and *Piedmont,* which he moored as storeships off the end of the pier (106).

As Henry Beach's frustrations with *Apollo* demonstrate, the shifting of the waterfront out into the cove could quickly shift a lot's value. On August 3, Messrs. Stevenson and Parker, old hands who had bought many of the lots in the area, advertised them in the *Alta* as "desirable business locations for sale or lease—Water lots on Sacramento, Front, and Davis streets, substantially piled and capped ready for erection of stores, having free use of wharf in front and rear, besides water communication." Three weeks later, on August 23, most of the lots had sold, and Stevenson and Parker's attorney, Henry Gordon, was down to offering just one "prized and capital water-lot, on the corner of Front and Sacramento streets, with one hundred and eight foot frontage, 64 feet on Sacramento street, 60 feet on Front street and 60 feet on Central wharf basin, having deep water and substantial free wharf on each of its fronts . . . For a large mercantile establishment or a first class hotel this lot presents unusual advantages. Vessels of 200 tons can discharge alongside, and lighters find access to its 3 fronts at all sides." This last lot sold quickly because submerged land was highly desirable in this new mercantile core.

On September 27, the editors of the *Alta* commented that the extension of Battery Street from Market Street to California Street was progressing rapidly. "The completion of this work will greatly enhance the value of real estate in the vicinity, and give access to a large number of water lots." By November 1, they saw the new mercantile district and its wharves as true signs of progress, because of the "vast amount of business transacted. . . . A great deal of labor and money has been expended . . . and we are happy to find that their enterprising proprietors are likely to reap most grateful rewards for their energy, while every facility thus given the commercial interests of our harbor and the state, add to the credit and wealth of the city . . . and the permanent good of commerce in its widest range" In a marked departure from Reynolds's May advertisement for a storefront on Montgomery Street, another, unnamed entrepreneur advertised in the *Alta* on November 3 for any "corner water lot . . . between California, Washington, Battery and Montgomery streets," by then the most desirable property in town. This waterfront entrepôt, with its "strange spectacle" of three hemmed-in and surrounded storeships, remained the center of San Francisco's mercantile activity. Consequently, it was also the most desirable real estate in town and attracted intense real estate speculation and construction activity until it was destroyed by the May 4, 1851, fire. After the fire, the mercantile core shifted east, following the transient shoreline as it advanced into the bay.

THE MAY 1851 FIRE

The fire on May 4, 1851, was one of several that ravaged San Francisco during the Gold Rush. Fires on December 24, 1849 May 4, 1850, June 14, 1850, and September 17, 1850 consumed wide areas of the downtown, killing many people and destroying millions of dollars in property and merchandise. The fires occasioned massive rebuilding efforts, and "it would be difficult to overestimate the influence of fire in the total development of San Francisco" (Lotchin 1974:18). The fires pushed development eastward, out into the bay, where buildings on pilings, surrounded by water, were better protected from fire, although not always. The fact that real estate on the water provided better access to goods—easier loading and unloading from ships—was another inducement. The fire of May 4, 1851, the largest in the city's history until April 1906, demonstrated that even these structures were vulnerable, but the effect was still the same. After the fire, development continued east, past Battery Street and into deeper water (18–19).

The fire began just before midnight on May 3 on the south side of Portsmouth Square and burned out of control until well into the next day. After the discovery of the fire, the flames spread rapidly, fanned by a northwest breeze. Because "the buildings in the vicinity" of the initial fire were "all of wood and extremely combustible, the fire spread up Clay street, back towards Sacramento, and down Clay towards Kearny with frightful rapidity" (*Alta*, May 4, 1851). The area south of Kearny began to burn in the early morning hours, with the wind fanning the flames, the fire burnt out five square blocks between Pine and Jackson streets, moving to Montgomery and taking another six square blocks as the flames continued toward Sansome Street. By 5:00 A.M., thirteen blocks were gone, and the fire was moving to the wharves, the piling-elevated buildings alongside them, the storeships, and ships anchored nearby. When the fire finally went out in the late morning, another four blocks had burned down to Battery Street. The fire had raged for ten hours, destroyed between one thousand and two thousand buildings, and destroyed some $12 million in property; the city never made an accurate count of the dead (Bancroft 1888:204–206).

Contemporary accounts of the fire mention not only its duration and impact but also its intense heat and ferocity. "We have never seen flames spread so rapidly" (*Alta*, May 4, 1851). Barry and Patten describe a firestorm. "Its progress was so rapid that people occupying houses a block away were unable to remove their goods. The roofs of buildings, seemingly too remote for danger, caught fire like powder, the flames creeping from street to street like a laid train, finding fresh combustible . . . and the wind—sleeping at the fire's commencement—now roaring like a pyromaniac, tossed the blazing brands and glowing embers far away, igniting new fires upon distant roofs, till people thought incendiaries were consummating preconcerted deviltry" (1873:72). The fire from the hills above "was low and darkly red, like a great bed of lava, and the black smoke rolled over the bay, as silent as a picture" (81).

Another contemporary account reported that the wind was "raised to a hurricane by the action of the flames," and the heat was so intense that water pumped by firefighters on the flames "dissipated into clouds of mere steam" (Soulé, Gihon, and Nisbet 1855:331). The firestorm "greedily sucked in the fresh air," and "the hollows beneath the planked streets were like great blow-pipes, that stirred the fire to fearful activity. Through such strange channels, too, which themselves became as dry and inflammable as tinder, the flames were communicated from street to street, and in an amazingly short time the whole surface, over a wide region, glowed, crackled, and blazed, one immense fiery field . . . On all sides in the doomed city was heard the fierce roar, as of many storms, that drowned the shouts of men" (331). As the fire swept out along the waterfront, the wind transmitted flames beneath the piling-elevated structures and tossed embers in the air, setting some structures and the wharves on fire from below.

Merchant Alfred DeWitt described loading a lighter [barge] with a hand-pumping fire engine to float underneath the burning district to fight the fire. As the men pumped, they "obtained water to play on the piles and timbers under the stores, also I sent men in a boat under the stores with a bucket to swash water on the burning piles" (1890). As men tore down and blasted buildings on land to make firebreaks, and others chopped up the wharves to halt the fire's advance, the efforts of firefighters like DeWitt eventually stopped the fire. Accounts of the fire by people on the waterfront are rare, other than DeWitt's, and I have been unable to locate any accounts of the burning of *General Harrison* or of the neighboring storeships *Niantic* and *Apollo* other than immediate postfire accounts indicating that the three vessels burned up.

When the fire ended, it had affected some twenty-two square blocks, "weakened by lack of ready materials, and checked on one side by the waters of the bay, where the wharves, broken into big gaps, interposed a shielding gap" (Bancroft 1888:205). A map in Bancroft shows the burnt district and includes *Apollo, Niantic, Georgian,* and *General Harrison* (204). However, the toll is listed at three storeships, suggesting that *Georgian* survived. "The store-ships *Niantic, Gen. Harrison,* and *Apollo* were wholly or partly destroyed" (206).

FILLING THE BURNT WATERFRONT

The May 4 fire swept the old waterfront clean, leaving behind "a melancholy array of charred posts. All the sleepers are burnt off, and in many instances the piles are burnt down to the water's edge" (*Daily Herald*, May 8, 1851). A lithographed view "the morning after the great fire of May 4th . . . taken from the corner of Broadway & Sansome" shows a flat expanse of bay bottom punctuated by stubs of piles in regular rows. In the middle of that expanse, awash at high tide, was the half-burned hull of *General Harrison* (Justh & Co. 1851). The mass of "charred posts" and debris in the shallows made the burnt area unusable and required that it be filled.

To fill the waterfront, entrepreneurs turned to a mechanized process. The "steam paddy" (a steam shovel so nicknamed because it ostensibly displaced Irish laborers) cut into the sand hills that lined the waterfront. From it, hopper cars running along temporary rail lines carried the sand to the water, where it was dumped. A May 31 account in the *Alta* describes the rail-and-car system on Battery Street, noting that the railway "is now extended to California street, upon a slightly inclined plane, so that the carts loading from the steam excavator with dirt, go by their own weight along the descent, and precipitate their loads directly into the water." A later account, in 1854, noted that the "cars laden with sand ran on a railroad of descending grade along Battery Street, disposing their freight from California to Clay streets. The stagnant water which accumulated in the docks above the newly formed streets became very offensive, giving rise to immense quantities of sulpheretted hydrogen gas, which blackened the painted signs along Sansome and Battery streets to render them nearly illegible" (Le Count and Strong 1854:20).

Within a month of the fire, work to fill the shallows below Montgomery Street began, as did work closer to Market Street. The *Evening Picayune* reported on June 16, 1851, "The extension of Battery Street is progressing surely, though not very rapidly, while in the neighborhood of Clay, Sacramento, California and Market streets, lots are being filled in, in every direction." However, work to extend the streets and fill into the deeper water waited a bit longer, partly because of a change in the patterns of redevelopment. On September 24, 1851, the *Evening Picayune*'s editors commented, "There are still streets along which the ravages of the flames are still distinctly visible. On some streets which before the fire of the third of May were completely built up, hardly a house has been re-erected. Even in Sacramento street, which at one time gave promise of being the first business street in town, large gaps, disfigured with blackened chimneys standing like grim sentinels, may be seen; and in the upper part of it the major part of the property is unoccupied."

The *Evening Picayune*'s editors suggested in the article that the city had learned a great deal in coping with its many fires and now required "rarely more than a week" to rebuild. "Besides," said the editors,

> the merchant who was content to do business in Sacramento street as long as his old building stood, and who was able to transact his affairs in Jackson street, because the length of time during which he had stopped there had given his locality a prestige, when he was compelled to move, preferred the more eligible sites which the steam excavator, and the hammer of the pile driver were continually making in the harbor, and even at a higher rent erected his warehouse in the deep water. The city is moving bodily into the bay, and the fact of vacant lots being observable in the upper part of the city is no more to be wondered at than there should be unimproved property on Telegraph Hill. One end of Pacific street has suffered, but the other has improved; what Dupont street has lost, Battery has gained; the city is nearly as large as ever it was, although it is a little more spread out.

Spreading out required more landfill. On October 7, the *Alta* reported that the streets running east into the bay were advancing, and "as the wharves run out the steam paddy empties the sand in between them, and where vessels floated a few months since, merchandise is being dragged by drays, and stately structures stand." Just a day earlier, the *Alta* had noted that "Sansome street, which has but recently been filled in is nearly planked" and that "work has been commenced upon Battery, which is now planked between Sacramento and Commercial streets, up to which latter thoroughfare only, the steam paddy has thus far carried it." The filling of the shallows probably began with the capping of the old wharf alignments to make the streets solid ground, and then, with the streets planked, the infilling of the lots between the streets could proceed. An article in the *Alta* on October 9 gives a more detailed view of the landfilling:

> We notice that the laborers are filling up Pine street, between Sansome and Battery streets. The lots on California street, reaching from Sansome nearly to Battery, have just been filled, and the work on Pine street will about complete the reclamation of the entire blocks between Battery and Sansome stretching from Bush to Commercial streets. The steam paddy does not, it seems, work expeditiously enough to suit Los Yankees, so they must need [to] keep hundreds of dirt carts running at the same time. Taking it all in, it is found to be much cheaper actually to fill in the lots with sand than it is to pile them and then build. . . . the burnt district is rebuilding, but no part of the city is improving so much, and with such astonishing rapidity as the "water lot" section of San Francisco. For the considerations of health, if nothing else, we are glad to see the solid earth going on the water lots rather than the steam pile driver at work there. An effluvium arises from those mud lots which have not as yet been filled in, which is not only disagreeable, but actually deleterious to health.

The fill reached and covered the remains of *Apollo* by August and buried *General Harrison* by late October or early November. A brief article in the *Alta* on October 26 reported, "The property holders on Battery street have petitioned the Council for permission to complete the filling in, with sand, of Battery street, from California to Broadway. . . . The Common Council granted their petition last night, and we may expect to see the work done in the course of a few days. Some of the citizens owning lots between Battery and Sansome will find their cellars all dug for them."

At least half of the six-block stretch between California and Broadway had already been filled, and the filling of Commercial (a half block from *General Harrison*) to Broadway was only four blocks, which meant that the *Alta*'s estimate of a few days' work was reasonable. The comment that "some citizens owning lots between Battery and Sansome" found "their cellars all dug for them" may be a reference to the partially burned hulks of the storeships *Apollo* (at Battery and Sacramento) and *General Harrison* (at Battery and Clay). This reference might also suggest that at or around that time, the hulks had been cleared during salvage activity. The filling that followed would have happened quickly, given the mechanized nature of the process.

THE "OLD WATERFRONT" VANISHES

By the end of 1851, the burned-over waterfront was filled. The 1852 U.S. Coast Survey map of San Francisco, surveyed in February, shows that the line of fill roughly followed Battery Street, pushing east half a block toward Front Street between Pine and California, and then to the Front Street alignment from California to Clay, before angling westward to the corner of Battery and Washington streets. The water lots between Sansome and Battery streets and Washington and Jackson streets remained unfilled, but the lots immediately south of them were now dry land, with new structures built over the now-buried remains of *Niantic, Apollo,* and *General Harrison.*

The filling of the cove now assumed a regular pace, accomplished with "planned precision" (Dow 1973:45). The typical process of redeveloping the old waterfront—through the engagement of contractors—is documented in a July 21, 1852, contract between Halleck, Peachy & Billings, attorneys, and G. C. Potter. The contract spells out the filling arrangements:

> We will pay you eight thousand dollars for filling with sand, water lots 502, 503, and 504 at the corner of Pine and Front Streets, on the following conditions. 1st the lots to be filled within 3 feet of the grade of Front Street. 2nd

the part of Pine Street opposite these lots to be filled to its grade. Front street, opposite the lots and to connect with California Street Wharf, to be filled to its grade 20 feet in width at top, and to be filled to grade to the middle of the street where the lots opposite are filled in. The payments to be made as follows, 1/3 when the work is half done, 1/3 on completion of the work, and 1/3 [illegible] work is completed. The work is to be done by [illegible] September (Halleck, Peachy & Billings 1852).

Rapidly, and systematically, the waterfront shifted farther east as the dumping of sand and rock into the shallows continued to fill Yerba Buena Cove. Ultimately, at least 22 million cubic yards of fill completely erased the former outline of the cove (Dow 1973:47). The commercial heart shifted with the landfilling, and the addition of flat, dry land provided more room for the mercantile community to construct more solid, and ostensibly more fireproof, brick buildings on it. The city and its port were becoming more permanent. Yet the storeships persevered for a while. Owners of storeships changed tactics after 1851; forgoing the old model of beaching and conversion to shift the moorings of ships, following the old real estate maxim of "location, location." For example, the owners of the storeship *Thames*, moored off Central Wharf in May 1850, had relocated it to a water lot at the northeast corner of Jackson and Front streets by the end of 1851.

In November 1851, the deputy harbormaster of San Francisco counted 148 storeships on the city waterfront; another 30 lay off the river port of Sacramento, and a dozen others were moored off the smaller ports of Benicia and Stockton (*Alta*, November 1, 1851). The use of storeships was then in decline. By late 1851, bulkheads had been built along the waterfront, streets were paved, and construction of permanent brick warehouses ashore provided more commodious and drier storage facilities. Yet as early as January 1851, advertisements announced "Storage at Reduced Rates" aboard a variety of storeships, including the ship *Noble*, which promised the "lowest rates." (*Alta*, January 9, 1851). Around the same time, other advertisements offered "Store Ships—A hull of a ship 325 tons, storage capacity 750 tons, price $1000. A brig of 200 tons, well found, 600 tons storage capacity, price $800" (*Daily Herald*, February 20, 1851).

A year later, San Franciscans saw the storeships as nuisances. In a notice in the *Alta* on January 9, 1852, the harbormaster listed the vessels in the harbor as "not moored in accordance with the regulations of the port . . . thereby endangering themselves and others, near them, besides risking the loss or damage of their cargoes." He then listed forty-five offending vessels, most of them storeships. In the summer of 1852 (July 17), the *Alta* editors commented, "We are glad to see the movement commenced of hauling away hulks that are being surrounded by buildings. Many . . . will be great annoyances in a few months. One was hauled away yesterday, and we notice the places of several others vacant."

On July 10, the editors commented on the changes the waterfront had witnessed and the demise of the storeships. "We believe the hulk which, if standing now, would be farthest up among the houses, was the old *Niantic*. We can hardly realize ourselves that, before she was burned in one of the conflagrations, she was standing . . . on the corner of Clay and Sansome streets. The fourth of May fire destroyed a large number of hulks, which would otherwise have been a nuisance, surrounded by filled-in lots, and far up in the city. A conflagration was one way to get rid of them." They pointed out that a number of ships had been hauled away "before they were hopelessly aground" and "burned" at Rincon Point, but "we notice that there are several so completely surrounded by houses it is impossible to draw them away."

On July 19, the *Alta* reported plans to burn a removed hulk off Rincon Point. "She will be placed that no danger be apprehended from fire, and we mention the fact that an alarm not be raised." Despite the fact that storeships were no longer seen as a desirable aspect of the waterfront, the July 7, 1852, edition of the *San Francisco Prices Current and Shipping List* enumerated 164 storeships in San Francisco—by name and with their general locations, many of them off Pacific and Market streets' wharves. After 1852, many older storeships were shifted south of Market Street, away from the active business core, to lie off Rincon Point, the haven of the shipbreakers. A daguerreotype panorama of the city from late 1852 shows a number of vessels lying in haphazard abandonment, including one hulk with the legend "storage" painted on her bulwarks, next to another vessel with a housed-over "barn" on her deck (Harmon 1964).

Ships that could not be shifted because they were blocked in by landfill or construction were broken up where they lay. On February 9, 1853, an article in the *Prices Current and Shipping List* remarked on the dismantling of the storeship *Thomas Bennett,* which had been shifted at least twice in her career on the waterfront, once to Howison's Pier and then,

in March 1850 [an error, as the ship was still off Howison's Pier in August of that year], the *Thomas Bennett* was hauled on the flats near what is now the corner of Sacramento and Front streets, but which at that time was in the harbor, beyond the end of Long Wharf. A pier was built to the ship, and she was covered and built around with stores, the whole being known as *the Thomas Bennett* Dock and Warehouse. Since then great changes have taken place . . . and a block of brick buildings has been put up below and on each side of the *Thomas Bennett*. In these circumstances, the ship, after a careful survey, being considered no longer land worthy, was sold, and is now being broken up. The *Thomas Bennett* was substantially built of live oak and cedar, well fastened throughout, and every part of her appears as sound and perfect as when first put together. The breast hooks, transoms, and lower deck frames, were extra heavy, and most of the deck stanchions butted the floor timbers. It is to be regretted that such a ship should have to be broken up, as she would have been a good vessel for many years, and worth at home at least $20,000.

At this time, so-called hulk undertakers purposely scuttled a number of former storeships to establish title to certain water lots.

Between June 14, 1851, and January 30, 1852, a court order required the sheriff to auction off approximately 2,000 acres of property so that the city could satisfy a $64,000 judgment against the City and County of San Francisco. The judgment was in favor of Dr. Peter Smith, who had provided medical care to the city's indigents. The city was, in fact, paying Smith for his services by selling off water lots that had gone un-sold when the lots were first surveyed. Dissatisfied with the progress of the city's payments, Smith sued. With the settlement, he then bought many of the lots at bargain prices.

Arguments about the legality of Smith's sales continued for years but ultimately were settled in favor of Smith and many of his influential back-ers. The "Peter Smith sales" spurred the development of the post-1851 waterfront, extending the city front into the former deepwater anchor-age, and created a substantial flat area for the hitherto-nonexistent ware-house and commercial district. The former waterfront of 1849–51, now several blocks from the sea, ceased to be the center of activity. Ironically, many of the formerly valuable storeships, rendered redundant by the new development and the rise of brick and stone warehouses on the new wa-terfront, found a new purpose. Enterprising individuals scuttled some storeships close to shore to form bulkheads or the base of wharves. Other ships, bought at low prices, were scuttled simply so that their owners could hold title to a lot by fixing "real estate" on it until landfilling commenced.

The principal figure in this "hulk undertaking" was Captain Fred Law-son, who had paid $3,500 for three of Smith's lots. This amount was a bargain price and one that historians Roger and Nancy Olmsted believe to be "indicative of the lack of confidence that the doctor himself had in the title to the lands he had picked up in his own sheriff's sale" (Olm-sted, Olmsted and Pastron 1977:448). During the early 1850s, the customary real estate value of a block on the city front would have been at least half a million dollars, the price paid for several blocks adjacent to Lawson's property in 1853 (Hittell 1878:199–200).

Lawson was prepared to operate on the premise that possession is nine-tenths of the law. Moreover, he had developed the strategy of scuttling hulks to establish possession in the face of opposition from wharf owners (the franchised operators of city-street extensions), whose berthing spaces would be filled up with buildings that Lawson erected on pilings or on landfill within his properties that lay alongside their piers. After purchasing a floating hulk, Lawson employed a large gang of men to ballast the vessel heavily with stone. Under the cover of darkness, Lawson's men would drill a series of holes into the ship, which they plugged temporarily while they moved the hulk to the desired location. When the hulk was in place, they removed the plugs, and the hulk sank. The next morning, Captain Lawson would state that the scuttled hulks had foundered accidentally but assert that they constituted "improvements" comparable to "permanently" moored storeships.

Lawson's opponents, who were by no means prepared to accept this ploy as a substitute for legitimate improvements, immediately cried foul. Anyone even vaguely familiar with the nature of wooden ships knew that the old "tubs" that had survived arduous journeys to California were not likely to sink accidentally, especially at an auspicious moment and at a precise spot in a calm, sheltered anchorage.

Lawson scuttled four hulks in 1852. He first scuttled the former storeship *Noble*. When the Pacific Wharf Company tried to tow away the sinking ship, Lawson cut the towline and defended the vessel with his pistol. He then purchased the English brig *Hardy* (also spelled *Hardie*) for the same purpose. One can almost see the gleam in Lawson's eye as he describes the sinking *Hardy*: "When I sunk the *Noble* the Pacific Wharf Company objected so strongly that we made a sort of compromise, and I brought in the *Hardie* to help remove the *Noble* from her position. The company furnished the men for the work, and besides their pay they received all the free drinks that they wanted. The first day the tide was too low to move her and on the night of the second day a norther came up and somehow . . . the little *Hardie* had to sink, and that settled my title to the property" (*San Francisco Examiner*, August 3, 1890).

The Pacific Wharf Company, unwilling to accept Lawson's claim to the land, continued to fight. When Lawson tried to surround the wharf with pilings, the company pulled them up at night. He then sunk the ships *Inez* and *Bethel*, which "cost me $450. We exchanged a few shots before she went down. That is, I mean the Wharfinger and myself did. I had a line fastened to the wharf to steady her, and he started to cut it so she would drift away. I yelled at him to drop the knife, but he didn't, so a bullet took it out of his hand . . . I stayed with the *Bethel* until she sank, when I rowed away from her; but I didn't get her in the right place. She got on to Miller, Hough & Casserley's property, so I sold her to them" (*San Francisco Examiner,* August 3, 1890). At this point, the wharf company gave up. By the end of 1852, filling of the lots had begun, and the wharf shifted farther east as the port gradually assumed the proportions and form of the modern San Francisco waterfront.

Despite the work of Lawson and other hulk undertakers, and efforts to clear out the hulks, some storeships remained in use on the waterfront at least until 1856. Photographs of the last unfilled portion of Yerba Buena Cove from that year show two storeships lying along the alignment of Steuart Street (Fardon 1856:plate 22). A February 2, 1855, advertisement in the *Daily Herald* noted that the "Store-Ship *Ilzaide* . . . has taken a permanent berth alongside Mission street wharf," a location well outside the commercial heart near the expanding industrial area of the city. The Mission Street locale, in the shallows of the unfilled southern portion of Yerba Buena Cove, was close to the temporary moorage of some two hundred hulks, many of them former storeships, that the harbormaster had parked to clear the working waterfront. These ships, dismantled by shipbreakers, gradually disappeared. By 1857, the breakers had torn apart the last Gold Rush ships on the waterfront.

FROM WATERFRONT TO ARCHAEOLOGICAL SITE

By 1860, San Francisco was the twelfth-largest urban center in North America and America's principal port on the Pacific. A bulkheaded waterfront with a massive seawall bristling with piers enclosed the acres of loose sand that now topped the Peter Smith lots. Ships connected San Francisco with an active coastal and Pacific trade, including a growing trade with Australia, which was experiencing a gold rush of its own; and with the Pacific Northwest, which would also blossom thanks to trade in lumber and the discovery of gold in British Columbia in 1858. Between 1860 and 1869, San Francisco and its port repaid the efforts of global maritime capitalists and entrepreneurs, who had built up the city from nothing, at great expense and through economic hardships and fires.

The development of the San Francisco waterfront during the Gold Rush fit within the overall development of European and American economic interest in the Pacific as the world system used maritime trade to incorporate this peripheral zone. While aided by the Gold Rush, San Francisco's development, in the context of the *longue durée*, was a critical phase in that long-standing process of incorporation. The waterfront of San Francisco was an interrelated system of water lots, piers, and structures that included storeships. Even the storeships, in the context of the *longue durée*, echoed a European—especially British—mode of incorporation.

The storeships and the waterfront that housed them are artifacts of the incorporation of San Francisco into the world system. This waterfront, which is now an assemblage of archaeological sites, is the result of massive development and change in the tight temporal framework of 1849–51. The waterfront that had evolved by early 1851 was partially destroyed by fire in May 1851. The fire was critical in creating the archaeological site that lies beneath modern San Francisco, part of a dynamic process of site formation. The development of the Gold Rush waterfront dramatically transformed the formerly undeveloped shores of Yerba Buena Cove into a densely developed maritime landscape of piling-supported wharves and buildings, bulkheads, and "permanently" and temporarily moored storeships.

The ongoing redevelopment of this waterfront gradually introduced fill, in the form of siltation and in the form of sand, debris, and discarded merchandise dumped into the shallows. As a result, the shoreline of the cove changed, as did water depths. This gradual filling was capped, literally and figuratively, however, in the summer and fall of 1851, after the catastrophic fire of May 4. The fire, on top of the initial, intensive process of development, spurred the transition of Yerba Buena Cove into a maritime archaeological site, depositing additional and substantial cultural remains into the cove. In its wake, the material remains of the maritime aspects of the California Gold Rush vanished beneath the urban landscape of the redeveloped city of San Francisco and became a substantial archaeological site awaiting future study.

CHAPTER 5

The Commission Merchants

Adopting Braudel's concept of the *longue durée*, I have assessed the centuries-long integration of the Pacific into the world system through maritime trade and commerce. The China trade, the Northwest Coast's maritime fur trade, and the California hide and tallow trade were part of that process, and various commercial entrepôts dominated by European interests such as Hong Kong, Sydney, and Valparaíso were players in this system. Another *événement,* to use Braudel's term, is the incorporation of San Francisco into the world system by the commission merchants of San Francisco, specifically those who operated the storeship *General Harrison*. By exploring these merchants' participation in the world maritime system and their role in building the infrastructure of San Francisco, we can see the forces at play in this global event

Through their participation in maritime trade, a variety of global partners with commercial interests abetted San Francisco's rise as a port. These players in the world maritime system—linked to Europe, the Pacific Rim, and the eastern seaboard of the United States—integrated San Francisco into their system through maritime trade and commerce. Commission merchants were essentially agents, *négociants* who handled the freight, transfer, and insurance of goods shipped from one point to another. As such, they were agents of the world system (Wallerstein (1980:234), because they controlled the flow of commodities as peripheral zones were incorporated into the core.

Commission merchants played a critical role in building the American frontier in the trans-Mississippi West between 1820 and 1860 because the frontier's economic life was built "around the collecting and processing of raw products and the exchange of these for manufactured goods in distant markets" (Atherton 1971:133). This process essentially added the trans-Mississippi peripheral zone to the core economy on the eastern seaboard. The key to the success of Mississippi Valley commission merchants was their use of the Mississippi River as their primary means of transport, an approach that I view as a template for San Francisco's commission-merchant system: "They were fully acquainted with the organization of transportation. These firms also owned warehouses in which goods consigned to their care could be stored until shipping arrangements were complete. Furthermore, they maintained connections with similar companies in other cities, which assured them of a share in the business passing through their own city. Companies in different towns consigned goods to their associates' care, a practice that contributed to the more efficient handling of shipments." In addition to handling such transactions, "men who had such connections were also well equipped to carry out commissions," selling daily to merchants who made regular visits to their warehouses to see goods for sale. But of equal significance, these "forwarders," with space for storage and "acquainted with conditions in other markets," became merchandisers on their own account (134).

The commission merchants who came to San Francisco were not graduates of Mississippi and other river trade. Though the processes were similar, the commission merchants of San Francisco represented international, oceanic aspects of trade. I specifically shall examine the representative firm of E. Mickle & Co., which had garnered similar experience outside the United States and was fully acquainted with the organization of transportation by sea. Founded by a former ship's captain who had engaged in South American coastal trade (Edward Mickle), the firm had traded in and out of Ecuador, Peru, and Chile for several years before the Gold Rush. It owned at least one vessel, the clipper ship *Ann McKim*, and chartered other vessels. The firm clearly maintained regular communication by sea between San Francisco and Valparaíso, given records of its regular shipments between the two ports. The partners probably had connections with commission merchants in other cities, because goods were dispatched to their care from New York and Baltimore, the latter the port city where Mickle was born. Moreover, vessels touching at Valparaíso from these ports, as well as from London and Canton, took on goods for delivery to San Francisco care of Mickle & Co. Edward Mickle had immigrated from Baltimore to Valparaíso, and his parents and brother, Robert, who was a banker, remained prominent residents there.

Although Mickle & Co. never advertised overseas connections other than the office in Valparaíso, other commission merchants in San Francisco advertised business relationships with commission merchants in Hawai'i, China, Chile, Panama, New York, and London and with banking houses in London, Paris, New York, and almost every major port city on the East Coast of the United States. Advertisements for some of the city's Gold Rush commission merchants illustrate their widespread networks. Commission merchants Joseph E. Dall and H. S. Austin listed partners in Canton, New York, Boston, Baltimore, Philadelphia, and New Orleans, for example, and commission merchants William Jewell and Charles Melhado advertised connections to Panama, London, New York, Philadelphia, Boston, Baltimore, Norfolk and Richmond (Virginia), New Orleans, and Portland (Maine) (*San Francisco Daily Alta California*, October 29, 1849).

One key to these merchants' success was their access to an international network via relatively easy and speedy communication by sea. In 1848, New York was only three weeks' sail from London (Albion 1939:331). Via overland travel or communication, San Francisco was several months' distance from New York. Merchants did not enough ships, nor the incentive to add them, before the Gold Rush to speed up the oceanic lines of communication. On January 11, 1848, the *New York Herald* advertised the latest dates of newspapers and correspondence received from foreign ports: news from Pacific ports was only a few months old, with the latest news from Sydney, Australia, dated August 13 and the latest from San Francisco dated September 18, the same date as news from Manila in the Philippines; Valparaíso's news was from October 26. The four- month gap between New York and San Francisco closed dramatically during the Gold Rush. On April 14, 1852, the *Herald* was able to report news from San Francisco dated March 17 and from Valparaíso dated February 26, whereas Sydney's news was from December 15 By 1851, a commission merchant in San Francisco could regularly dispatch orders by ship to New York, where goods arriving direct from London could be transshipped, and the return cargo would arrive in San Francisco approximately three to four months after placement of the order. The return was even faster from a closer port such as Valparaíso, which was a month's sail from California.

The commission merchants of San Francisco were an important, if not dominant class. In an 1850 San Francisco business directory, some 31

percent of businessmen adopted the secondary title of "commission merchant" (Hattori and Kosta 1990:93). Similarly, the San Francisco city directory of 1850 lists twelve commission merchants out of thirty-four businesses within a two-block radius of Central Wharf (Kimball 1850). This
area was the heart of maritime mercantile activity in Gold Rush San Francisco. Commission merchants, active in the creation of the entrepôt and
its infrastructure, had been key partners in building Central Wharf and
in operating some of the most prominent waterfront warehouses and
storeships (like Cross, Hobson & Co.) as well as in beaching and converting the *Niantic* storeship, the city's first "permanently moored"
ship/building. Also active in civic politics, commission merchants dominated public life, including through merchant William Tell Coleman's
notable leadership of the committees of vigilance in 1851 and 1856 (Scherer 1939).

I have argued elsewhere that the rise of the commission merchants in
Gold Rush San Francisco stemmed from the haphazard and chaotic conditions that resulted when a glut of certain commodities created an influx of cargoes (Delgado 1990a:89). "The cost of storage being greater
than their actual or prospective value, they could be turned to no greater
use than fillage. Thus entire lines of sidewalks were constructed of expensive merchandise in bales and boxes" (Scherer 1939:81)

The glut of commodities was an inevitable consequence of the world
market's response to the Gold Rush. The commission merchants of San
Francisco, especially those already established in the city and those who
came in the first year of the rush, could not control the influx of ships
but could try to control the flows of commodities (Wallerstein 1980:238).
But their control was not absolute, nor could it be. Though merchants
could count on a regular influx of goods in response to market conditions advertised months earlier, they could not always foresee local fluctuations in the market. Moreover, the world system advanced by industrial Europe and the United States at times overwhelmed the local market
economy. The archaeological record reflects this fact not only through
the discovery of discarded or unsold commodities but also through the
study of the *Niantic* and *General Harrison* storeships. These vessels are
quintessential artifacts of Gold Rush San Francisco's waterfront, having
once enabled commission merchants to regulate the flow of commodities.

A key element of success for a commission merchant was to warehouse
goods as they came in, not only to stow them safely and arrange them
for sale, or to store them for consigners, but also to hold goods that were
perhaps too widely available until demand increased and drove up the

potential for profits. As we have seen, in a booming city like San Francisco with valuable real estate and expensive construction costs, storeships provided an expedient means of warehousing. Mickle & Co. initially owned a store with limited storage space in San Francisco, but in May 1850, the firm acquired *General Harrison* to warehouse goods consigned to its care until the partners could complete shipping arrangements or sell the goods at auction. This strategy was abetted by the company's modus operandi in which the partners not only sold goods on commission but also on their own account, in their case probably the goods shipped directly from their home port and headquarters, Valparaíso. The main office would purchase and ships goods to them in their own chartered vessels along with cargo for ships passing through with other goods consigned to the office in San Francisco. In short, like the successful forwarders and commission merchants of the trans-Mississippi frontier, Mickle and other commission merchants in California, acquainted with other markets and well supplied with goods, became merchandisers on their own account. They were able to play this role because of their business connections, their use of ships as freighters, and their use of ships as warehouses where goods were easily off-loaded, transshipped, stored, and sold.

THE CHILEAN CONNECTION

Mickle & Co.'s ultimate ownership of the storeship *General Harrison* and the record available through subsequent archaeological excavation make the firm an excellent focus for examining the development of the San Francisco entrepôt. In particular, the firm represents San Francisco's link to the earlier Pacific entrepôt of Valparaíso. Mickle & Co. was just one of several Chilean firms that carried on regular trade between Valparaíso and San Francisco during the Gold Rush. Chileans were among the first commercial interests to arrive in San Francisco and were key players in developing the port. Their activities predate the arrival of the majority of fortune seekers by several months. On December 1, 1848, Cross, Hobson & Cia. of Valparaíso, a merchant firm with long-standing maritime interests on the coast, advertised in Valparaíso's English-language newspaper, the *Neighbor,* that it had established in San Francisco and Valparaíso "houses for the transaction of commission business." The ad then noted that the firm and potential customers would benefit from the "many years experience of the several members of the firm in the trade of the Pacific." The company was soon joined in San Francisco by Mickle

& Co.; Alsop & Co.; Loring, Sartori & Co.; Waddington, Whitehead & Co.; Daniel Gibb & Co.; and A. Hemenway & Co, all Valparaíso commission merchants (Cornejo 1930:51–52).

Most of these Chilean firms were founded by commission merchants with long-standing family and business ties to the United States and Europe. Alejandro Cross and William Hobson, the first of Valparaíso's commission merchants to establish an office in San Francisco, had been residents of Chile since the late 1830s and were tied to Glasgow. William Hobson served as U.S. consul. Elishu Loring, member of a prominent New York and Connecticut banking family, arrived in the 1830s to work as a shipping agent. These agents were there partly because of a shipping-business strategy to send partners, relatives, or junior employees to establish a foreign office and handle the business at other ports "and thus keep all the profits and commissions under control" (Albion 1939:237). Although this practice ostensibly sought to expand the firms' business, and build a port, it also had the broader effect of expanding the world maritime system.

Valparaíso's mercantile houses played a significant role in the development of San Francisco's mercantile community, and Chile was one of Gold Rush San Francisco's major trading partners, establishing fortunes that outlived the Gold Rush. These merchants were described in May 1851 by Canadian argonaut and merchant William Perkins with a mixture of praise and condemnation: "Men of all classes have come from there; for Chile is not only a seaboard country, but its people are infinitely more enterprising than any other of the Spanish Republics of South America; and they have a very respectable marine. It has consequently been no difficult manner for Chilenos, of even the lower class, to make their way to California. The lower orders are sturdy miners, and the better classes, sharp merchants. The latter class is seldom seen at hard work, but have made large fortunes in commerce" (Morgan and Scobie 1964: 222). Valparaíso was the first foreign port to learn about the California gold discovery because of regular sailings to and from it to Yerba Buena, Monterey, and San Diego.

The Hobson-owned Chilean bark *J.R.S.* brought the first gold to Chile when she arrived at Valparaíso, and although the shipment was not cause for much comment in the press, among the city's merchants, it undoubtedly was. By the spring of 1848, the news had spread, and the initial sailings of Chileans for California had begun, along with shipments of some cargoes to serve the needs of California's market. The pace picked up in the fall of 1848: between September 12, 1848, and January 19,

1849, 511 to 736 Chileans (the statistic varies, the first number being a count of the official passports issued and the second being the unofficial tally of a waterfront shipping merchant) sailed to San Francisco in response to news of the gold discovery (*Neighbor*, January 29, 1849). The number would swell to the thousands within the next year, and Chilean historians later estimated that 30,000 Chileans made their way to California during the Gold Rush (Cornejo 1930).

By March 1849, the *Neighbor* reported:

> California affairs appear to absorb almost all interest and attention from other branches of business, and the greater part of our commercial activity . . . The tonnage of vessels sailed for that destination ascends to 3597 tons register, and mostly with full cargoes—and there are about 3000 tons on the beach loading. The gold imported within this month amounts to about half a million, and nearly an equal amount of specie arrived on the steamer. Our money market is overflowing for exportation . . . Our bay has been and is now covered with shipping from all parts (March 1, 1849).

By the early summer, the full impact of the rush to California was apparent in Valparaíso. "The opening of California has brought to the Pacific the presence of the United States . . . Chile is the country which has felt this contact most of all; her speculations have been aroused; her productions have found exportation, and their returns in gold have rapidly created fortunes" (*Neighbor*, June 29, 1849). This report no doubt caught the attention of Edward Mickle, a Valparaíso commission merchant in the firm of Mickle y Compañía.

Mickle was an American immigrant from Baltimore who had married the daughter of General Ramón Herrera Rodado (1799–1882), a veteran of South America's wars of independence from Spain. Mickle was active in maritime trade by the mid-1840s. His activities extended beyond local or regional boundaries. In August 1844, Denmark named Mickle its consul for Guayaquil (Ministerio de Relaciones Exteriores 2005). The posting aimed to promote and encourage trade between Denmark and Ecuador and is reflective of Europeans' interest in South American trade (which the Americans shared). In 1847, the Valparaíso newspapers mentioned Mickle as master of the Ecuadorian brig *Eduardo*. Sometime that year, he also went into business as a shipping agent and founded the trading firm of Mickle and Polhemus with Charles Polhemus, a twenty-nine-year-old native of Burlington County, Vermont, who had arrived in South America in February 1836. Polhemus left in 1848 to start his own firm and in 1849, sailed to San Francisco to represent the banking firm of Alsop & Co. Mickle's new partner was his father-in-law, General Herrera. As Mickle y Compañía, the partners traded out of Valparaíso, Guayaquil, and Panama. In 1848, the firm established a San Francisco office with Etting Mickle in charge. The precise nature of his relationship to the family is unknown.

MICKLE & CO.'S OPERATIONS, 1848–1850

Etting Mickle's San Francisco business partner was William H. Tillinghast, a twenty-five-year-old native of Pennsylvania and another Yankee who had settled in Valparaíso and now had come to California. Mickle apparently joined one of the first groups of Chileans to sail from Valparaíso to San Francisco in the summer of 1848, for by November, the firm was in business with the bark *Tasso* already bound for Valparaíso, having been dispatched from San Francisco in late September. On November 29, the *Neighbor* advertised that the *Tasso* would make a return voyage to San Francisco as soon as she took on more cargo. On December 5, the paper announced that *Tasso* had arrived at Valparaíso from San Francisco, via San Diego, sixty-six days out and with a cargo of "talloco and 3968 ounces gold."

On December 3, 1848, the *Neighbor* reported that Mickle y Cía had dispatched the clipper *Ann McKim* to San Francisco via Guayaquil. The clipper was part of a regular series of Mickle sailings. *Tasso* arrived two days later on the December 5, and on the 21st, the company dispatched the schooner brig *Progreso,* which sailed with a large cargo and passengers (*Neighbor,* December 5 and 21, 1848). The following month, Mickle y Cía dispatched the schooner *Dominga* with an assorted cargo to Guayaquil, maintaining its earlier maritime supply line with the Ecuadorian port. Throughout the firm's California enterprise, the cargoes shipped to and sold in San Francisco included Ecuadorian products as well as Peruvian, Chilean, and European goods (*Neighbor,* March 23, April 29, and June 29, 1849).

The *Daily Alta California* of January 25, 1849, announced that Mickle and Tillinghast "have this day established themselves in this place for the transaction of a general agency and commission business under the firm of E. Mickle & Co." Operating out of Sherman & Ruckle's warehouse at the corner of Clay and Montgomery streets, the partners advertised on February 8 that they had just received "a large and excellent assortment of Carre & Goods" from *Ann McKim,* just arrived from Valparaíso after a January 9 departure from Chile. The connection between Valparaíso and San Francisco was working well, with regular dispatches by a fleet of vessels contracted to or owned by Mickle. Through its control of the vessels, Mickle & Co. was able to avoid the problems of crew desertion and vessel layups that were already plaguing American ships arriving in San Francisco.

On February 13, the *Neighbor* reported that *Huntress* had arrived a week earlier, sixty days out of San Francisco, in ballast (empty) but carrying a consignment of $100,000 in "gold dust and grains for Mickle y Cía." Mickle quickly loaded *Huntress* and returned her to San Francisco; the ship cleared Valparaíso on March 19 with a cargo of "assorted goods" consigned to Mickle & Co. The next return from San Francisco, via *Ann McKim* on April 15, brought $80,000 in gold. Business was good in California; *Ann McKim* also brought news that prices were "still exorbitantly high," with lumber selling "as high as $350 and even $400 a thousand" (*Neighbor,* April 29, 1849).

As for Mickle & Co. in California, on March 22, 1849, the firm advertised in the *Alta* as "Importers and Commission Merchants" in both San Francisco and "Benicia City." On April 12, another advertisement touted the company's "new and superb goods," which were a "great attraction at Benicia" as *Tasso* and *Progreso,* "just arrived from Valparaíso" landed their cargoes. The firm advertised that "to accommodate purchasers from the interior, the most extensive arrangements have been made for the conveyance of goods from Benicia to Sacramento City, Stockton and other points, at one half the rate of freights now charged from San Francisco on goods destined for the same places."

Regular connection with Mickle y Cía in Valparaíso maintained the home office's fortunes and kept the San Francisco partners stocked with goods. Summarizing these shipments reveals a pattern in which Mickle & Co. imported little in the way of "luxuries" and instead focused on the commodities required by a growing city and by the camps in the hinterland: food, clothing, building supplies, hardware and equipment, coal, furniture, furnishings, and other domestic items such as blankets and soap (see table 1).

The only problem was keeping the supply line open. The demand for Chilean vessels to carry cargoes to San Francisco was great. On June 29, 1849, the *Neighbor* reported that the Gold Rush was overwhelming Valparaíso. "In one day passports for a hundred persons have been asked. Persons from the interior are continually coming to take passage. Every vessel that touches here from America has crowding applications. Ships are scarce for the demand. Freights have risen to 40 and even 45 dollars a ton, for this to San Francisco. It is calculated that about three thousands

TABLE I. COMMODITIES IMPORTED BY MICKLE & CO., 1849–1851

Food	Barley, beans, beef (mess), butter, candies, cheese, chocolate, coffee, currants, dried fruit, eggs, flour, fruitcake, ginger, hams, lard, macaroni, meal, molasses, olives, oranges, oysters, pickles, pork, potatoes, preserves, raisins, rice, sardines, sauces, sausages, spices, sugar, sweetmeats, syrup, tea, vinegar, walnuts
Alcohol	Ale, anisette, arrak, bitters, brandy, cherry brandy, champagne, claret, cognac, cordials, frontignan, gin, Hock, Madeira, marsala, port, porter, rum, sherry, stout, whiskey, wine
Hardware and equipment	Axes, bolts, brooms, brushes, canteens, carpenter's tools, copper, fire engines, furnaces, harness, hinges, iron (bar), knives, locks, oars, screws, stills, stoves, tin plates, tinware, wagons
Building supplies	Boiled oil, bricks, cement, iron houses, lumber, nails, paint, planks, rope, shingles, tacks, tents, white lead, window glass, wood houses, zinc
Miscellaneous	Beads, cigars, coal, combs, hay, launches, medicine, paper, powder, tobacco
Clothing and footwear	Bluchers, boots (gaiter and winter), brogans, domestics, drawers, fabric, flannels, handkerchiefs, sashes, shoes, silks, shawls, shirts (cotton), straw hats, undershirts
Domestic Items	Baskets, bedsteads, blankets, books, bookcases, boxes, candles, carpeting, ceramics, chairs, couches, curtains, cutlery, earthenware, glasses, hangings, lamps, lacquerware, matting, mattresses, oilcloth, piano, pictures, prints, settees, side tables, soap, straw mats, tables, trunks, tumblers

SOURCE: *San Francisco Daily Alta California.*

and five hundred [persons] have sailed from this port alone." The conditions and the need to keep the San Francisco partners supplied led the firm to send some goods via foreign vessels bound for San Francisco that had stopped in Valparaíso for rest, provisions, or repairs, as well as to sign on as agents to sell the rest of that vessel's cargo, on consignment, once it arrived in California.

One example of such an arrangement was Mickle & Co.'s work with the ship *Montreal* in August 1849. Owned by Henry Peirce and James Hunnewell, *Montreal* was a veteran of Pacific and China trade, now sent to California by her owners to participate in the Gold Rush. Two receipts in the papers of Josiah Belden, from an auction on August 8, show that Belden bought three dozen "silk hose" and one dozen "straw hats," as well as a crate containing thirty-three muslin dresses at $4.25 each, for a total of $140.25, all of these goods presumably from *Montreal*'s cargo (Belden 1849).

By that time, Mickle & Co. had relocated from Sherman & Ruckle's warehouse to its own building on the Clay Street wharf. The waterfront location was choice, as shown by the company's *Alta* advertisement selling a lot with "a large and commodious store, with a good dwelling house in the rear" on Kearny Street near the corner of Sacramento. Though this lot was a good piece of property, it had less value to the partners than their lot on the wharf. There, at the water's edge, in a rapidly developing commercial district of wharves, warehouses, and auction houses, they were in the thick of the action and the potential for profit. The Kearny lot, farther up the street and closer to the plaza, did not provide the same opportunity.

The partners remained busy. On August 23, they advertised goods from *Ann McKim, Norman, Connecticut, Ocean,* and *Montreal,* as well as "other vessels," in one of a series of regular advertisements in the *Alta.* On September 13, they advertised in Spanish that the Chilean bark *Carmen* would sail for Valparaíso and Talcahuano in two days. On November 1, they advertised the sale of "sawed pine lumber" from the British bark *Ennerdale,* from Auckland, New Zealand. Five weeks later, they advertised passage and freight on *Ennerdale,* now bound for Callao. On November 8, they offered for sale fresh flour and barley "just arrived" from Valparaíso in *Bingham* and *Ann Smith,* as well as dry goods, clothing, food, "scales and weights, 1,500 canteens, 20 large tents . . . also 2 excellent frame houses, complete, size 25x35 and 15x35 feet" from the *Francis Ann,* just arrived "from Boston and Valparaíso." On December 6, they advertised sugar, lumber, and barley from four vessels just arrived from Buenos Aires and Talcahuano. They also advertised the impending sailing of *Ennerdale* for Callao. Despite their Chilean connection to the parent company, the partners also handled ships bound for other ports; on November 15, they advertised freight and passage on the Dutch bark *Drie Gebroeders,* bound for Hong Kong and Manila.

The ship *Probus,* which arrived on December 9 from New York and Valparaíso, brought Mickle & Co. a cargo of prefabricated iron houses, stoves, furnaces, tinware and lumber, which the firm advertised for sale on December 15. On December 24, an advertisement offered "passage or freight" in the British bark *St. George,* bound for Valparaíso. On January 7, 1850, the partners advertised passage to Valparaíso on the Chilean bark *Fanny,* "100 tons dead weight, freight free." January was a busy month for the firm; on January 28, the partners ran five advertisements for goods, and the next day they informed the *Alta*'s readers that they "wanted to purchase" a fast sailing schooner or brigantine even as they advertised someone else's ship, in this case the bark *E. H. Chapin,* for "freight or charter." On February 18, they advertised their dispatch of the bark *Hamburg* "for freight, (merchandise or treasure) or passage."

The ship *General Harrison,* 185 days from Boston, and 58 days out of Valparaíso arrived on February 4 (*Alta,* February 5, 1849). This ship, its cargo consigned to Mickle & Co., represented a turning point in the company's affairs. Nearly three weeks passed before Mickle & Co., which had taken on the ship's cargo on commission, could begin landing *General Harrison*'s cargo. On February 23, the firm advertised the sale of the ship's cargo in the *Alta,* along with cargo from the Chilean ship *Carolina,* just in from Valparaíso, and the cargo of the *Nathaniel Hooper,* just in from New York.

Mickle & Co. also advertised the sale of *General Harrison:* "500 tons, well found and in complete order" (*Alta,* February 23, 1850). The market was not good for ship sales at that time, however. An advertisement for the storeship *Georgian,* moored off the foot of Jackson Street, praised that vessel's 450 tons of storage capacity and "excellent accommodations for a large number of persons" but noted the owners were willing to sell the ship on terms of "half cash, and the balance at 60 days" (*Alta,* January 31, 1850). On these terms, the ship did sell, and it remained in business as a storeship through the May 4, 1851, fire.

Mickle & Co.'s regular advertisements in the *Alta* provide a sense of the goods that moved in and out of *General Harrison* after her conversion (see the summary in appendix 3). The first cargo to be landed, stowed in the storeship, and then sold was probably the goods from the ship

Pacific, which had arrived from Valparaíso. The goods had been off-loaded by August 7, when Mickle & Co. advertised *Pacific*'s return voyage to Valparaíso. The partners then offered goods from *Sir George Pollock,* a July 31 arrival from Hong Kong with "silks, satins, crepe shawls, superior sweetmeats, trunks and teas." They repeated and augmented the ad on August 16: "white embroidered crape shawls, col'd d[itt]o, assorted damask d[itt]o, d[itt]o scarfs, crimson cord sashes, silks, satins and saranets of ass'd colors and styles, figured camlet, check'd and satin gauzes, black silk and satin hdkfs, figured and checked d[itt]o, black Levantine d[itt]o, preserved ginger, oranges, & c. teas, superior, in 5 and 10 lbs. caddies. Also, an assortment of lacquered ware, table and hanging solar lamps."

The auction attracted the positive attention of the editors of the *Alta,* always eager to promote the business of the town and the larger goal of transpacific trade with Asia. On May 16, an *Alta* story had noted, "The rage for China Goods seems to be on the increase . . . the avidity with which these curiosities are brought up on the occasion of public sales, has given an impetus to this particular trade." On the auction of *Sir George Pollock*'s cargo, an August 5 story in the *Alta* said, "The sale of Chinese goods, at the warehouse of E. Mickle & Co., Clay street wharf, deserves the attention of all desirous of purchasing this description of goods. The assortment has been well selected, and comprises some of the richest descriptions ever imported into this market. The sale will commence at ten o'clock this morning."

Auction sales were generally monthly. On September 19, the firm offered goods that were not identified with specific ships and were apparently unsold merchandise from *Pacific, Sir George Pollock,* and perhaps even earlier arrivals. Though unsold goods occupied space that might otherwise be rented out, having a storeship nonetheless enabled Mickle & Co. to hold goods and sell them later if the market and the prices were not right when a ship arrived with a cargo consigned to the firm.

Space was still at a premium, and Mickle & Co. did not want to pack *General Harrison* full of unsold or stored goods. When an economic downturn hit the city in September and continued through the fall, one bank, Naglee & Company, closed after a run on it (Soulé, Gihon, and Nisbet 1855:289). The extension of credit for unproductive property included credit for merchandise—a "glut of goods . . . coming in faster than it could be sold except at a loss," held in warehouses and storeships on credit in a cash-strapped market (Johnson 1964:41).

Not surprisingly, therefore, on September 21, Mickle & Co. advertised in the *Alta* to tell consignees of the ship *John Marshall,* "The ship is ready to discharge her cargo, and they [consignees] are requested to call at our office, pay the freight, and receive orders for their goods without delay." Mickle & Co. advertised the cargo of *John Marshall* again on September 29 and October 5 and 7. Mickle's ad exhorted consignees of some of the goods on *John Marshall*—namely, lumber and shingles shipped for Smith & Bennett and lumber, shingles, and boxes shipped to John A. Sheaf—to pay for them before the firm had to sell them at auction for freight and charges.

On October 20, in one of several *Alta* ads that aimed to clear unsold merchandise, Mickle & Co. announced a variety of goods "per late arrivals." The push to sell those items may have come from knowledge of the impending arrival of the bark *Equator,* a regular sailer from Valparaíso, which came in a week later. A month after *Equator*'s arrival, on November 25, Mickle advertised goods, "which will be sold low to close invoice," from the recently arrived three-masted schooner *Spray* from Paita, Peru, and the ship *Powhattan* from Baltimore. These cargoes included the usual assortment of goods from South and Central America such as 360 bags of Chile beans (modern "chili beans" owe their name to the predominantly Chilean origin of these nineteenth-century exports; people named products to reflect their point of origin) and four cases of straw hats—but also a variety of cigars and wines and liquor. On December 9, the firm advertised even more "segars" and tobacco, "just received, per *Baltic,*" and on the 19th, more goods from Valparaíso landed by *Justine.* At the end of the year, the partners advertised for freight or charter the ship *Lady Amherst,* a November 19 arrival from London via the Falklands that had sailed into town with 50 coffins, 40 casks of porter, 3 iron houses, 2 wooden houses, 27,000 bricks, 1,000 casks of ale, and 40 bales of dry goods.

The town and its businesses quickly recovered from the slight depression of the fall. By year-end 1850, the owners of Mickle & Co. were listed among the millionaires of San Francisco based on their city taxes. Paying $750, Mickle & Co. was in the middle ranks of the city's "wealthiest portion" (*Alta,* December 14, 1850). In the new year, though, Tillinghast left the firm to begin a new career as a banker. On January 3, Mickle announced in the *Alta* that "the term of co-partnership of the firm of E. Mickle & Co., commission merchants, having expired this day, Mr. Wm. H. Tillinghast has retired from said firm, and J. M. de Satrustegui has joined the new co-partnership, commencing from this date.

The business of the house will be conducted as hitherto, and under the same style, San Francisco, Jan. 1, 1851."

The new year of 1851 also started with an advertisement that Mickle & Co. had "just received an invoice of China goods" (*Alta*, January 1, 1851). On January 10, Mickle advertised goods from two arrivals: the *Oscar* from China and the brig *Erato* from Callao. Mickle was not alone in selling goods from *Oscar*. Commission merchants Macondray & Co. advertised three types of tea, whereas Mickle advertised a larger and more diverse sale of coffee, tea, eggs, pork, "Manila segars," furniture, rope, oars, oilcloth table covers, matting, silks and satins, rice, molasses, wine, spices, preserves, Collins's axes, trunks, and gunny bags. The goods from *Erato* were the usual shipments of sherry, cognac, Chile flour, chocolate and sugar, as well as "looking glasses, undershirts, drawers, hose, towels, oilcloths, segar paper, hock &c &c" (*Alta*, January 10, 1851).

On February 8, Mickle & Co. advertised a variety of goods in the *Alta* without citing a specific ship's cargo. Though some of the items were leftovers from the recently arrived *Oscar*'s cargo, such as "China goods, furniture & c." and "20 casks Tennent's draught ale," the rest of the list follows a pattern that recurred throughout the company's ads, reflecting the typical makeup of the firm's regular shipments from South America. While Mickle was handling and selling cargoes taken on consignment for absent owners, the firm was also relaying orders to Valparaíso for regular shipments of goods that were popular in San Francisco, like the alcohol, tobacco, and food staples advertised on the 8th: port wine in casks, sherry, "superior wine in cases," "spirits in demijohns," "Havana and Esmerelda segars," and "Peruvian and Chile chocolate." Another indication of the firm's regular connections to Valparaíso was an advertisement in the February 10 and March 1 editions of the *Alta*, announcing that the ship *Pacific*, which had previously arrived in 1850, had returned from another voyage, to Valparaíso, and "consignees of cargo are requested to call without delay at the office of the undersigned, pay freight, and receive orders for their goods."

March was a busy month for the firm. On March 7, the partners joined Daniel Gibb in selling goods from the brig *Huntress,* just arrived from Valparaíso. They were not the agents for the brig, however, and handled only a portion of the cargo. On March 25, another commission merchant, Sage & Smith, advertised in the *Alta* that *Huntress* was ready to discharge cargo and invited consignees to call, pay freight, and "get an order for delivery."

Mickle & Co. ran a similar advertisement the same day for the ship *Emily,* just arrived from Valparaíso, and on the following day advertised that another vessel in its care, the schooner *Holder Borden,* was ready to discharge. The *Alta* reported that the schooner was sixty days from Valparaíso and had a cargo of 50 barrels of mess beef, 356 kegs of lard, 40 barrels of rum, 1,119 bags of Brazil sugar, and 690 bags of flour. On March 29, Mickle advertised the sale of the mess beef and 63 bales of Virginia tobacco, apparently all that were left of the 100 bales brought in by *Huntress.* The firm also offered "dried fruits and potatoes, Claret in cases, and a variety of desirable goods."

On April 5, Mickle advertised the availability of goods from the brig *Jackin,* which had arrived on April 3, 130 days from Sundsvall, Sweden, via Valparaíso (53 days out) under the command of Captain Lidquist. An *Alta* report on the ship's arrival described the cargo as "21,200 lbs bolt iron, 16,000 bricks, 2 kegs cognac, rope, wine, flour, sherry, straw mats and barley." Mickle's advertisement on April 5, even before the cargo was unloaded, was more specific: "21,000 lbs. Swedish bolt iron, from ½" to 1"; 16,000 bricks; 33 doz Arrak punch; 100 doz 3 inch planks, boat spars, spare timber; 80 cases sherry wine; 50 cases Paxarere (sweet sherry;) 25 cases Frontignan; 100 kegs sherry wine; 9 gals ea; 300 half sacks flour; 187 bags beans, 49 bags barley &c &c." The cargo of *Jackin* was the last to be off-loaded into *General Harrison.* The fire of May 4, 1851, destroyed the storeship.

Mickle & Co. remained in business after the fire. On May 6, the partners advertised in the *Alta* that they would "commence business in a few days upon their Clay street property; until a building can be run up, they will be found at Edmund Scott's, Dupont st, near Sacramento st." The next day, they advertised "100 doz. Straw mats, good for bedding; 275 hf bags Chile flour; 44 cases sherry wine; 25 cases sweet wine; 25 casks sherry wine; 33 doz arrak punch; 18,000 lbs. round Swedish bolt iron; 600 lbs copper bolts; 18,000 segars, Panama hats, &c." Some of the items offered for sale were from *Jackin*'s cargo, which survived the fire, perhaps because not all of the cargo had been off-loaded into *General Harrison* at the time of the fire.

On May 24, an advertisement in the *Alta* announced, "E. Mickle & Co. have rebuilt their house on Clay st. wharf and resumed business. They offer for sale—iron, Panama hats, domestics, drills, carpeting, Havana segars, first quality; port and sherry in casks, champagne, cherry cordial, lard, flour &c. &c." The partners worked hard to get the business back on its feet. Just a few days earlier, on May 20, the firm had advertised the impending departure "For Hong Kong—To sail on the 24th May, the new Swedish clipper brig JACKIN, 260 tons. For Freight or Passage apply to E. Mickle & Co." The loss of *General Harrison* was a major blow to the fortunes of E. Mickle & Co. The firm remained close to its original location, listed at 144 Clay in Parker's 1852–53 directory and at 146 Clay in A. W. Morgan & Co.'s 1852 directory. However, the firm is not listed in city directories. thereafter. The firm may have overcapitalized with the purchase of a water lot and the purchase and modification of *General Harrison* into a storeship. Although the influx of funds to the company was substantial, as reflected by the recorded remittances of gold to the parent office in Valparaíso, Mickle & Co. apparently did not have the means or the desire to capitalize a new warehouse on the San Francisco waterfront.

Etting Mickle retained property in nearby Benicia, which he did not liquidate until the mid-1850s, and Edward Mickle emigrated to San Francisco. Edward remained active in local affairs and was an officer in San Francisco's Spring Valley Water Works until his death in 1865. The Mickles did not go bankrupt, but they dropped out of the commission-merchant business. Nonetheless, the career of E. Mickle & Co., as reconstructed through the firm's newspaper advertisements, offers a detailed example of commodity flow and the way in which the maritime system worked through commission merchants to create the entrepôt of San Francisco.

ANALYZING MICKLE & CO.'S BUSINESS

Mickle & Co. remained active as commission merchants in San Francisco for more than three years between September 1848 and early 1852. Its total profits are unknown, because no one has located the company's business records. However, the partners did well enough, by the end of 1850, to rank among the millionaires of San Francisco (*Alta*, December 14, 1850). The pattern of shipping and commodities offers another indication of their relative success and of the way in which they conducted their business. Beginning at the end of 1848, the firm dispatched at least two vessels between Valparaíso and San Francisco each month, on an alternating schedule.

For example, on December 5, 1848, the company's chartered bark *Tasso* arrived in Valparaíso, and on December 21, it sent the schooner *Progreso* to San Francisco. As *Progreso* sailed north, the company's brig *Huntress* was heading south for Valparaíso, having cleared San Francisco on December 13. Just before *Progreso*'s arrival, on January 9, 1849, Mickle dispatched the ship *Ann McKim* to San Francisco. Over the next two years, with the number gradually declining after mid-1850, Mickle advertised eleven vessels. Some, like *Huntress, Progreso, Virginia,* and *Tasso,* had multiple sailings, and *Ann McKim* sailed regularly through September 1851.

These regular sailings of company-owned or chartered vessels largely brought gold dust back to Chile and carried basic Chilean commodities like barley, butter, flour, beans, wine, and fresh and dried fruit to California—along with diverse goods that had come to Valparaíso from other Latin American countries, such as tobacco from Cuba and Ecuador, sugar from Brazil, coffee from Ecuador, chocolate from Peru, and straw hats from Panama and Ecuador. Also shipped on the company's vessels were items from Europe, Asia, and America that, like the Latin American goods, had probably initially come to Valparaíso because the port was the southern Pacific's most active entrepôt. This activity suggests that in response to regular communication from Mickle & Co. in San Francisco, Mickle y Cía in Valparaíso was diverting goods arriving from abroad to the local (California) market instead of transshipping them to other South American ports or to Australia or China.

The Mickle advertisements also suggest that the company extended its business beyond its own ships and its home port of Valparaíso to vessels from foreign ports. In these cases, as forwarding and commission merchants, the partners either handled the sale of the entire cargo or, as the ads indicate, handled a portion of a ship's cargo in tandem with other commission merchants. Mickle was not alone in advertising goods from some vessels, as we can see from its sharing of the *Oscar*'s cargo with Macondray & Co. and *Huntress*'s cargo with fellow Chilean commission merchant Daniel Gibb.

Between January 1849 and May 1851, a period of twenty-eight months, Mickle & Co. handled cargoes from twenty-three vessels from New York, Canton, Australia, Baltimore, and London. Only seven (33 percent) of these vessels sailed to San Francisco via Valparaíso, where Mickle y Cía loaded goods on them. This activity is probably indicative of Mickle's global connections. These vessels and their owners and masters had either made previous arrangements with Mickle or had negotiated deals in Valparaíso after their arrival. In one case, that of the Danish ship *Cecrops,* a prior arrangement may have been in place, given Edward Mickle's long-standing relationship with Denmark through his previous role in Ecuador as the Danish consul. The others may be the result of successful hustling on the Valparaíso waterfront, but the fact that the other fourteen vessels that Mickle advertised in San Francisco came directly from other ports, and yet were consigned to Mickle & Co., suggests that the world maritime system was at work through Mickle's global business relationships.

The commodities shipped in these vessels are also suggestive of Mickle's communication to foreign partners of market conditions and requirements. The booming community of San Francisco required building materials, so *Cecrops* arrived with 75,000 feet of pine boards and window glass; the British bark *Ennerdale,* from Auckland, New Zealand, brought "sawed pine lumber"; and *Probus* brought Mickle & Co. prefabricated iron houses, stoves, furnaces, tinware, and lumber. *John Marshall* brought, among other items, 50,000 shingles, 140 boxes of stoves, 50,000 bricks, and 130,000 feet of lumber. *Lady Amherst* brought 3 iron houses, 2 wooden houses, and 27,000 bricks. *General Harrison*, solely handled by Mickle, came to San Francisco with 250,000 feet of "superior planed and matched pine boards, of all sizes; 100,000 best shaved shingles; 10 two story frame houses, 20x20, complete; 1 do 18x28 do; 1 do 15x32 do; 75,000 bricks; 1500 fire bricks; 200 bbls. Extra cement, metallic paint, nails, carpenter's tools, boil'd oil, brushes, etc.," all for building; as well as "25 tons Lackawanna coal," a much-needed commodity, and "3 new and superior launches, well adapted to the river trade, with masts, sails and rigging complete," perfect and highly salable craft to work the trade between San Francisco and Sacramento.

These cargoes reflect an important aspect of Mickle's role in the San Francisco economy and highlight the impact of regional and global processes on the city's market economy. The global nature of the maritime system meant that cargoes from all over the world—Swedish steel, French and German wine, Spanish raisins, Belgian carpets, Peruvian chocolate, Cuban cigars, French tinned sardines, preserved eggs from China, spices from Indonesia—were being shipped from smaller ports like Sundsvall, Marseilles, Callao, Havana, Malaga, Antwerp, Nantes, and Canton to larger ports (entrepôts) like London and New York, and from there to Valparaíso and San Francisco. These goods were luxury items intended for the gold-glutted market of San Francisco, which was described by an outraged minister in 1855: "I have seen purer liquors, better segars, finer tobacco, truer guns and pistols, larger dirks and bowie knives and prettier courtesans here than in any other place I have ever visited; and it is my unbiased opinion that California can and does furnish the best bad things that are obtainable in America" (Helper 1855:68)

But this market entailed more than the pursuit of luxury goods arriving from foreign ports in response to the gold.

The Mickle advertisements reveal consistent shipments of commodities that aimed to serve the actual needs of the growing city and region rather than the gold-frenzied market of conspicuous consumers that many outsiders envisioned. Though traders shipped and sold items such as alcohol and cigars, the majority of shipments to Mickle were not luxury items but staples and basic commodities that spoke to the need for food, shelter, and clothing, as well as industry. A comparison of Mickle's advertised cargoes with other advertised cargoes between November 1850 and November 1851 shows, for example, thirty-two cargoes with barley and forty-four cargoes with bricks versus only four cargoes with perfume (Rasmussen 1966:360, 361, 372).

AGENTS OF THE WORLD SYSTEM

The industrialized world (system) created mass-produced goods—machine-cut nails, bricks, milled wood, steel tools, machinery, and even prefabricated houses and other buildings—and shipped them to build San Francisco. These goods, as well as the other bulk commodities required to feed the city, show up frequently in Mickle's advertisements. The regular shipments of beans, barley, coffee, butter, hams, and mess beef from Chile and other centers were, with alcohol, the mainstays of Mickle's shipments. The local economy could not and did not provide these items, so, like building materials, they had to be shipped from elsewhere. These shipments are the significant *événements* we can identify in Mickle's advertisements, and they support Wallerstein's observation that in flows of commodities, "in the long run, staples account for more of man's economic thrusts than luxuries" (1974:42). Mickle and his fellow commission merchants, as well as their consignees and partners around the world, recognized this fact and realized that the much-needed goods would sell for maximum profit.

The commission merchants of San Francisco established themselves on the waterfront at a critical junction, and from there they could control the flow of commodities. From this central point—where ships docked and goods were unloaded for transshipment to the interior and to the mines or for sale to the city's market—the merchants not only controlled the movement of commodities but also influenced market conditions, through warehousing in large facilities dockside such as piling-supported buildings or storeships.

With regular and relatively quick communication to an international network of other commission agents and partners in other ports, commission merchants in San Francisco could respond to the ebbs and flows of the city's and region's commerce. Mickle, for example, imported Indian trade beads in 1849 (*Alta,* April 5, 1849), which apparently did not sell and which the company never again imported or advertised. The probable remains of that unsold shipment of beads was excavated in 2001 from the *General Harrison* storeship, where it had been stowed two years after its arrival. The storeship was Mickle's way of handling unsalable merchandise and slow-moving goods.

Goods in high demand commanded high prices until the market was glutted, at which point their value dropped. This cycle occurred with flour and lumber on more than one occasion. Commission merchant Joshua Norton attempted to corner the market on rice but overcapitalized by borrowing and investing all he had in successive cargoes, which he stowed aboard his storeship (McGloin 1978:84). Norton was ruined when several cargoes of rice arrived at once, saturating the market and driving down the price. Bankrupt and insane, he reemerged in public life as a publicly popular and tolerated beggar with delusions of grandeur, the self-styled "Norton I, Emperor of the United States and Protector of Mexico," until his death in 1880.

Not every commission merchant gambled or overextended to Norton's extent. But others did risk losing their heavy investments in one of the city's frequent fires, especially if they stashed all their inventories, including goods belonging to others, in one locale. After two and half years of success, Mickle & Co. was finally caught in this trap, as were others. But while individual merchants faltered, failed, and withdrew, others thrived. Investing their profits in more shipborne cargoes, but also in real estate and more permanent infrastructure, they continued to capitalize San Francisco as an entrepôt and growing urban center. Their contributions not only enhanced the city but also fueled the world system's expansion into the Pacific. The outward flow of gold and the inward flow of the industrialized output of the eastern United States and Europe integrated San Francisco into the world system, first as a semiperipheral zone and then as part of the core.

By the late nineteenth century, San Francisco was a principal player in integrating the broader Pacific as a peripheral zone, importing resources such as copra, rubber, oil, and the goods of the China trade from across the Pacific. From San Francisco, these goods headed to the east by rail or to Europe by ships. This integration of the city and expansion of the

role of the Pacific were the legacies of the Gold Rush commission merchants. Despite individual travails, the merchants persisted as a cohesive
force, overcoming risks and occasional disasters, such as fires, to develop
a permanent base for trade. In time, this trade would control more than
the flow of commodities in and out of California's gold mines, towns,
and cities, eventually governing the flow of commodities throughout the
Pacific Rim.

Opium hulks at Shanghai, late nineteenth century. The British and American hulks in China were templates for San Francisco's storeships. (Author's collection.)

Long Wharf, the maritime heart of San Francisco's waterfront, 1850. (Courtesy of San Francisco Maritime National Historical Park, A11,16,350n.)

Niantic and *Apollo* on the waterfront, spring of 1850. (Courtesy of San Francisco Maritime National Historical Park, A11.15,693n.)

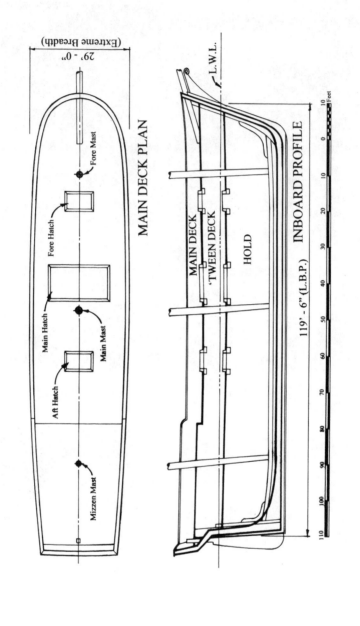

(Extreme Breadth)

29' - 0"

Fore Mast

Fore Hatch

Main Hatch

Aft Hatch

Main Mast

Mizzen Mast

MAIN DECK PLAN

L.W.L.

MAIN DECK

'TWEEN DECK

HOLD

119' - 6" (L.B.P.)   INBOARD PROFILE

110   100   90   80   70   60   50   40   30   20   10   0   10   Feet

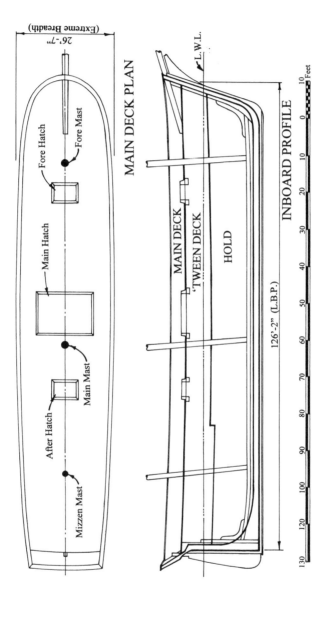

(Extreme Breadth)
26'-7"

Fore Mast
Fore Hatch

Main Hatch

Main Mast
After Hatch

Mizzen Mast

MAIN DECK PLAN

L.W.L.

MAIN DECK
'TWEEN DECK
HOLD

126'-2" (L.B.P.)

INBOARD PROFILE

130 120 100 90 80 70 60 50 40 30 20 10 0 10 Feet

Profile views of *Niantic* as built, 1835, and *General Harrison* as built, 1840. (John W. McKay.)

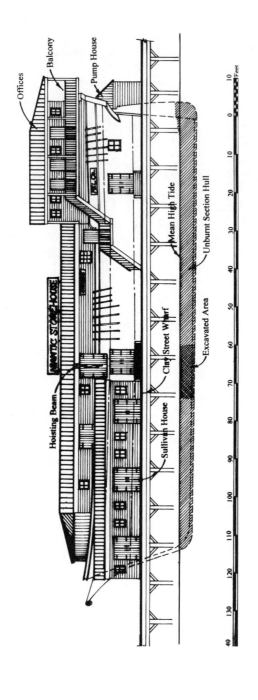

Profile view of *Niantic* as a storeship, 1850. (John W. McKay.)

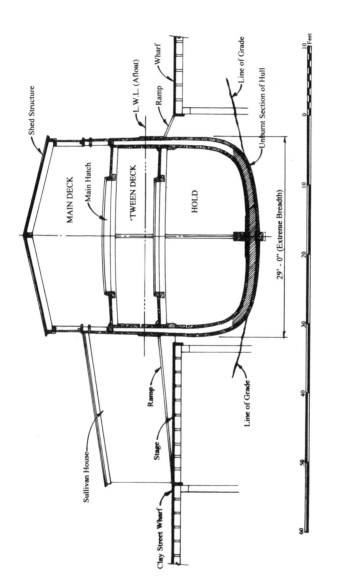

Midship section, the *Niantic* storeship. (John W. McKay.)

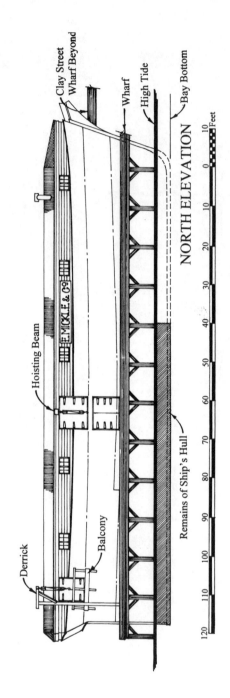

Derrick

Balcony

Hoisting Beam

E. MICKLE & C°

Clay Street
Wharf Beyond

Wharf

High Tide

Bay Bottom

Remains of Ship's Hull

NORTH ELEVATION

120 110 100 90 80 70 60 50 40 30 20 10 0 10

Feet

Profile view of *General Harrison* as a storeship, 1850. (John W. McKay.)

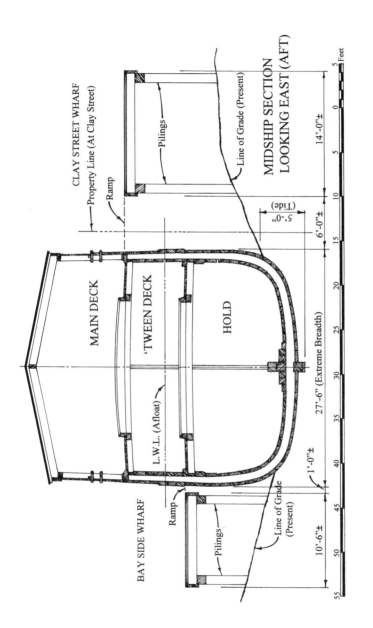

Midship section, the *General Harrison* storeship. (John W. McKay.)

The "Forest of Masts" panorama of the Gold Rush waterfront, December 1850 or early January 1851. *Niantic, Apollo,* and *General Harrison,* along with Hoff's Store and the buildings at the 343 Sansome site, are all visible. (Courtesy of the Bancroft Library, Zelda McKay Collection.)

(Detail) *Niantic* and *General Harrison,* from the "Forest of Masts" panorama. The circle on the left is *General Harrison;* the circle on the right is *Niantic.*

(Detail) *Apollo* (lower circle) and Hoff's Store (upper circle), from the "Forest of Masts" panorama.

(Detail) The storeship *Georgian* (circled), a typical floating depot on the waterfront, with her yards cockbilled on the masts, from the "Forest of Masts" panorama.

The San Francisco waterfront, 1851, from the U.S. Coast and Geodetic Survey chart.

The fire of May 4, 1851, from Soulé, Gihon, and Nisbet, *The Annals of San Francisco*. (Author's collection.)

Gold Rush ships about to be scrapped at Rincon Point, 1853, showing former storeships and a representative bark, possibly the 1849 arrival *Harvest*. (Courtesy of San Francisco Maritime National Historical Park, A11.4,528.03n.)

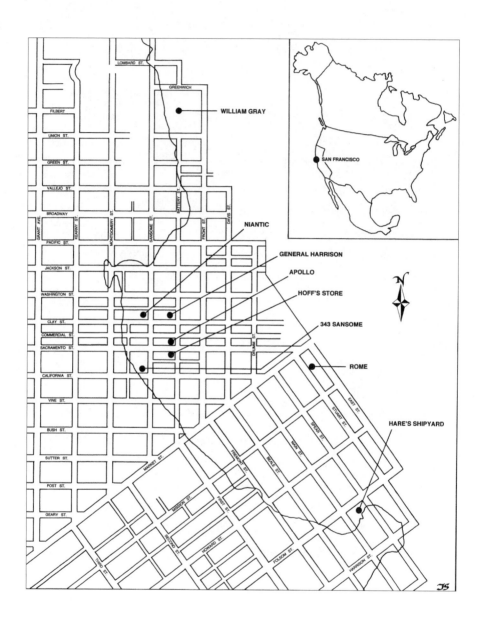

LOMBARD ST.

GREENWICH

FILBERT

WILLIAM GRAY

UNION ST.

GREEN ST.

VALLEJO ST.

BROADWAY

GRANT AVE.
KEARNY ST.
MONTGOMERY ST.
SANSOME ST.
BATTERY ST.
FRONT ST.
DAVIS ST.

PACIFIC ST.

NIANTIC

JACKSON ST.

GENERAL HARRISON

WASHINGTON ST.

APOLLO

HOFF'S STORE

CLAY ST.

COMMERCIAL ST.

343 SANSOME

SACRAMENTO ST.

DRUMM ST.

CALIFORNIA ST.

ROME

VINE ST.

BUSH ST.

EAST ST.
STUART ST.
SPEAR ST.

HARE'S SHIPYARD

SUTTER ST.

MAIN ST.

MARKET ST.

POST ST.

FREMONT ST.
BEALE ST.

GEARY ST.

MISSION ST.
FIRST ST.

THIRD ST.
SECOND ST.
HOWARD ST.

FOLSOM ST.

HARRISON ST.

SAN FRANCISCO

N

JS

Locations of excavation sites on the San Francisco waterfront. (Jack Scott.)

Construction workers hacking at the exposed remains of the *Apollo* storeship, 1921. (California Historical Society, FN-22384.)

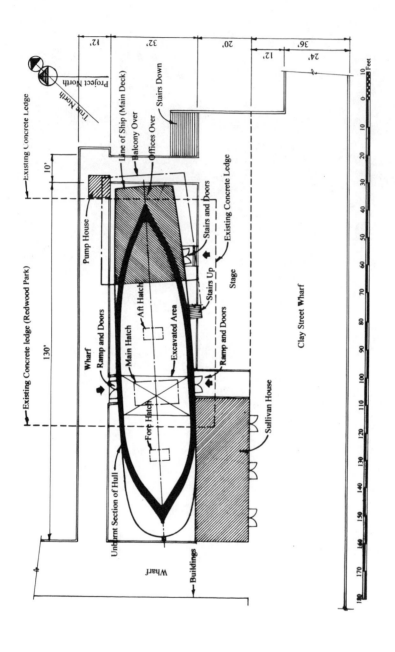

Conjectural site plan of the *Niantic* excavation, 1978. (John W. McKay.)

Aerial view of *Niantic*'s exposed hull, May 1978. (Courtesy of U.S. National Park Service.)

Niantic's stern lying in at the bottom of the excavation at 505 Sansome, 1978. (Courtesy of U.S. National Park Service.)

Volunteers racing against the clock to excavate *Niantic*'s midship area, 1978. (Courtesy of U.S. National Park Service.)

The Hoff's Store site, January 1986. (Photograph by author.)

Unit 3N, Hoff's Store, showing barrels of salt pork, round-point shovels, and tin-plated wares, January 1986. (Photograph by author.)

Artifacts from the Hoff's Store site: imported olives, boxed snuff tins, match-books, imported mustard, patent medicines, and butter-filled ceramic crocks. (Photograph by Jerre Kosta, Archeo-Tec.)

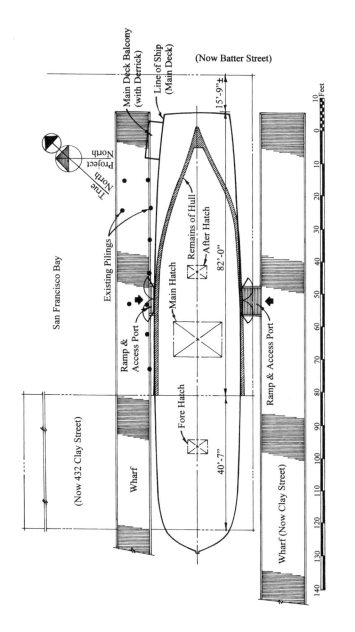

Conjectural site plan of the *General Harrison* excavation, 2001. (John W. McKay.)

View from the stern of *General Harrison* during excavation, September 2001.
(Photograph by author.)

Partially burned, empty cask from the stern area of *General Harrison*. (Photograph by author.)

The excavation and documentation of *General Harrison*'s hull. (Photograph by author.)

An intact crate of white wine from the redeposited, partially burned contents of the *General Harrison* storeship. (Photograph by author.)

Alcoholic beverage bottles from the *General Harrison* site, with their contents. (Photograph by Eros Hoagland, Archeo-Tec.)

The Archaeology of Gold Rush San Francisco's Waterfront

A historical overview of the development of historical archaeology in San Francisco—specifically the sites associated with the city's maritime origins and buried waterfront—is critical to understanding the impacts of ongoing urban development and showing the potential for archaeology. The rapid pace of change and the massive amount of physical redevelopment of Yerba Buena into San Francisco completely erased most traces of the Gold Rush city. Several catastrophic fires, as well as the dumping of 22 million cubic yards of landfill (Dow 1973:47–48) to create a new waterfront over the burnt remains of the city's first working port, left a massive archaeological assemblage beneath the downtown core. Subsequent urban development has both filtered (with the removal of some material culture) and scrambled this assemblage. Although these activities have damaged and diminished the archaeological record, they have also illustrated the research potential of the assemblage, thereby inspiring the passage of protective legislation and spurring efforts to mitigate the archaeological damage.

The earliest recorded adverse impacts were in the last quarter of the nineteenth century with the unearthing of the remains of the storeship *Niantic* by construction workers. Burned in the May 4, 1851 fire, *Niantic* yielded some of the cargo stowed in the hold when first dug into in 1872 and again in 1907 (Bullen 1979; Delgado 1979; Smith 1981). The storeship *Apollo,* also burned in the fire, was exposed and haphazardly cleared out in 1901, 1921, and 1925 (Delgado 1986). No one un-

TABLE 2. GOLD RUSH SITES EXCAVATED ON THE
SAN FRANCISCO WATERFRONT, 1872–2006

Site Name	Date(s) of Excavation	Percent of Site Excavated	References
Niantic storeship	1872, 1907, 1978	68	Smith 1981
William Gray (hulk)	1980	5	Pastron and Prichett 1979
Hoff's Store	1986	100	Pastron and Hattori 1990
Hare shipbreaking yard	1988, 2005	75	Pastron and Delgado 1990; William Self Associates 2006
343 Sansome	1989	50	Dames and Moore 1989
Rome (hulk)	1994	15	William Self Associates 1996
General Harrison	2001	70	Delgado, Pastron, and Robichaud 2007

SOURCE: *San Francisco Daily Alta California.*

earthed any other major site affected by the May 4 fire until urban re-
newal and major construction projects began in the 1960s. By this time,
the damage to the buried waterfront was substantial.

Beginning in 1978, a series of exposures and excavations of sites coincided with the passage of protective laws and the development of historical archaeology on the old waterfront (see table 2). This work, which I
summarize subsequently, has yielded a more comprehensive understanding of the Gold Rush waterfront.

UNEARTHING OF *NIANTIC* AND
OTHER BURIED SHIPS, 1872–1900

Even during the height of the Gold Rush, the citizens of San Francisco
were aware that the rapid pace of growth, landfilling, and the numerous
conflagrations were leaving an archaeological record beneath the city's
streets

> At some future period, when the site of San Francisco *may be* explored
> by a generation ignorant of its history, it will take its place by the side of
> Herculaneum and Pompeii, and furnish many valuable relics to perplex
> the prying Antiquarian. Buried in the streets, from six to ten feet beneath
> the surface, there is already a stratum of artificial productions which the
> entombed cities of Italy cannot exhibit. Knives, forks, spoons, chisels, files,
> and hardware of every description, gathered from the places of several con-
> flagrations. Masses of nails exhibiting *volcanic* indications, stove plates

and tin ware, empty bottles by the cart-load and hundreds of other misc-
ellanies, lie quietly and deeply interred in Sacramento street, and perhaps
will be carefully exhumed in days to come, and be distributed over the
world as precious relics! (*San Francisco Evening Picayune*, September 30,
1850).

Forty-niner Howard C. Gardiner (1970:116), referring to the burning
and burial of *Niantic* remarked, "It may be that long years hence, when
the early history of San Francisco shall be forgotten, some future gener-
ation shall unearth her timbers and the archaeologists vainly endeavor
to form a reasonable hypothesis to account for their presence."

In August 1872, demolition of the Niantic Hotel at the corner of Clay
and Sansome streets unearthed the hull of *Niantic*, which formed the foundation of the building (*San Francisco Daily Alta California*, August 2,
1872). San Franciscans T. A. Barry and B. A. Patten (1873) recalled in *Men
and Memories of San Francisco in the Spring of 1850* that the demolition
uncovered the lower hull of the ship and thirty-five "baskets of champagne," identified as Jacquesson et Fils, "a superior wine, very popular
in California." When excavated, the champagne effervesced "slightly on
uncorking, and was of very fair flavor" (Barry and Patten 1878:135–136).
Champagne tasting at an end, construction soon buried *Niantic* again.

In May 1882, the *Alta* offered a three-part reminiscence of "the Pioneer Storeships," and the "Old Hulks and Storeships" in response to a
recent unearthing. Among the vessels remembered was the "Old Ship"
Arkansas. Partly broken up and then "scuttled and sunk . . . if we mis-
take not, the quarterdeck and other portions of her are still there" The
Alta story then mentioned, "A brig on the corner of Battery and California streets was closed in, and our new-comers will be astonished on
passing over that spot to reflect that there is A VESSEL BURIED BENEATH
THEM" (May 22, 1882).

The *Alta* also reported on the fate of other old ships, explaining that
the ship *Globe* had been scuttled with the hull resting beneath Davis Street
and that another ship, whose name was not known, lay to the west of
Globe. Beneath the southeast corner of Battery and Green streets lay a
brig on whose deck the Bay Hotel had been built. Landfilling had
trapped and then buried the brig (May 22, 1882). A week later, at the
series' conclusion on May 29, the *Alta* also mentioned the buried *Al-
mandralina* at the corner of Pacific and Front streets, the landfilled hulk
of *Elmira* at the corner of Pacific and Davis streets, and *Inez*, an old New
Bedford whaler sunk and then filled over on Drumm Street.

In 1886, historian Hubert Howe Bancroft, in his seven-volume his-

tory of California, commented, "As late as Jan '57 old hulks still ob-
structed the harbor while others had been overtaken by the bayward
march of the city front and formed basements or cellars to tenements
built on their decks. Even now remains of the vessels are found under
the filled foundations of houses" (Bancroft 1888:168). A discovery in June
1890 bore out Bancroft's comment. Workers excavating along Pacific
Street, between Battery and Front streets, hit a buried hulk. "Even in its
decay sufficient of the wreck remains to give a fair idea of what it was
once like. Part of the main deck was exposed to view, as well as the
beams . . . A CHRONICLE reporter came across the queer old relic, and
after inspecting the worm-eaten timbers and the rusted and bent chain
bolts, set about to find out something of the identity and history of the
ancient craft" *(San Francisco Chronicle,* June 9, 1890).

The discovery set off a spate of letters to the editor in which old-timers
familiar with the forgotten vessel explained it was the "old ship"
Arkansas. The exposure of the buried ships along the former waterfront
inevitably inspired romantic recollections of the city's Gold Rush past,
even though the remains of the ships were cut up, hauled out, or reburied.

THE EARLY TWENTIETH-CENTURY UNEARTHING
OF *NIANTIC, APOLLO,* AND *GENERAL HARRISON*

The Niantic Building, completed in 1873, was badly damaged by the
earthquake of April 18, 1906. During redevelopment of the site in 1907,
construction again exposed the buried remains of *Niantic.* Just a few years
earlier, excavation for the foundation of a new building at the northwest
corner of Sacramento and Battery had revealed part of the hull of *Apollo*
(Wiren 1910). The next discovery came with a 1912 construction project,
during which workers encountered a ship that proved to be the storeship *General Harrison,* though details of the discovery are not available
and the buried vessel was at first misidentified as another ship *(San Francisco Bulletin,* May 10, 1912). The discovery of these buried ships, though
only briefly noted in the newspapers of the time and considered an anti-
quarian curiosity, was seen as a hindrance to progress and the construction of modern high-rises.

Perhaps the most illustrative case of this perception of the buried ships
as hindrances is the unearthing of the storeship *Apollo,* which had burned
and then been sepulchred in the May 1851 fire. The encounters with
Apollo's remains in 1901, 1907, 1921, and 1925 underscored the long-
standing view that discoveries were romantic encounters for pioneer rem-

iniscences and relic hunting. A *Chronicle* article on January 15, 1921, during the excavation looked back at the 1901 discovery of the ship during the installation of an elevator shaft in a building at Battery and Clay. At that time, "part of the old ship was cut away to permit the excavation of the shaft." The 1907 exposure of part of the hulk resulted in the recovery of "a large copper bolt" as well as "some oak lumber" from which souvenirs were made (Wiren 1910). *Apollo* was subsequently exposed in 1921 during excavation for the Federal Reserve Bank, which remains on the site. Workers encountered the bottom of the hull as well as the burned-off pilings from the wharves that once surrounded the ship. The *Chronicle* article on the 1921 excavation indicates that it rested 30 feet beneath street level and lay upright in the mud, bow pointing west. The records describe the hull as "much rotted, although the stem is in fair preservation."(January 15, 1921).

The *Chronicle* misidentified the hulk as *Euphemia,* San Francisco's Gold Rush jail, which had been moored next to *Apollo* in 1849 and 1850 but was later shifted to North Beach and ultimately hulked and buried there. The former prison brig appears as an outline on the 1853 Coast Survey map near North Point and appears in an 1856 published photo of the area taken by George Robinson Fardon (Fardon 1856:plate 18). Workers reportedly encountered *Euphemia*'s remains during construction in the early 1960s near Columbus and Bay streets, close to where historians Roger and Nancy Olmsted and archaeologist Allen Pastron suggested the ship might rest, on or about the line of Jones Street between Francisco and Bay (Olmsted, Olmsted, and Pastron 1977:609–610).

Notwithstanding the 1921 misidentification of the hulk of *Apollo* as *Euphemia,* the *Chronicle* reported, "From the size of the stem, some three or four feet of which remain intact, and the slope of her sides it is evident that she must have been eighty or ninety feet in length . . . A number of bronze spikes, once used to hold the timber of the hull, have been recovered from the mud. The spikes are about six inches long and in perfect preservation. A large copper spike, more than a foot in length and an inch and half through still held fast in the stem when the remains of the vessel were unearthed" (January 15, 1921).

In later years, *Chronicle* reporter William Martin Camp reminisced about the discovery and identification of the ship in 1921:

The new bank building needed an especially deep foundation, and the steam shovel had worked its way to a considerable depth when it hit a snag. Workmen tried every means of removing the obstacle before they discovered they were digging into the stem piece of a ship. They went to

work with pick and shovel and finally uncovered the entire keel and a considerable part of the planking and flooring of the ship. When the timber
was sawed up it was found to be as sweet and hard as the day it entered
the water . . . The discovery sent a thrill through the scores of idle watchers
who stood around the protective railing surrounding the excavation (Camp
1947:77).

Despite the construction and the hacking and sawing reported in 1921,
portions of *Apollo*'s hull and the Gold Rush material culture associated
with it remained beneath the Federal Reserve Bank.

In 1925, excavation for an underground garage behind the bank again
hit the hulk. On May 5, 1925, the *San Francisco Bulletin* reported, "A
treasure ship" of "the days of old that sailed during the craze for gold
in the days of '49 was unearthed . . . below the ground at Sacramento
and Sansome streets today." The excavation exposed *Apollo*'s rudder.
According to a May 5 report in the *Bulletin*, "Among the rotting timbers
were coins of 1840, an American penny of 1825, a British penny of 1797,
a large nugget, a sextant, ship's fittings and pieces that are a delight to
those rare things. The treasure is now in charge of Captain John P. Healy,
head of the Federal Reserve guard forces, who remembers when, several
years ago, huge beams believed to have belonged to this same ship were
unearthed when the bank foundation was being laid." Bank officials displayed these artifacts in a glass cabinet mounted atop a copper-clad section of the ship's sternpost, apparently cut free of the exposed hull in
1925. Also in the cabinet were souvenir wooden forks and spoons carved
from the ship's timbers by a bank officer. In 1980, when the bank relocated to another building, Federal Reserve officials donated these artifacts to the National Maritime Museum in San Francisco (Delgado 1986).

The *Apollo* assemblage, which is undoubtedly a very limited sample
of the items excavated in 1921 and 1925, now comprises twenty-eight
artifacts, some of which are on display at the museum. The artifacts include items from the ship's construction, navigational instruments, tools,
personal effects, and one culinary item. The construction-related items
are the small section of the copper-sheathed and fastened sternpost, two
fragments of copper drifts for fastening large timbers, four yellow metal
spikes, and five small boat nails. The navigational instruments comprise
one nearly intact sextant and two fragments of another sextant. The tools
are the metal bit of an auger, the wooden handles for two small awls,
and a pair of scissors.

The personal items recovered from *Apollo* include a small brass cross,
all that remains from what was apparently an ornate crucifix; a small

round brass box, perhaps for pills; and a small ceramic pipe bowl with the legend "—A—COGHILL" on one side and "GLASGOW" on the other. In addition, excavators found a partially melted American eagle brass-cap badge, possibly of Mexican War issue but too badly obscured to identify it conclusively. A single brass cup weight from a gold scale completes the small assemblage of personal items. The single culinary item, a burnt brass label for a box of sardines, has the surviving legend "J. COLIN A NANTES—SARDINES J COBO HUILE—RUE DES SAR-R-S NO. 9." This type of label originally adorned a tin containing sardines packed in oil.

This small group of artifacts offers a hint of a potentially diverse and rich archaeological site. Though they are unfortunately not an archaeologically documented assemblage and are the result of a very selective process of recovery, these items are the largest group of artifacts left from the chance exposures of the buried Gold Rush fleet that occurred before the 1970s.

FROM BOTTLE DIGS TO URBAN ARCHAEOLOGY, 1963–1977

Despite the 1948–49 commemoration of the Gold Rush centennial, Gold Rush discoveries and urban archaeology did not take place in San Francisco. However, commemoration and site development at state parks took place, specifically at Coloma, site of the January 1848 gold discovery (Heizer 1947; Neasham 1947; Fenenga 1967), Sutter's Fort in Sacramento (Gebhardt 1955a, 1955b; Olsen 1959a, 1959b, 1961; and Payen 1960, 1961), Old Sacramento (Landberg 1967; Praetzellis, Praetzellis, and Brown 1980; Schulz and Rivers 1980; Honeysett and Schulz 1990), and in the mining districts of the Mother Lode (Heizer 1948; Payen, Scott, and McEachern 1969; Ritter 1970). In the 1960s, San Francisco entered a period of urban redevelopment, undertaking several large projects such as the downtown excavation of the Bay Area Rapid Transit (BART) system and the Municipal Railway (MUNI) system and the demolition of many older structures to make way for high-rise hotels and offices such as the Golden Gateway, the Embarcadero Center complex, and the Transamerica Pyramid.

This redevelopment transformed the old downtown into the Financial District. The construction also provided a boom time for Bay Area bottle collectors. "Digging in downtown San Francisco was a bottle digger's, coin and relic hunter's dream come true in the mid 1960s though the late 1970s. The Great Bottle Rush got its start in the Golden Gateway Redevelopment project [which began around 1965] . . . The major excavations started in the areas of Drumm, Sacramento and Clay, Davis, Sansome, Front and Battery Streets" (Whited 2004).

As these construction projects transformed the physical landscape to create the Financial District, they unearthed considerable buried remains of the Gold Rush city, unfortunately without consistent archaeological control or documentation. In addition to uncovering the "relics," the 3.5 million-square-foot Golden Gateway excavation exposed a large number of burnt-off pilings in 1967 (Whited 2004). Had someone mapped the locations of the pilings, we would have a physical outline of the piling-supported streets and buildings of the waterfront destroyed in the May 1851 fire.

In 1963, San Francisco Maritime Museum librarian Albert Harmon, curator Harlan Soeten, and director Karl Kortum prepared a detailed map of downtown San Francisco that documented the historically cited locations of forty-two "Gold Rush Vessels Beached, Scuttled and Broken Up" and some of the major wharves. The museum's research indicated that as many as forty of the ships might still lie buried beneath the modern city. The Maritime Museum map, an excellent interpretive tool and the first comprehensive effort to identify the probable locations of the city's buried hulks, served as the basis for subsequent maps and provided a tool for predicting future exposures due to construction. Such predictions have not always been accurate, however. In 1967, much anticipation accompanied the extension of the BART tunnel along Market Street, but workers encountered no buried ship; excavation revealed only bottles and ceramics in landfill.

Excavations for the foundation of the Transamerica Pyramid at Clay and Montgomery streets in December 1969 reached 52 feet down into the old shoreline. Though workers found no ships, they encountered a broken spar from a ship and Gold Rush artifacts, and although no archaeologist was present, a sketch map and notes by a diligent local historian resulted in registration of the destroyed site in the California State archaeological database. One of the finds at the site was a seaman's or forty-niner's trunk, intact and complete with its belongings. The contents were donated by Thomas Thormahlen to the Maritime Museum, where they are now on display. These specimens include gold scales; a fragmentary sextant manufactured by James Bassnett of Liverpool; navigation instruments, including the remains of a parallel ruler; a "pepperbox" pistol, powder flask, and bullet mold; and a chronometer manufactured by Bliss & Creighton of New York. Former Maritime Museum curator Harlan Soeten (personal communication, 1979) identified these artifacts as the "surviving contents of a sea chest stored in the hold of one of the storeships known to have been moored in this area." Because of the find's proximity to the site, Soeten also believes that the spar—the broken end of a yard– might have been discarded during the conversion of *Niantic* into a storeship in 1849.

The Maritime Museum enlisted the aid of the California Historical Society and bottle hunters to rescue what it could from the construction of the Embarcadero Center Three complex in 1972–73. Again no archaeologist was present, but the bottle hunters, according to the *Santa Rosa Press Democrat* of August 20, 1972, recovered more than twenty-five hundred items, including "hundreds of bottles, a ship's sextant, a chronometer dated 1841, a derringer, silverware, remains of muskets, lanterns, ship gear and myriad other items lost or purposely thrown into the bay during the early 1850s."

The *Press Democrat* also noted that cranes were pulling out "hundreds of pilings, some of them 70 feet long" that had once supported Central Wharf. Although the excavation did not disclose any buried ships, it did uncover a fragment of a dismantled Gold Rush vessel and turn it in to the Maritime Museum, where it is still on display. The identity of this ship remains unknown.

THE *NIANTIC* REDISCOVERY OF 1978

With ongoing redevelopment of the old waterfront in the 1970s, it was only a matter of time before excavations encountered a buried hulk. In May 1978, historians Roger and Nancy Olmsted, working with archaeologist Allen Pastron, reviewed the *San Francisco Prices Current and Shipping List* article of July 7, 1852, that enumerated 164 storeships. They noted that "not half of them are accounted for by vessels known or believed to have been left in place, burned or dismantled by the already active shipbreakers at Rincon Point, or refitted for sea" (Olmsted, Olmsted, and Pastron 1978:39). Based on this information, they estimated that as many as 75 ships lay buried beneath downtown San Francisco. As they wrote their report, construction excavation at 505 Sansome Street, at the northwest corner of Clay and Sansome, unearthed the remains of the *Niantic* storeship.

The discovery of *Niantic* caught the government and the historic-preservation community off guard. The City of San Francisco's Landmarks Advisory Board, and the Department of Planning assumed that 1872 and 1906 construction activities at the site had destroyed the vessel's remains (Smith 1981:1). To comply with federal and state historic preservation laws, the planning department prepared a preconstruction review of the possibility of archaeological remains at the site as part of an environmental impact report (EIR) prepared in early 1978 (San Francisco Department of Planning 1978).

The preservation laws, particularly the California Environmental Quality Act of 1970, the National Historic Preservation Act of 1966, and the Archaeological and Historic Preservation Act of 1974, were enacted in response to increasing public demand for the preservation of historical and archaeological resources to prevent additional destruction of standing historic structures and buried archaeological features (King 2004). The new laws required the preparation of EIRs and provided for the use of mitigative measures if significant resources were perceived to be at risk. However, such measures could be limited and ineffective for projects that did not involve government lands, funding, or participation. Whereas government agencies, especially federal agencies, operated under stringent guidelines, owners of private lands and developers largely had limited responsibilities, primarily needing to prepare EIRs. Any mitigation that followed depended upon the goodwill of the developer. The *Niantic* discovery clearly demonstrated this fact.

The EIR for 505 Sansome sidestepped the question of whether *Niantic*'s remains were present at the site (Smith 1981:1) and made the following recommendation: "If any material of potential archaeological or historical importance should be found . . . the contractor would be legally bound to stop construction to permit professional evaluation of the find. The San Francisco Maritime Museum would be notified regarding excavation dates and specific excavation plans in order that a qualified historian or archaeologist could be present if necessary" (San Francisco Department of Planning 1978).

This statement was a reactionary response, and despite the obligation to stop construction, the contractor and developer were not legally obligated to do anything other than notify the Maritime Museum. The museum would then conduct the ill-defined "professional evaluation" and develop an excavation plan, without regulatory requirement to specify a minimum amount of time or an adequate amount of funding (San Francisco Department of Planning 1978). Nor did the EIR establish standards for a principal investigator of the site, leaving the evaluation and excavation, if deemed necessary, to a "qualified" historian or archaeologist. The EIR did not specify who would determine necessity. For all these reasons, the report placed the San Francisco Maritime Museum, which had passionately pursued its interest in the city's Gold Rush past and buried hulks, in a difficult situation.

Following demolition of the buildings on the site in April 1978, excavation of a large area for the foundation of the new structure encountered the remains of the ship either late on April 27 or on the morning of April 28, 1978 (Mahoney 1978). Work continued to clear the surrounding area to the level of the top of the exposed hull. Then, as required by the EIR, the developer, J. Patrick Mahoney, delivered a letter to Karl Kortum, director of the San Francisco Maritime Museum (Mahoney 1978). On May 3, museum staff members, including curator Soeten and the museum's photographic archivist, Isabel Bullen, were allowed on the site to examine the vessel. Construction work continued but at a slower pace, and the contractor's workmen had cleared almost all the mud and sand deposits above and in the hull except for a small area at the west end of the site. Here the remaining 2 feet of fill over the floor of the vessel reached to the top of the frames (ribs). This fill extended about 18 feet from the west end of the site (Bullen 1979:326). At that time, 73 feet of the lower hull, which extended some 7 feet down, lay exposed on a bed of bay mud with the bottom of the keel lying some 19 feet below the street grade (Smith 1981:4, 20). The remains were parallel to Clay Street, with the stern at Sansome Street and the bow apparently under the Transamerica Building's Redwood Park to the west (Bullen 1979:326). Others later determined that 38 feet of the forward hull remained buried beneath the park, where it remains to this day. The site is now listed in the National Register of Historic Places (Delgado 1986).

The vessel remains that were examined on May 3, 1978, exposed the outline of 68 percent of the original hull length. For a majority of the vessel, "all that remained . . . was the bottom of her hull—keel, frames (ribs), bottom planking with copper sheathing, partial ceiling (inner planking) and part of her keelson" (Bullen 1979:326). The excavated hull was empty of artifacts, and much of the interior planking and portions of the keelson had been removed. The building contractor indicated that the workers had encountered nothing other than sand fill in this area of the hull. The lack of artifacts was later explained as the probable result of the 1872 and 1906 exposures; an 1878 reference to the 1872 exposure commented that the hull had been "dug out" to allow for construction to proceed (Hittell 1878:166). No other reference to the 1872 and 1907 exposures provides any detail on impacts to the site. It was impossible to determine how much of the site had been exposed at each time in the past and how much had been removed. What was known was that artifacts and ship timbers had been removed in 1872, 1907, and 1978 by construction workers, despite assurances to the contrary (Smith 1981:19).

The undisturbed western portion of the site had survived with some level of archaeological integrity because the earlier construction had occurred on lots that covered only 73 ft on Clay Street, leaving "a substantial portion of the storeship's remaining length . . . beneath adjacent lots." Smith calculated that 9 feet of hull was "newly exposed along the east-west axis" (Smith 1981:20). Bullen's report noted that some 18 feet of hull contained undisturbed cultural materials (1978b:6). This suggests that the building(s) in this area lacked basement(s) or foundation(s) deep enough to affect the *Niantic* remains (Smith 1981:20). Smith estimated that the undisturbed cultural materials subsequently excavated from this area represented only 12 percent of the original archaeological matrix and assemblage that existed after May 4, 1851, and before 1872 (207).

On May 4, excavation of the interior of the hull commenced under the supervision of Bullen with the support of museum staff and volunteers. The dig began on the late afternoon of a Thursday after construction work ended for the day, and it continued through the weekend with a deadline for completion of Monday, May (Bullen 1979:328, 330; Thomsen 1978a). The *Niantic* excavation was marred by late-night raids of relic seekers who removed an unknown quantity of artifacts, including an intact wooden crate of champagne bottles, which the raiders broke into and demolished for its contents (Bullen 1979:328, 330; Thomsen 1978b). Meanwhile, government representatives, the developer, and museum officials met to decide the fate of the ship and artifacts. The cost estimates for removing the hull remains intact ran to $630,000 — including the costs of shoring up the unstable mud and sand fill that surrounded the site and of reimbursing the developer for construction delays at $16,000 per day (Mulhern 1978). Despite public appeals, the money was not forthcoming. On May 10, working with a grant from the National Trust for Historic Preservation, Kendiah Jeyapalan of Fresno State University measured the exposed hull with photogrammetric stereo photography (Rosato 1978).

On May 11, construction resumed as workers cut away a cross-section of the midships portion of the hull with jackhammers and lifted it onto a flatbed truck for transportation to the Maritime Museum. The developer donated the equipment and labor and then, after bulldozers had cleared away the remaining hull, also pulled the intact stern and rudder from the mud and donated them to the museum. Bulldozers pushed piles of broken frames and planking into dump trucks, and a crane pulled the stern and rudder free of the mud (Todd 1978).

All of this work occurred without formal excavation or examination of the area immediately outside the hull for artifacts, portions of the ship that had fallen during the fire, or evidence of the surrounding wharf or piling-supported structures. Nor was any opportunity afforded ongoing archaeological monitoring as construction continued on the site. The bow, however, survives intact, because the hull structure continued beneath the retaining wall into Redwood Park.

Following excavation and curation of the *Niantic* collection by the Maritime Museum, Mary Smith, a graduate student at San Francisco State University, received permission to analyze the artifacts as part of her MA thesis project (Smith 1981). The National Maritime Museum Association, which helped finance museum activities, and the National Trust for Historic Preservation assisted Smith's work through a grant for the project. Smith's research, after initial cataloguing, focused on a series of questions about the ship, its construction and modification into a floating building, and the function and use of the storeship. She then expanded her goals to look at *Niantic*'s role in San Francisco's overall mercantile and trade patterns. The *Niantic* assemblage represented the use of the storeship as a warehouse, indicating that the ship held goods for established San Francisco businesses and may have provided personal storage along the lines of today's storage-locker business. Smith was able to ascribe the majority of the goods to specific businesses: a wine and liquor merchant, a crockery merchant, a merchant who dealt in furnishings, and a stationery and office-supply merchant (210–212).

The stationery supplies came from a variety of sources—bound journals and daybooks manufactured by William C. Rose, a New York stationery supplier and bookbinder; lead pencils manufactured by William Munroe of Concord, Massachusetts, E. Wolff & Son of London, and A. W. Faber of Germany; brass pen nibs manufactured by Richard Mosley & Co. of London; and English ink bottles and printed paper items (Smith 1981:83–100).

The wine and liquor merchant's goods revealed a diverse international market. The majority of recovered items were cases of champagne, identified as the Jacquesson et Fils brand from Reims (Barry and Patten 1873:135–136; Delgado et al. 1979; Smith 1981:146–147). Other bottles most likely contained porter from the Bristol Porter Brewery in England (Smith 1981:152). Madeira and "Old Xeres" or Spanish sherry came from Jerez de la Frontera (155). A German "Hock" or Riesling bottle, with a lead foil cap identifying it as the product of "Gerowoth" winery, also was in the assemblage, but it had been removed from the site before the excavation (Whited 2004).

The crockery, recovered in fragmentary form, did not offer diagnostic clues such as back stamps or other marks, but they bore transfer-printed patterns that Smith believed were of possible British manufacture. One fragmentary base shard contained a back stamp of Joseph Genella, a San Francisco merchant whose company remained in business on nearby Broadway Street. The 1852 San Francisco city directory identified him as a "wholesale and retail dealer in China, Glass and Britannia Wares, cutlery, lamps, etc." (Smith 1981:175). The implications of the assemblage were clear: San Francisco was not an isolated frontier town.

In summarizing her findings on the *Niantic* site, Smith argued that the storeship was an important individual site. However, she agreed with Hickman (1977:270–272) that "significance be assigned on the basis of a property's representativeness of a particular historical pattern during a particular time period" (Smith 1981:204). The *Niantic* site was valuable because it was likely representative of San Francisco's Gold Rush market and economy in May 1851, following Brown's (1979b:33) assertion that "with regard to urban historic archaeology, an individual site, to the extent that it is both representative and approached with well-defined research goals, can provide generalizations about a city as a whole" (Smith 1981:204).

Smith's work was important not only for her analysis of *Niantic* but also for her recognition of the wider context in which it occurred. Urban historical archaeological practice was shifting from archaeology in the city to "archaeology of the city" (Staski 1987). Her work provided background for future Gold Rush archaeological work, although some archaeologists have questioned the *Niantic* assemblage's value for comparative studies "due to the limited area of the storeship available for sampling . . . and the severely limited time available for archaeological investigation" (McDougall 1990:72).

Others believe, however, that despite the obvious problems in the recovery, the *Niantic* assemblage "is of particular relevance" (Pastron 1990:14) for interpretation, both in analyzing the Hoff's Store Site and other Gold Rush sites and subsequently in the interpretation of the *General Harrison* assemblage (Delgado, Pastron, and Robichaud 2007). The remains of *Niantic*'s hull and an analysis of the construction techniques have also provided useful comparative data for investigating other Gold

Rush hulks and wrecks in San Francisco and in the Sacramento River (James 1986a, 1986b; Smith et al. 1988; Pastron and Delgado 1990; Self 1996; Delgado, Pastron, and Robichaud 2007).

THE MODERN ERA OF ARCHAEOLOGY IN SAN FRANCISCO

The *Niantic* episode combined with newly passed local and state laws led the federal government to inaugurate the modern era of archaeological resource management in San Francisco, one requiring preconstruction site assessment, archaeological testing, and monitoring of construction sites in the historic core. This new approach was demonstrated in the three-year San Francisco Wastewater Program of large-scale sewer construction along the San Francisco waterfront (Olmsted, Olmsted, and Pastron 1978; Pastron, Prichett, and Zeibarth 1981). Archeo-Tec, a consulting firm of archaeologists led by Allen Pastron, was responsible for much of the archaeological work. Because the project covered miles of sewer trenches and borings, the archaeological team was able to record hundreds of sites, making the project the most extensive archaeological monitoring project yet undertaken in San Francisco. The team recorded a wide array of features, ranging from various phases of wood- and stone-bulkhead construction to a single buried ship. The sewer alignment ran from the end of Berry Channel, which now bisects largely filled Mission Bay, and then along the Embarcadero and along North Beach to the boundary of the Presidio of San Francisco at the Marina (Olmsted, Olmsted, and Pastron 1978; Pastron, Prichett, and Zeibarth 1981).

In June 1978 and February 1979, excavation for new construction uncovered two more buried ships. The first was the hulk of the abandoned whaler *Lydia,* sepulchred in 1906 and discovered when workers cut a sewer trench through it at King Street as part of the sewer project (Olmsted et al. 1981). The second was a Gold Rush storeship hulked and buried to form a wharf in the 1850s in the lee of Telegraph Hill. The latter ship was discovered during preconstruction historical assessment and archaeological testing for the construction of an office complex. However, though the hulk was largely intact, it was not fully cleared nor fully documented, because complete excavation was not necessary to allow construction to proceed. The exposure of the starboard bow, a portion of the deck, and historical research by Roger and Nancy Olmsted identified the ship as *William Gray,* a Gold Rush storeship subsequently filled with rock and scuttled to form the base of a dock in 1852 (Pastron and Pritchett 1979). This research was later synthesized, and I prepared a revised National

Register of Historic Places nomination form for the buried vessel (Delgado 1986).

Another Archeo-Tec project of importance and another one in which I participated was the 1988 excavation of Hare's shipbreaking yard near Rincon Point, which yielded the remains of several Gold Rush hulks (Delgado 1981b; Pastron and Delgado 1990). Charles Hare, an English-born shipbreaker, worked with San Francisco's Chinese community between 1851 and 1857 to scrap and salvage nearly one hundred vessels that had arrived in the harbor during the Gold Rush (Delgado 1981b). The excavation revealed more than one hundred hardwood timbers at the site of his shipbreaking yard. Maritime artifacts excavated at the site included various structural elements, fastenings, a small anchor, rigging elements, copper sheathing, and possibly the bedplate of a Gold Rush steamship.

The excavation of the site of the shipbreaking yard was particularly instructive for reconstructing the age and size of the last vessels broken up at the site, presumably in or around 1857 (Pastron and Delgado 1990). In 2005, construction at 300 Spear Street in San Francisco, on the lot across the street from the Archeo-Tec dig, exposed another significant portion of the Hare yard. William Self Associates, with maritime archaeologist James Allan, recovered forty-two ship timbers and the stern section of a partially dismantled hulk subsequently identified as the 1818-built ship *Candace,* one of the last vessels dismantled at the Hare yard. The excavation also revealed the foundation of a building constructed of dismantled ship parts that lay close by in piles of stockpiled fittings. This foundation is probably the remains of Hare's "store" and office where he transacted his business and sold the items he had salvaged (William Self Associates 2006). I participated in the postexcavation analysis and concluded that the stern section was most likely from *Candace* (Delgado 2005).

As excavations unearthed remnants of the Gold Rush waterfront through the 1970s and early 1980s, San Francisco's Department of Planning and the State Historic Preservation Office finally recognized the heritage value of the sites. As Pastron emphasized, the buried hulks were as part of a macroartifact that could provide for "archaeology on a grand scale along San Francisco's waterfront" (Pastron 1980). However, not until 1993 did another opportunity arise for archaeological study of a buried Gold Rush hulk. At that time, an underground tunneling project to extend MUNI encountered *Rome,* an intact sepulchred hulk filled with rock and purposely scuttled on a water lot in the early 1850s. Archaeologists documented a portion of the hulk as the tunnel project burrowed through the hull near the bow, leaving much of the vessel buried beneath the city's Embarcadero (Allan 1995; William Self Associates 1996). In 2001, as we will see later, another storeship, *General Harrison,* was excavated by Archeo-Tec.

THE HOFF'S STORE SITE

During the 1980s, archaeological monitoring and excavation encountered a series of Gold Rush sites but no new ships. This work, much of it performed by Archeo-Tec, revealed one exceptionally artifact-rich site: a piling-supported two-story wood frame building at Battery and Sacramento streets that had burned and collapsed into the bay during the May 4, 1851. This site was directly adjacent to the *Apollo* storeship and a block away from the site of *General Harrison* (Pastron and Hattori 1990). Known as the Hoff's Store Site, it included a large assemblage of materials and features. It added much to scholars' understanding of the nature and the development of waterfront infrastructure as well as the diversity of material goods—especially Asian trade goods and the strong role of maritime trade and commerce in the emerging city. As the consulting maritime archaeologist for the project, I participated in the excavation and analysis of the site (Delgado 1990a).

The preconstruction impact assessment first identified Hoff's Store Site as a potentially significant resource. A number of Gold Rush sites had been found in the 1970s – and 1980s, but "relatively few of these deposits are characterized by a high degree of stratigraphic and/or contextual integrity," as was Hoff's Store (Pastron 1990:6). The store was also one of a few sites on lots then untouched by the rapid pace of urban redevelopment, which had severely eroded the database of Gold Rush sites in San Francisco. The value of the site's material record was in "obtaining new data and/or supplementing or correcting the archival record," because it represented a brief time (1848–51) during the period of massive change in Gold Rush San Francisco. It presented an opportunity to assess the city's multinational and multicultural character through the material record. And, as Pastron noted in arguing for central themes for San Francisco's emerging urban archaeology, the site reflected the "rapid transformation from boomtown to urban center," with subthemes such as the chronology of urban development throughout the Gold Rush, social conditions, trade and economy, and sociocultural change (Pastron 1990:11). Finally, and most significant for this book, "While a number of residential deposits from the Gold Rush era have been encountered in

San Francisco, the Hoff's Store site is unusual in that it contains the remnants of a commercial establishment ruined by a single day's catastrophe. Accordingly, this deposit provides a unique opportunity for archaeologists to view the Gold Rush phenomenon from a singular perspective of a mid-nineteenth-century merchant and entrepreneur" (6). The occupants of this piling-supported building were the city's harbormaster, the government official responsible for maintaining order on the waterfront, and ship chandler William C. Hoff, a merchant with a maritime-based business at the port.

The Hoff's Store excavation revealed more than 5,800 artifacts of Hoff's business of supplying ships with goods, provisions, and equipment (Pastron and Hattori 1990). The materials recovered from the site are significant because they shed light on the crucial role of both "maritime commerce and ship chandlers in provisioning the Gold Rush and in bringing about San Francisco's rapid transformation from a small village to a great city. Supplies of consumer goods . . . were almost entirely dependent upon the arrival of ship-borne goods at San Francisco, a port which functioned as the primary commercial emporium and depot of the Gold Rush" (Delgado 1990a:25). Thus, Hoff's Store was tied to the global system, insofar as "the trade networks which developed [during the Gold Rush] were world-wide, and California's effect upon the international economy was substantial" (Pastron and Hattori 1990:13).

In my work at the site, I compared the Hoff's Store assemblage with a contemporary catalogue of a San Francisco ship chandler, Folger and Tubbs, and reconciled it against a detailed advertisement for the store in 1852. This comparison "reflected the basic nature of supply by ship in Gold Rush California . . . [and] . . . points to an actual booming port and maritime activity that responded to economic and social dynamics demanding regular supply, available only by ship" (Delgado 1990a:31). As well, "nearly every imaginable item could be found aboard a merchant vessel of the mid-19th century—as indicated by the catalogue of Folger and Tubbs . . . and the assemblage from the Hoff Store site . . . the goods sold by Hoff . . . provide a unique opportunity to assess the social and economic aspects of a maritime subculture in a city that depended upon the sea for its existence" (33).

However, viewing the store strictly as a maritime site because of the nature of Hoff's business resulted in too narrow a focus and missed an aspect that, in hindsight, seems to be the more significant one: how the site's assemblage underscores the nascent entrepôt's participation through maritime trade in the extension and modification of the world system then coming into play in the Pacific.

This global nature of the city's maritime supply is readily apparent in the analysis of the Hoff assemblage's bottled goods. The artifacts were primarily bottled medicinal supplies, bottled condiments, and alcoholic beverages whose origins ranged from the eastern United States to Europe. The bottles "seem to reflect the desires of the more affluent or sedentary population of San Francisco. . . . In addition, the bottled preserved foods strongly reflect an Anglo-Saxon taste preference . . . In this respect, the Hoff Store bottle assemblage is similar to the collection of bottled goods recovered from the storeship *Niantic*" (McDougall 1990:72).

The same diversity of supply held true for other foodstuffs at the site. In this category were barrels of salted pork, tinned oysters, barrels of hardtack biscuit, individually paper-wrapped cakes, a variety of fruit seeds, nuts, dried beans, peas, rice, coffee, wheat, tea, and stoneware pots of butter. Analysis indicated that the probable sources of manufacture and supply for these foodstuffs were China, India, Central and South America, Germany, Australia, Peru, Brazil, Tahiti, Hawai'i, Mexico, Chile, and Holland, apart from the known eastern United States suppliers (McDougall 1990:72).

Reliance on maritime trade, particularly with China, was explicit in the Chinese export porcelain from Hoff's Store and an adjacent store at the site. The porcelain assemblage "appear[s] to represent a new dimension of the West Coast China trade—a trade that was already well established in California prior to 1849, but which increased dramatically in the years following the discovery of gold" (Terrey and Pastron 1990:81). The Chinese porcelain assemblage also suggests that the site did not simply house one store (Hoff's) but was home to a mixture of stores adjacent to the *Apollo* storeship, which itself was occupied by various commission merchants.

The Hoff's Store Site demonstrates a "direct connection with suppliers on the eastern seaboard of the United States, Britain, China and possibly France and Germany . . . [in a] frontier outpost whose prime commerce revolved around transshipment to and from ocean going vessels and river boats" (Pastron et al. 1990:104). Left unsaid in the conclusion of the report but becoming increasingly clear was the idea that the Hoff's Store Site, like that of *Niantic*, marked this area of the waterfront as the center of a rapidly built entrepôt dominated by commission merchants. Though the analysis did not articulate this hypothesis specifically, it planted the seeds of the idea, which was ultimately tested and proved with the excavation of the nearby storeship *General Harrison*. Meanwhile, one more waterfront store site, which included the office of pioneer stevedore and storeship owner Philip Caduc, emerged from the fill during another downtown excavation.

343 SANSOME STREET SITE, 1989

The construction of a fifteen-story office building on a block bounded by Sansome, Halleck, Leidesdorff, and Sacramento streets in early 1989 revealed another fire-destroyed waterfront structure. The project, undertaken by archaeologists from Dames & Moore and under the direction of Michael S. Kelly, resulted from a preconstruction testing program conducted by Mason Tillman Associates. Archaeologist Richard Ambro, a veteran of Archeo-Tec's Hoff's Store excavation, developed the testing plan and drilled into the site with an auger at the end of October 1988. Three of the thirteen 2-foot-diameter borings reached through 1906 earthquake debris and sand fill to hit the original mud bottom of the bay between 16 and 18 feet beneath modern-day street level. The drilling recovered samples of wood, ceramics, glass, leather, and metal artifacts dating from the Gold Rush that lay within an apparently burnt layer 1 to 2 feet thick, although researchers could not conclude with certainty that the items came from burned and collapsed structures (Ambro 1988).

Subsequent testing by Dames & Moore opened a series of units in January, and those findings led to excavation of additional units and trenches in February. The excavation revealed a shallow layer of burnt material that was "rich with artifacts," including square nails, burned timbers, charcoal fragments (Dames & Moore 1989:8). In all, 5,977 artifacts were recovered, many of them in discrete concentrations such as a group of bitters bottles in the northwestern corner of the block, several hundred leather shoes and boots in the southeastern portion of the block, and corked ceramic "Refined Cider" bottles in the eastern portion (12). The number and concentration of these artifacts suggests that they were merchandise in storage. In addition, an iron cot, charcoal brazier, and small number of personal items—such as bone-handled shaving and toothbrushes, framed daguerreotypes, and a silver-handled pocket knife—in the southern end of the excavation suggest "the presence of a living area or residence, perhaps attached to a store" (15).

Most items in the 343 Sansome assemblage were glass, such as bottles, tumblers, and glasses for alcoholic and nonalcoholic beverages, medicines, and foodstuffs (preserves, pickles, and sauces). Ceramics—including stoneware, earthenware, and porcelain— clay tobacco pipes, and metal also accounted for large portions of the assemblage. The metal ranged from two 1846 U.S. one-cent pieces to square nails, hammers, broad axes, and tin cans, as well as a large (and empty) iron safe, its lock broken off and the door wedged open by a partially burned and battered ax. This find suggests that during or after the fire, the safe was broken into, perhaps by its owners, to retrieve what lay inside. Another evocative metal object was a branding iron "actually used for burning a manufacturer's or exporter's name into crates or barrels" (Dames & Moore 1989:50). Amazingly, the name on the iron, in raised 1-inch letters, was "P. CADUC," the stevedore and storeship owner who had built nearby Howison's Pier (8).

Ongoing flooding and slumping of the sand fill made the excavation difficult and ultimately ended the project, although postexcavation monitoring by the archaeologists revealed additional artifacts and a stone and wood retaining wall. The wall formed a bulkhead that initially supported the fill that created Leidesdorff Street. Unfortunately, the bulkhead was not documented.

Analysis of the assemblage suggested that the site was the remains of a single structure with two or more rooms, one of was for storing or selling merchandise or perhaps both. The artifacts that were in large quantities (shoes, cider, and bitters) as well as hardware (nested tinware pots and pans, axes, and hammers) and a large concentration of decomposed tin cans lay in close association, some in individual units. For example, all the shoes were in one unit, and most of the hardware and bulk household goods (mainly ceramics) came from two adjacent units (Dames & Moore 1989:57). The 343 Sansome excavation "documented a small commercial enterprise with a rather limited stock, primarily shoes, alcoholic beverages, patent medicines and a small supply of hardware and household goods" (58). It also revealed, through a 27-kilogram sample of butchered bone, an adjacent area that may have been a butcher or meat-storage facility

Ultimately, though the 343 Sansome site was not as diverse as Hoff's Store, it was a strong reminder of the potential of postfire waterfront sites to offer well-preserved remains, as well as strong historical associations. Researchers were able to make the connection with Philip Caduc, as well as other individuals at the site, through artifacts with his and others' names on them, such as the branding iron. The silver-handled pocketknife bore the name B. F. Hillard, an associate of Caduc's and a one-time habitué of the *Thomas Bennett* storeship (58). It is tempting to conclude that one of these men was the owner and inhabitant of the structure. In addition, the provocative discovery of the collapsed living quarters yielded three daguerreotypes that were well enough preserved to recover the family images on them. They literally put a human face on the site and the event. The next excavation, though lacking in images, made a strong connection to yet other merchants on the Gold Rush waterfront.

THE *GENERAL HARRISON* SITE, 2001

When the development of the corner of Clay and Battery streets, site of the buried *General Harrison* storeship, occurred in 2001, Pastron was selected as the project archaeologist. I was the project's maritime archaeologist, and Rhonda Robichaud directed the fieldwork. Though test borings at the site in June 2000 failed to locate the buried hulk, deeper drilling in August 2001 made contact with subsurface wooden remains. including a section of a futtock and treenails (Delgado, Pastron, and Robichaud 2007). Another boring encountered a 0.33-meter-thick matrix of fire-affected cultural materials similar to the black layer at the Hoff's Store Site. The archaeologists interpreted these materials as burned cargo.

Excavation began on August 3, 2001, and continued until the vessel was completely exposed. The test borings had indicated that the interior was likely devoid of the burnt layer and filled with sand, which largely proved true, although the excavation revealed some individual artifacts and features. At the southern end of the hull, the vessel's proximity to the southern property line and supports for the adjacent sidewalk and Clay Street did not allow excavation. Thus, our team realized that the project would not be able to find burnt-off pilings or other remains of the Clay Street wharf. Similarly, excavation did not proceed on the western edge of the site when workers discovered that the vessel's remains continued beyond the boundaries of the site and beneath an adjacent building.

We designated two concentrations of artifacts as feature 2 and feature 3 (Delgado, Pastron, and Robichaud 2007). Feature 2 was a concentration of penny pipes, iron bars or drifts, and a pile of discarded leather footwear. Feature 3 appeared to contain material both from the 1851 fire—a mix of partially burnt rigging elements and cargo—and from the 1906 earthquake rubble, a wooden half barrel, and the badly corroded remains of a round-point shovel. The barrel was from the Gold Rush, and the round-point shovel was post 1906, presumably from the time of the vessel's partial unearthing by construction in 1912. These artifacts indicated that the interior of the vessel did not represent a completely undisturbed deposit of materials from the May 4, 1851, fire. Following the complete exposure of the interior of the hull in September 2001, further documentation of the vessel's construction by San Francisco Maritime National Historical Park, led by John Muir, yielded a series of measurements and offsets to create a set of profiles and body lines for the hull. This work, as well as observations by the park staff, proved invaluable in the analysis of the vessel's construction and salvage (Canright 2001).

As documentation of the hull proceeded, excavation of the area outside the hull to the north revealed the upper portion of the burnt layer. This area was excavated using wet site-exposure techniques, including both water hoses and wet screening. Burnt glass, charcoal, and oxidized materials formed much of the layer's matrix, although our team recorded a concentration of glass beads, textiles, and seeds (feature 1). Logistics prevented excavation of the entire burnt layer, so we devised a sampling strategy.

Backhoes excavated horizontal trenches along the starboard side of the hull in 3-meter sections for a total area of 135 square meters. The trenches were the width of four backhoe buckets, or approximately 3 meters wide. The trenches revealed that the burnt-layer deposit was a continuous layer that followed the curvature of the hull, which indicated that the deposit stemmed from a single event, the fire that destroyed *General Harrison* and the surrounding docks. The trenches exposed the outer hull to enable profiling and to expose and plot the pilings from the structure that was now clearly a Gold Rush–era wharf that had burnt along with *General Harrison*. All material from the trenches was wet screened and sorted, and diagnostic artifacts were retained for analysis.

Water-hose excavation of the trenches revealed a partially burnt wooden door with a wooden brass pull ring from one of the ship's companionways or cabins (feature 4). Beneath the door lay a series of partially burnt wooden crates, one of which contained intact, straw-packed wine bottles with corks and liquid. Wet site-excavation techniques allowed us to wash away the sand fill to reveal the entire hull and the surrounding burnt layer without disturbing its vertical profile. Analysis of the hull revealed that it had been cleared after the fire and partially salvaged. As a result, we reevaluated the burnt layer as the redeposited burnt remains of the storeship and its "cargo," which we concluded had been cleared out of the hold and dumped alongside during the postfire, prelandfilling salvage project.

We sent a variety of artifacts, including fabrics, liquid contents of intact bottles, seeds, wood, and samples of the pine resin that coated the exterior of the hull to a variety of laboratories for specialized analysis. A cross-disciplinary group of experts also consulted on other aspects of the assemblage. The results of these studies allowed full identification of the cargo of *General Harrison*. The cargo proved to be a diverse mixture of hardware, building materials, comestibles, alcohol, and clothing. By examining newspaper advertisements of the time, we traced these goods to shipments from around the world, but with many transshipped through Valparaíso, Chile, by commission merchants Mickle & Co., owners of the *General Harrison* storeship. The excavated material proved to be unsold cargo, some of it dating to a year before the fire, that had been stored and advertised for sale by Mickle & Co. The diversity of the material, and the opportunity to link recovered merchandise in the burnt layer to specific shipments provided an opportunity for interpretation not available with any other excavation, including that of Hoff's Store.

The analysis of the *General Harrison* data provided a detailed look at the vessel's architecture and its related infrastructure as a floating building. This level of detail greatly augmented the sparse archaeological record of *Niantic*'s physical characteristics and filled in a number of gaps in researchers' understanding of the processes of converting vessels into storeships on the Gold Rush waterfront.

CHAPTER 7

Gold Rush Cargoes

Evidence of the World Maritime System

If San Francisco is a product of the maritime system, then the cargoes sent to California between 1849 and 1851 should reflect 1) a global system of supply by sea, 2) evidence that this global system responded to the Gold Rush by sending goods specific to San Francisco and California's market needs, and ideally, 3) patterns showing connections to the networks of the world system, such as the diversion of goods from entrepôts in the core to the semiperiphery of San Francisco. If merchants' intent was to create, enhance, or support the rise of San Francisco as an entrepôt, these goods or commodities should represent more than a market response to the conspicuous consumerism of a gold rush boom economy. They should also represent an effort to meet the needs of an urban population for food, clothing, and increasing permanence.

I now draw on the archival record to identify the patterns of shipping in San Francisco, including ports of origin, and to assess whether these patterns link the city to the world system and its subset, the maritime system. By evaluating an archival data set, examining the advertisements of commission merchants E. Mickle & Co., and analyzing the material-culture assemblages from the *Niantic,* Hoff's Store, 343 Sansome, and *General Harrison* sites, I have been able to identify the types of goods being shipped in and out of San Francisco and glean clues to the city's role in the larger maritime system.

As we have seen, the voyages of exploration, the annexation of the Spice Islands, the Northwest Coast maritime fur trade, and the establishment of entrepôts at Nagasaki, Macau, and Hong Kong were all *événéments* of the longer process of history playing out in the Pacific (Gibson and Whitehead 1993; Perry 1994). The same processes are evident in the flows of commodities—porcelain, tea, spices, opium, silver, gold, sea-otter pelts, *beché de mer,* and others—and the control of these flows.

The expansion of trade was slow between the sixteenth and early nineteenth centuries. However, the pace picked up dramatically in the mid-nineteenth century as the industrial age brought steam-powered iron- and steel-hulled vessels, which could be linked to ports by railroads, and as mechanization gave rise to factories that mass-produced goods. To feed the factories and the emerging global economy, steamships expanded trade and naval control into the Pacific, seeking greater quantities of goods such as tea and silk and pursuing new profitable commodities.

Beginning in the mid-nineteenth century, gold became one of these critical new commodities, and fresh discoveries accelerated the incorporation of California (1848–56), Australia (1852–56), British Columbia (1858–65), and the Klondike/Yukon (1898–1904) into the world market. Indeed, the rise and stabilization of San Francisco had more to do with long-standing desires for a Pacific entrepôt linked to the core in Europe and the United States than it does with the accident of the Gold Rush. The industrial revolution abetted the city's development into a world trading center through the establishment of regular steamship lines and ultimately, a transcontinental railroad.

SHIPPING DIVERTS TO SAN FRANCISCO

Historical accounts mention the influx of ships to San Francisco from all over the world as people flocked to join the Gold Rush. William Heath Davis, a contemporary observer, described the crowded waterfront. "An immense fleet of vessels from all parts of the globe, numbering eight to nine hundred, were anchored in the bay east of the city, between Clark's Point and the Rincon, presenting a very striking picture—like an immense forest stripped of its foliage" (1967:333–334).

Other accounts remark on the large number of vessels that played a role in the Gold Rush. Goodman (1987) lists 762 vessels that cleared North American ports for San Francisco between December 5, 1848, and December 31, 1849. The number of foreign ships reportedly equaled the number of North American vessels, and in all, some 1,400 vessels sailed to California in the first wave of the Gold Rush between 1848 and 1850 (Delgado 1990a:19, 23).

Most of these vessels carried passengers. The editors of the *San Francisco Daily Alta California,* working from the harbormaster's records, reported that 39,888 persons had arrived in San Francisco on 805 vessels between April 1849 and January 1850 (January 31, 1850). A review of vessel arrivals reported in the *Alta* confirms that nearly all these vessels carried cargoes (Delgado 1990a:43–44). Excluding small amounts of goods from local suppliers, all merchandise and foodstuffs imported into California arrived in the holds of vessels. The range of places from which these vessels departed demonstrates the global nature of San Francisco's maritime activity. My tabulation of *Alta*-reported vessel arrivals that indicate the port of origin yielded 795 arrivals in 1849. In that year, the paper listed 76 separate points of departure that encompassed European, North American, Central and South American, Pacific, and Asian ports.

The United States' eastern ports were the largest participants in the rush, with ships sailing from Connecticut, Louisiana, Maine, Maryland, Massachusetts, New York, Pennsylvania, Rhode Island, South Carolina, and Virginia. New York, with 16 percent of the 1849 arrivals, dominated the sailings, followed by Boston at 6 percent. North American sailings accounted for 38 percent of the total, and sailings from smaller Canadian and other U.S. ports on the eastern seaboard and in the south constituted 20 percent of these North American sailings. Sailings from Central and South America constituted 32 percent. The dominant port was Valparaíso, followed by Panama and Mazatlán. "Country trade," a contemporary (1849) term for trade with Oregon, British Columbia, Russian Alaska, and various California coastal ports, accounted for 11 percent of arrivals. Pacific ports, notably Honolulu and Sydney, accounted for another 11 percent. Europe, led by Liverpool and London, and Asia, primarily Hong Kong, each accounted for 4 percent (table 3).

The 1849 patterns of shipping suggest a consistent flow of commodities from San Francisco's closest ports—namely those on the Pacific coast from Sitka to Valparaíso, from Hawaii, and from the eastern seaboard of the United States, primarily New York. The smallest numbers were vessels direct from Europe and Asia, followed by vessels from the wider Pacific, including Australia, New Zealand, and Tahiti (in aggregate, 11 percent). On December 26, 1850, the *Alta* provided a month-by-month tabulation of American arrivals (which appear to be those from the eastern seaboard) and European arrivals, apparently neglecting those from Central and South America and Asia (table 4).

TABLE 3. PORTS OF ORIGIN FOR VESSELS ARRIVING AT SAN FRANCISCO, JANUARY 1–DECEMBER 31, 1849

Port of Origin	Arrivals	Percent of Total Arrivals
Acapulco	3	<1
Auckland	10	1
Baltimore	14	2
Boston	54	6
Buenos Aires	8	1
California coast	52	7
Callao	22	3
Columbia River	35	4
Guayaquil	5	1
Le Havre	7	1
Hobart	10	1
Hong Kong	17	2
Honolulu	44	6
Lahaina	7	1
Liverpool	9	1
London	3	<1
Mazatlán	35	4
Nantucket	4	<1
New Bedford	17	2
New York	125	16
Panama	44	6
Philadelphia	15	2
Río de Janeiro	12	2
San Blas	12	2
Sitka	2	<1
Sydney	14	2
Tahiti	8	1
Talcahuano	10	1
Valparaíso	107	14
Misc. Europe	15	2
Misc. North America	53	7
Misc. Central and South America	13	2
Misc. Pacific	6	1
Misc. Asia	3	<1
Total	**795**	**101**

SOURCE: *San Francisco Daily Alta California*.
NOTE: Percentages do not add to 100 because of rounding.

TABLE 4. SAN FRANCISCO PORT
STATISTICS, 1850, "AMERICAN" VERSUS
"EUROPEAN" ARRIVALS

Month	American	Percent*	European	Percent*	Total
January	50	91	5	9	55
February	44	96	2	4	46
March	51	94	3	6	54
April	45	90	5	10	50
May	70	93	5	7	75
June	82	96	3	4	85
July	61	98	1	2	62
August	51	94	3	6	54
September	37	95	2	5	39
October	42	86	7	14	49
November	44	80	11	20	55
December	21	66	11	34	32
Total	598	91	58	9	656

SOURCE: *San Francisco Daily Alta California,* December 26, 1850.
*Percent of total arrivals for the month.

In its summary of 1850 arrivals, the *Alta* noted the likelihood of in-accuracies, "as the books from which they are compiled have at times been loosely kept." The exclusion of Latin American, Asian, and trans-pacific arrivals may stem from the article's stated intent of showing that "but a very small portion of the direct arrivals have been foreign." The records are not complete, either in the newspapers or in customhouse ac-countings for 1850–51, because of the two major fires that destroyed San Francisco and its government offices, including that of the harbor-master. Working from a variety of sources, however, one can reconstruct the arrivals in 1850. By adding arrivals from Central and South Amer-ican, Pacific, Asian, and Pacific Coast ports to the *Alta*'s December 1850 tabulation of 598 "American" sailings and 58 "European" sailings, I have come up with an estimate of 800 vessels overall (table 5).

The reconstructed 1850 patterns of shipping indicate that the major flow of ships was from North American ports, which represented 75 per-cent of the total. Central and South American, Pacific, and Asian ports accounted for 18.6 percent of arrivals, and European ones accounted for 7.3 percent. The role of specific American ports within the North Amer-ican total is not as easy to discern. Vessels from Pacific Coast ports (which the *Alta* called the "California Coast" and the "Columbia River" in its lists of vessel arrivals) were, as coastal traders, bound by law to be ves-sels bearing the U.S. flag, and they were part of the *Alta*'s "American"

TABLE 5. ARRIVALS AND PORTS OF CALL, 1850

Port	1850 Arrivals	Percent of Total
Acapulco	4	1
Auckland	3	<1
Callao	6	1
Canton	1	—
Guayaquil	1	—
Guaymas	3	<1
Hobart	5	1
Hong Kong	4	1
Honolulu	7	1
Lahaina	7	1
Launceston	5	1
Macao	1	—
Manila	2	—
Mazatlán	9	1
Montevideo	1	—
Paita, Peru	1	—
Panama	50	6
Pernambuco	1	—
Port Adelaide	2	—
Río de Janeiro	5	1
San Blas	3	<1
Sitka	1	—
Sydney	9	1
Talcahuano	2	—
Valparaíso	12	2
Misc. "European"	58	7
Misc. "American"	598	75
Misc. Central and South America	2	—
Total	**803**	**100**

SOURCES: *San Francisco Daily Alta California*; Rasmussen 1966.
NOTE: *Alta* notices use the terms *European* and *American* to classfy ship arrivals.

category. Working from the *Alta*'s arrival notices between January and December 1850, which again are not complete, I found that 180 of 244 arrivals, or 73 percent, were from U.S. ports, a number that close matches the reconstructed statistics for the year (table 5).

Of this sample of 180 U.S. vessels, New York sailings dominated, followed by sailings from Boston, Baltimore, Charleston, and New Orleans (51 percent of the U.S. total). Country trade on the coast accounted for 3.8 percent of the total. New York sent a third more ships to San Francisco in 1850 than did closer-proximity American ports. Comparing 1849 patterns of shipping with those of 1850 shows a 29 percent increase in vessels from North American and European ports and a corresponding

TABLE 6. PORTS OF ORIGIN, 1849–1850
(percent of arrivals)

Region	1849	1850	Change
Asia	4	0.5	-3.5
Central and South America	32	12.7	-19.3
North America including Pacific coast	49	75.0	+26.0
Pacific (foreign)	11	4.8	-6.2
Europe	4	7.0	+3.0
Total	100	100	

SOURCE: *San Francisco Daily Alta California.*

net drop in arrivals from Asia, the Pacific, and Central and South America. Latin American sailings showed the greatest decline, 19.3 percent (table 6).

The rise in North American and European sailings between 1849 and 1850 reflects the maritime system's response to the California Gold Rush. Another pattern is also apparent—namely a change in the ports that sent the most ships and by extension, the most cargoes. The dominant ports in the first year of the rush were New York and Valparaíso, followed closely by California coastal locations, Panama, the Columbia River, and Mazatlán.

In 1850, New York retained its domination of the California trade, augmented by other U.S. ports. Panama essentially qualified as a U.S. port because it was a major point in a U.S.-financed and -controlled trans-isthmian link connected by steamships on both coasts and a railroad then under construction (Kemble 1943). After these American-dominated ports came South America's dominant port, Valparaíso, and one of Europe's, Liverpool. In determining the relative importance of ports, we need to consider whether a link exists between cargo levels and the percentage of sailings from a point of origin. If so, we would expect that U.S.-manufactured goods would account for 50–75 percent (the 1849 and 1850 percentages) of the material record; Central and South American goods, 13–32 percent; European goods, 4 to 7 percent; and Asian goods, a mere 0.5–4 percent.

FROM CARGOES TO ASSEMBLAGES, 1849–1851

The excavation of the San Francisco waterfront provided assemblages from *Niantic,* Hoff's Store, 343 Sansome, and *General Harrison* sites with which to test the points of origin of the commodities that arrived in San Francisco. Ideally, matching the *Alta*'s merchant advertisements against the three assemblages would provide another source, in addition to the arrival notices, for comparison, but detailed advertisements do not exist for *Niantic,* Hoff's Store, or 343 Sansome. However, regular advertisements by Mickle & Co. provide both additional and comparative data to assess the *General Harrison* assemblage.

Like other urban sites, the San Francisco waterfront encapsulates materials that were deposited in landfill. However, the San Francisco waterfront is unique in that this process occurred within a brief twenty-four-month period between mid-1849 and May 1851. The *Niantic,* Hoff's Store, 343 Sansome, and *General Harrison* assemblages, while associated with waterfront businesses that were destroyed on a specific day, reflect that two-year time span. The patterns of merchandise in San Francisco's sites are characteristic of many dry goods store sites in western North America. The key is to look beyond goods' point of manufacture to identify patterns of supply and document the rapid delivery by sea to San Francisco within that brief period. Though the cargoes represent a short period, they fit within the patterns of global trade's centuries-long entry into the Pacific.

The Niantic *Assemblage*

The 1978 *Niantic* excavation yielded 3,948 artifacts that represented a minimum of 1,509 items (for example, not every fragmentary artifact could be linked to an item, such as isolated nails and other fasteners and fragmented bottle glass) (Smith 1981:213). Smith broke the collections into groups by their assumed cultural uses (table 7). She attributed both possible and known points of manufacture to artifacts in the assemblage, identifying pencils from Germany, London, and Concord, Massachusetts (86); brass pen nibs from London (92); a British gun and an American Hall's Model 1840 carbine (110–114); a Connecticut-manufactured steel axe (104); floor coverings that were either Belgian or British (130–131); French champagne from Reims (145–146); ale or porter from Bristol, England (151); Madeira and Spanish sherry (148); ceramics from the United States and England (169–176); a catsup bottle from New York (155); tin-packed truffle sausages from Brittany (184–185);and a spoon from Connecticut (163).

The artifacts were from a diverse group of businesses that were using the vessel as a storeship. Their names and businesses were unknown at

TABLE 7. *NIANTIC* ARTIFACT CATEGORIES

Activities Category	Number	Percent of All Artifacts
Stationery and printing	284	7
Tools	70	2
Arms	25	1
Architectural components	1,006	25
Furnishings	76	2
Kitchen	2,035	52
Comestibles	89	2
Storage	337	9
Apparel	20	1
Personal items	6	<1
Total	3,948	101

SOURCE: Smith 1981.
NOTE: Percentages do not add to 100 because of rounding.

the time of Smith's 1981 analysis except for the names of one commission merchant, Van Brunt, and a crockery merchant, Genella (211). The *Niantic* storeship was "a midpoint in the mercantile continuum that starts with producers . . . to eventual consumers" (214). The artifacts therefore represent merchandise selected by a segment of that continuum, likely wholesalers. They were unused items that were in storage for eventual sale, use, and discard and thus represent "the behavior of the merchant class and its definition of consumables" (215).

Smith assessed the product availability and diversity in the assemblage. The goods reflect a strongly male orientation with no ethnic or social differentiation, save a limited Anglo-Saxon cultural tradition (215–216). To Smith, they reflected the middle-class merchants of San Francisco, the city's "dominant cultural group," who used the ship and stored their merchandise in it (217). The storeship's assemblage represented their control over the distribution of mass-produced manufactured goods. Thus, the merchants "exercised a more influential role than other members of the middle class" (218). The goods in the assemblage suggested to Smith a flamboyant lifestyle and "even greater purchasing power than otherwise would be expected for typical consumers of the period," supporting contemporary accounts of San Francisco's conspicuous gold-fueled consumerism (219).

The *Niantic* assemblage did not reflect U.S. domination of commodities. Out of 1,509 artifacts, the combined percentage of imports outweighed U.S. manufactures ten to one (31.34 percent to 3.4 percent)

(Smith 1981:226). To Smith, this statistic demonstrated San Francisco's "dependence on the maritime sphere of trading and her linkage with national and international economies" (231). It also showed that San Francisco in 1851 had a "rather substantial dependence on imported manufactures" and was "tied to foreign markets and economies" just as it had been before the Gold Rush (228–231). Thus, Smith concluded that the *Niantic* assemblage was evidence that the accident of the gold discovery had served to "intensify the frontier process already in motion at this location" and represented not a radical transformation but rather "a more intense demonstration of previous beliefs and behavior patterns associated with capitalism" (232–233).

The Hoff's Store Assemblage

The assemblage of 5,806 artifacts excavated from a group of structures surrounding the ship chandlery of William C. Hoff was larger than that from the *Niantic* site. However Pastron's team could not analyze every artifact and die not report on every assemblage (Pastron et al. 1990:vi, 3). The team reported on firearms and other weapons, construction hardware, tools, bottles, comestibles, Chinese-export porcelain, and footwear (table 8).

The tools included round-point shovels stamped and identified as the product of the Ames Co. of Oliver, Massachusetts (Pastron et al. 1990:36–46). The furnishings were ten rolls and one fragment of a printed floor cloth similar to samples recovered from the *Niantic* site. The weapons were civilian and military arms, the majority of them U.S.-manufactured Mexican War surplus (Delgado 1990b:48). Embossed specimens of bottles were from a Bristol, England, glass factory; a Baltimore, Maryland, firm; and Altona, Germany (60). An intact black glass bottle, embossed "John Dove's Celebrated Ale Glasgow" was also recovered (62). Though the majority of wine bottles had contained champagne, the excavation also uncovered four Bordeaux bottles, one with a lead-foil cap embossed "Nelson Dupoy/A Bordeaux," and the base of a fragmented Hock bottle embossed "J. & W. Peters, Hamburg."

Most of the culinary bottles contained ground black pepper when found, the majority of them also retaining foil-cap labels embossed "Wells, Miller & Provost 217 Front Street New York" (63–64). Another group were embossed 'Wm. Underwood & Co. Boston" (64), and a third group of fragments bore no name but had a picture of Baltimore, Maryland's Washington Monument, which helped identify them as products

TABLE 8. HOFF'S STORE ARTIFACT CATEGORIES

Artifact	Number	Percent of All Artifacts
Tools	133	2
Arms	100	2
Architectural components	3,350	58
Alcoholic beverages	401	7
Kitchen	272	5
Comestibles	202	3
Footwear	1,131	20
Furnishings	10	<1
Medicine	182	3
Personal items	25	<1
Total	5,806	100

SOURCE: Pastron et al. 1990.

of the Baltimore Glass Works. Others carried the marks of "S Wardell," a New York pickle grocer; "Wm. Bodman," a Baltimore-based pickling merchant; and "Lewis & Co., Boston" (65–66). Medicinal bottles included specimens embossed "Ayer's Cherry Pectoral" or "No. 1 Shaker Syrup, Canterbury, New York" (69–70). Most toiletry bottles had cathedral-style and other decorations (including an image of the Madonna and Child), but only one bottle was embossed with a name, a small 1-ounce specimen marked "Lubin Parfumeur A Paris" (70). Two shards of soda-water bottles were embossed "Clarke & Co. New York" and were the only identified specimens from this group (71).

At least five Chinese underglaze blue porcelain toiletry sets were also recovered from the Hoff's Store Site. These sets included the remains of basins, water bottles, brush boxes, and soap dishes (Terrey and Pastron 1990:75). The specimens matched museum examples of items from the China trade in the eastern United States and were identified as Chinese-manufactured export ware. The toiletry sets may have been the property of an Anglo-American *négociant* or broker who handled Chinese goods rather than that of a Chinese merchant. They probably represented a new dimension of the West Coast's China trade, "a trade that was already well established in California prior to 1849 but which increased dramatically" with the Gold Rush (80–81).

The comestibles at the Hoff's Store Site included the remains of three barrels packed with salted pork, marked with the name of a New York manufacturer, paper-wrapped cake and bread embossed "T Carracas," and twenty-nine paper-wrapped biscuits, some of which were embossed with the name of Bent & Co., a Milton, Massachusetts, firm (Hattori and Kosta 1990:82–88). Two bundles of mat-wrapped rice were attributed to China (88). The excavation also revealed fruit seeds, including peach pits and grape seeds, shells of walnuts and hazel nuts, small quantities of wheat and flour, peas, dried beans, coffee beans and ground coffee, and tea packed in lead-lined caddies. Although researchers could find no definitive link to a country of origin, contemporary advertisements in the *Alta* suggested Central and South American, Tahitian, Hawaiian, German, Oregonian, and Chinese origins (89–91). Three brass labels, one for a New York–manufactured oyster tin, and two from sardine tins packed in Nantes, France, were also recovered (91–92).

The footwear included one specimen marked "F. Dane," a Boston shoe manufacturer. The assemblage also included bound stacks of other specimens bearing leather tags with the name of another Boston shoe manufacturer (Huddleston and Watanabe 1990:96–97). The excavators attributed the majority of the footwear assemblage to a U.S. manufacture, specifically one in the Massachusetts area, which was a major shoe-manufacturing center and the region "responsible for much of the California trade" (98).

From their examination of the Hoff's Store assemblage, the researchers concluded that by mid–1851, "California was still an isolated outpost, almost entirely dependent on logistical support from outside" (Pastron et al. 1990:101). Hoff's Store was filled with basic commodities suited to those "frontier conditions" but on a "frontier tamed" (102). In 1990, the excavators noted that those artifacts with a directly attributable point of origin demonstrated a direct connection with "suppliers on the eastern seaboard of the United States, Britain, China, and possibly France and Germany" (103). The trade represented in the assemblage was also indicative of San Francisco's maritime connections and its commercial role, which "revolved around transshipment to and from ocean going vessels and river boats" (104).

Although the Hoff's Store assemblage came from diverse points around the globe, unlike that from *Niantic,* it still showed overall U.S. domination of commodities. Of the 5,801 artifacts, the number attributable to U.S. manufactures outweighed foreign exports four to one, 1,806 to 452 (table 9).

Most of the artifacts in the assemblage, notably the building supplies, are unattributable. The supplies may be from the United States, in which case U.S. manufactures would constitute 88 percent of the assemblage. Also unknown is the total count of the various seeds, nuts, beans, and

TABLE 9. POINTS OF ORIGIN,
HOFF'S STORE ASSEMBLAGE

Point of Origin	Number	Percent of All Artifacts
United States	1,806	31
Unattributable	3,543	61
Europe	273	5
Central or South America	179	3
Total	5,801	100

SOURCE: Pastron and Hattori 1990.

other commodities, which might be Latin American or Pacific products. Nor is any quantifiable means of integrating the rice and tea, both Asian products, into the artifact count.

The 343 Sansome Street Assemblage

Excavation of the 343 Sansome Street site in 1989 produced an assemblage of 5,977 artifacts (Dames & Moore 1989:15). Excavators initially grouped the artifacts by material, sorting by the following categories: glass (1,728 items), ceramics (2,163), metal (914), leather (382), wood 101), bone (523), and other (166) (18). For comparative purposes, I have grouped them into functional categories (table 10). Some error is possible because the grouping by material does not necessarily allow differentiation by function. For example, "metal" objects include square nails and nested sets of tinware as well as tin cans, but because many of the metal artifacts are "fragmentary and unidentifiable," only 76 of them are enumerated and identified in sufficient detail to allow a functional classification (46). I have therefore counted only the identified artifacts in the function table, which reduces the count to 2,340 identifiable artifacts.

The tools recovered from the site were a round-point shovel, two broad axes, one common "American broad ax," and three "Pennsylvania-style" claw hammers (Dames & Moore 1989:43). Three brass powder gauges for loading weapons made up the arms group. The alcoholic-beverage bottles included a variety of Bordeaux, Hock, and brandy-styled bottles, as well fourteen champagne bottles with foil-covered corks wired in place. One bottle was marked "IOH: von Pein, Altona [Germany]" and was identical to a specimen from Hoff's Store (21), whereas another was marked "Dixon & Co., Liverpool." The largest number of alcoholic-beverage bottles (842) were stoneware containers stamped "Refined Cider" (29)

TABLE 10. 343 SANSOME STREET ARTIFACT CATEGORIES

Activities Category	Number	Percent of Artifacts
Tools	6	<1
Arms	3	<1
Architectural components	3	<1
Alcoholic beverages	938	40
Kitchen	44	19
Comestibles	517	22
Footwear	325	14
Furnishings	1	<1
Medicine	48	2
Personal items	54	2
Total	2,340	99

SOURCE: Derived from Dames and Moore 1989.
NOTE: Percentages do not add to 100 because of rounding.

Nonalcoholic-beverage bottles included seven soda or mineral-water containers, one marked "J. Boardman & Co., New York, Mineral Water. This Bottle is Never Sold" (21). Three fragmented examples were marked "Lynde & Putnam, Mineral Waters, San Francisco, Cal.a, Philadelphia," whereas two fragments of sarsaparilla bottles were each marked " . . . nsend . . . S..rilla" and "H. Bull, Extract of Sarsaparilla," the first being "Old Dr. Townsend's Sarsaparilla" from New York, and the other being A. H. Bull's extract, a product of Hartford, Connecticut (21).

Culinary bottles were represented by forty-seven examples from the site, including fruit or preserve bottles, one marked "William H. Davis, No. 57 Broad St., Boston." Other preserve bottles retained foil labels, two of which were from the New York firm of Wells, Miller and Provost. Unlike the Hoff's Store example of the firm's labels, the 343 Sansome examples were marked "Fresh Blackberries" on one label and "Fresh Wortleberries" on the other (25). One other Wells, Miller and Provost artifact, a tin can with a lead label, contained oysters. A similar label was found at the Hoff's Store Site. In addition, the remains of wooden crates filled with deteriorated tins held "remnants of a granular substance identifiable as ground coffee" (43).

Other bottles included unmarked pepper sauce and pickle containers, glass and ceramic ink bottles, and forty-eight bottles, including one still corked with contents intact, of "Clifford & Fernald's Original Indian Vegetable Bitters, Boston, Mass" (23). Fragmentary remains of other, unmarked patent-medicine bottles also emerged from the site. Other glassware included 343 fragments of pressed-glass goblets, wineglasses, and tumblers (27).

The large and diverse group of ceramics from the site, in addition to the bottles, stoneware jugs, and crocks, included fragmented earthenware, and the remains of cups, bowls, plates and saucers, all of them either in the blue-on-white, brown-on-white, plain white, or transfer-print styles. All were imports from Great Britain, with maker's marks for Davenport Ironstone of Longport, Staffordshire, England; Francis Morley & Company, which manufactured Mason's patent ironstone china in Shelton, England; James Edwards Ironstone, also from Longport; Thomas Walker's Tiger Hunt ironstone from Tunstall, Staffordshire; and Thomas Shirley & Company's Clyde pottery of Greenock, Scotland (34). Among 173 fragments of porcelain were 2 examples with the remains of hallmarks for "Imperial French Porcelain" (36). The examples may be white ironstone, perhaps of English manufacture, and inexpensive "knockoffs."

Leather from the site came from 325 fragmentary shoes. A study of 60 soles revealed the marks "A. H. Boston," "Wm. Bent," "Boston," and "A. H. & P. Boston" (Dames & Moore 1989:53). A rare sample of a rubber shoe sole, marked "Perpetual Gloss, Goodyear's patent, Ford & Co. Manufacturers, New Brunswick," is the only artifact yet found in any of the waterfront sites with a Canadian origin (53).

Among the other finds were over 4,350 animal bones, more than half of them butchered remains of cattle, but geese, sheep, deer, grizzly bear, elk, and even dog bones also appeared in the group. Many of the cuts were high quality; others were for soup. These remains suggested to excavators that a butcher or meat-storage locker was present at the site (56).

For the excavators, the crowded and probably cold and damp quarters built over the water that they exhumed in 1989 spoke of a difficult life and work with the moderating influence of imported wines, liquors, oysters, preserves, and fine cuts of meat (59). Additional analysis of the assemblage, particularly a comparison with the other 1851 fire assemblages, shows that the artifacts at 343 Sansome fit into the general pattern of goods present in the city at the time of the fire. The comparative analysis of origin is skewed by the large number of unattributable artifacts (61 percent). With acknowledgment of that fact, we can note that the number of U.S. goods is nearly equal to the number of foreign goods, with a slightly larger percentage of European manufactures (table 11). This calculation presents a very different picture from that of Hoff's Store. However, if the unattributable tins of coffee found with the Wells, Miller and Provost oysters were American and the cuts of meat were as well (as

TABLE 11. POINTS OF ORIGIN,
343 SANSOME ASSEMBLAGE

Point of Origin	Number	Percent of Artifacts
United States	435	19
Unattributable	1,428	61
Europe	474	20
Pacific, Central or South America	3	<1
Total	2,340	100

SOURCE: Dames and Moore 1989.

was true of the meats at Hoff's), the percentages might be closer to those of the other collapsed store's.

The General Harrison Storeship Assemblage

Excavation of the *General Harrison* storeship in 2001 produced an assemblage of at least 51,231 artifacts (Delgado, Pastron, and Robichaud 2007), which the excavation team sorted into architectural, kitchen, comestibles, storage, arms, apparel, and personal groups (table 12). Appendix 3 presents a detailed reconstruction of the assemblage based on Mickle's *Alta* advertisements and material record. The largest number of artifacts were architectural, represented by iron tacks (some 50,000) recovered from a large mass at the site. This mass skews the analysis of the sample and is extracted from the percentages table as are 334 architectural elements from the ship's construction. Excluding these items leaves 897 artifacts for analysis.

Analysis of the points of origin could not definitively assign a source to half the recovered artifacts, but the remaining artifacts split between U.S. (19.6 percent) and European (24 percent) points of origin (table 13).

This analysis is potentially skewed by the unknown total artifact count for barley and beans, observed in large quantities at the site but recovered only as small samples. These commodities which might represent Chilean products, but there is no quantifiable means to integrate them into the analysis. What does the assemblage suggest? The *General Harrison* assemblage is nearly equally split between United States manufactured and foreign exports at its simplest level.

Like the other three assemblages, the *General Harrison* assemblage demonstrates San Francisco's dependence on maritime trading, linking the city to national and international economies. Like the *Niantic* as-

TABLE 12. *GENERAL HARRISON*
ARTIFACT CATEGORIES

Activities Category	Number	Percent of Artifacts
Arms	6	1
Architectural components	175	20
Kitchen	340	38
Comestibles	125	14
Storage	117	13
Apparel	5	1
Personal items	129	14
Total	897	101

SOURCE: Delgado, Pastron, and Robichaud 2007.
NOTE: Percentages do not add to 100 because of rounding.

TABLE 13. POINTS OF ORIGIN,
GENERAL HARRISON ASSEMBLAGE

Point of Origin	Number	Percent of Artifacts
United States	174	20
Unattributable	491	55
Europe	214	24
Pacific, Central or South America	10	1
Total	889	100

SOURCE: *San Francisco Daily Alta California.*

semblage, it also shows that San Francisco in 1851 was heavily dependent on imported manufactures and was not yet self-sufficient.

CARGOES AND POINTS OF ORIGIN

Table 14 compares the points of origin of the 10,539 artifacts in the four
assemblages. A comparison of these numbers with data on ship arrivals
reveals that the assemblages have a smaller percentage of U.S. commodities and a smaller percentage of Pacific and Central and South American commodities than one would expect from analyzing shipping data
alone (table 15). The percentages are nearly a match for European commodities and within the range for Asian commodities.

These discrepancies have several possible explanations. One is that
the majority of the unattributable items in the assemblages—such as barley, beans, nuts, fruit pits, coffee, and tea—are U.S., Central or South

TABLE 14. POINTS OF ORIGIN FOR SAN FRANCISCO WATERFRONT ASSEMBLAGES

Ship	Date	Port of Origin	Cargo
Pacific	July 10, 1850	New York via Valparaíso	Alcohol, barley, building supplies, butter, cigars, dried fruit, dry goods, footwear, preserves
Sir George Pollock	August 5, 1850	Hong Kong	Fabric and clothing, handkerchiefs, oranges, preserved ginger, sweetmeats, tea, trunks
Virginia	August 13, 1850	Valparaíso	Barley, cement, coal, fruit
John Marshall	September 19, 1850	Baltimore via Valparaíso	Bricks, building supplies (shingles and lumber), cement, dried fruit, 2 fire engines, 1 frame house, hardware, lard, oysters, shoes and boots, soap and candles, stoves, straw hats, tea, 6 wagons
Equator	October 25, 1850	Valparaíso	Alcohol, barley, carpeting, cigars, coffee, dried fruit, flour
Spray	November 12, 1850	Paita, Peru	Assorted goods, beans, cigars, eggs, flour, onions, peas, pumpkins, sweetmeats, sweet potatoes
Lady Amherst	November 19, 1850	London via the Falkland Islands	Alcohol, bricks, coffins, dry goods, 3 iron houses, 2 wooden houses
Justine	December 19, 1850	Valparaíso	Alcohol, barley, chocolate, cigars, sardines
Oscar	January 2, 1851	Hong Kong	Bags, beef, cigars, coffee, eggs, furniture, molasses, oars, preserves, rice, rope, silks and satins, spices, sugar, tea
Erato	January 10, 1851	Callao, Peru	Alcohol, clothing, chocolate, flour, looking glasses, oilcloth, sugar
Pacific	February 10, 1851	Valparaíso	Alcohol, barley, beans, cigars, dry goods, hardware, sugar
Huntress	March 7, 1851	Valparaíso	Barley, ceramics, glasses, lard, tobacco
Holder Borden	March 23, 1851	Valparaíso	Alcohol, flour, lard, mess beef, sugar
Emily	March 25, 1851	Valparaíso	Alcohol, dried fruit, mess beef, potatoes, tobacco
Jackin	April 5, 1851	Sundsval, Sweden, via Valparaíso	Alcohol, barley, beans, bricks, flour, lumber

SOURCE: *San Francisco Daily Alta California.*

TABLE 15. POINTS OF ORIGIN:
ASSEMBLAGE DATA VERSUS ARCHIVAL DATA

Point of Origin	Percent of Assemblage	Percent of Total Ship Arrivals
United States	23	50–75
Unattributable	60	—
Europe	8	4–7
Pacific, Central or South America	2	13–32
Asian	<1	4–0.5

SOURCE: Ship arrival data from the *San Francisco Daily Alta California*.
NOTE: The ship arrival data show the range between 1849 and 1850. Percentages do not add to 100 because of rounding.

American, Asian, or Pacific commodities. The fragile or consumable nature of many of these commodities might also have affected the numbers: large amounts of flour, coffee, tea, rice, and other comestibles imported from Valparaíso, Panama, Mazatlán, or Callao may well have been consumed and therefore did not enter the archaeological record. The same is true for straw hats from Guayaquil, lumber from Sydney, and tobacco from Cuba.

The maritime system was complex, part of an international, interconnected web of trade. Various smaller ports dispatched local commodities not only to each other but also to larger entrepôts. These entrepôts accumulated commodities and dispatched them to other entrepôts. For example, Dutch ports predominantly fed Amsterdam, Amsterdam fed London, and London fed New York (Wallerstein 1989). Though individual merchant captains or companies could ship to foreign ports, by the nineteenth century, the costs and risks of such ventures were increasingly managed and controlled by consortiums and regulated by customs, excise, and insurance regulations. Large entrepôts had the facilities and the economic power to dominate global patterns of shipping.

The shipment of steel axes from Connecticut to Mickle & Co. in San Francisco illustrates this process. Shipped from Connecticut by rail or wagon to New York, the axes were loaded onto a ship that took them to Canton. From there, they were selected by a local commission merchant, probably one in communication with Mickle or another merchant in direct communication with California, who would select commodities likely to sell well in San Francisco and have them loaded into the *Oscar* for shipment to California (*Alta*, January 10, 1851). Perhaps not coincidentally, a Collins steel axe turned up in *Niantic*, two blocks way from the site where Mickle & Co. offloaded and sold his merchandise (Smith

TABLE 16. ADVERTISED ARRIVALS OF *GENERAL HARRISON*
WITH CARGOES FOR E. MICKLE & CO., MAY 1850–MAY 1851

Point of Origin	Niantic	Percent*	Hoff's Store	Percent*	343 Sansome	Percent*	General Harrison	Percent*	Total	Percent*
United States	52	3	1,806	31	435	19	174	20	2,467	23
Unattributable	984	65	3,543	61	1,428	61	491	55	6,446	61
Europe	472	31	273	5	474	20	214	24	1,433	14
Pacific, Central or South America	1	1	179	3	3	<1	10	1	193	2
Total	1,509	100	5,801	100	2,340	100	889	100	10,539	100

SOURCE: *San Francisco Daily Alta California.*
*Percent of all points of origin for preceding column.

1981:104). Mickle & Co. was not the only merchant to sell Collins axes, so no direct link can be determined between the Mickle axes and the axe from the *Niantic* assemblage. Nevertheless, the axe in the assemblage and the means by which Mickle obtained his axes for sale illustrate the maritime system at work.

The Mickle & Co. advertisements in the *Alta* offer a glimpse of San Francisco's role in the maritime system. The advertisements show a wide range of goods from around the world, specifically identifying products from Australia, Belgium, Brazil, China, Chile, Colombia, Cuba, Ecuador, England, France (specifically the regions of Bordeaux, Cognac, Champagne, Languedoc, and Provence), Germany (Rheingau, specifically Hockheim), Holland, India, Indonesia, Italy (specifically Marsala in Sicily and Venice), New Zealand, Panama, Peru, the Philippines, Portugal (Madeira and the Douro), Spain (specifically Malaga and Sevilla), Sweden, the United States (specifically Connecticut, Massachusetts, New York, Maryland, Pennsylvania, and Virginia), and the West Indies (specific islands unknown). However, not all these products came direct from ports in their home countries. Mickle & Co. never handled a direct shipment from Australia, Belgium, Brazil, Cuba, France, Germany, Holland, India, Indonesia, Italy, Spain, or the West Indies. The maritime system shipped the commodities from those countries to entrepôts in London, New York, and Valparaíso, from whence they were shipped to Mickle & Co. As Mickle & Co. was served by this system, so was every other merchant in San Francisco.

A review of Mickle & Co.'s advertisements in the *Alta* between May 1850 and May 1851, the year *General Harrison* was in operation, reveals a wide range of goods. The advertisements name the ships on which the goods arrived and the ports from which the ships sailed (table 16).

A majority of arrivals came direct from Valparaíso, or on ships that had stopped at Valparaíso on their way from other ports. Two vessels came from Hong Kong, two from Peru, and one from London. A close look at the cargoes from vessels coming direct from Valparaíso shows a mixture of local goods, such as Chilean produce, and goods manufactured elsewhere and then gathered and transshipped by merchants seeking to tap into the California Gold Rush market. Analysis of the Mickle & Co.-imported cargoes also confirms that other established entrepôts— London, Hong Kong, and New York—served as collection and redistribution points for merchandise and goods that made their way to San Francisco and into the storeship of Mickle & Co. and into the hands of many other merchants and consumers.

The activities of Mickle & Co. were not unique, and as we have seen, the Valparaíso connection was just one of several. New York was the principal entrepôt engaged in direct trade with San Francisco, dispatching 214 ships in 1849 (Albion 1939:356). New York had expanded its trade after 1815, and by 1860, it was "handling two-thirds of all the nation's imports and one-third of its exports" (386). The port's growth was already evident during the Gold Rush. At that time, "out of well over a thousand individual items distinguished in the customs reports, New York ranked first among the American seaports in all except seven articles of domestic export and twenty-four imported commodities. In the value of its imports and exports, as well as in the volume of shipping, which entered and cleared, New York not only stood an easy first among American ports; but in all the world only London and Liverpool exceeded it (386). New York was the initial point of entry for a variety of goods from other states and Europe, as well as from the Caribbean, that were then transshipped to California.

New York's role in such transshipments is clear from the list of items that came to Mickle & Co. via *Pacific* when it first arrived from New York via Valparaíso. According to the company's August 7, 1850, ad in the *Alta,* the cargo included 360 14-pound kegs of "choice Dutch butter," "Malaga raisins" from Spain, "8 cases English prints," "30,000 first quality Havana cigars" from Cuba, 10 cases of port from Portugal, 1,000 cases of "Claret" from Bordeaux, France, and 400 cases of French champagne. As the principal entrepôt in 1849–50, New York overshadowed Liverpool and London, the two largest (in terms of world trade) European entrepôts, which sent only twelve ships to San Francisco versus New York's 214 sailings to California during the same period. However, these English entrepôts participated in and profited indirectly from the San Francisco Gold Rush market, linked to it by the maritime system. They sent their goods to New York and to other ports that fed the growing California market.

Through this system, San Francisco, a peripheral zone in an intense stage of integration into the world system, was incorporated into the global market through its importation of mass-produced goods of the industrial age. Packed in the holds of hundreds of ships, these goods were shipped by the ton in exchange for gold. The people who communicated the market's demands, ordered the cargoes, and handled their sale on arrival were the *négociants,* or commission merchants, as represented by Mickle & Co. and its storeship *General Harrison.*

Like *Niantic, General Harrison* was a midpoint in the mercantile continuum. Along with the Hoff's Store and 343 Sansome assemblages, it represents the behavior of the merchant class through its definition and control of consumables. Gold Rush merchants were tied to mercantile partners with a stake in the emerging Pacific market. Having staked construction of the infrastructure of the new entrepôt of San Francisco, these individuals and new partners aggressively sought to import a wide range of goods, as demonstrated by the varied assemblages of the *General Harrison, Niantic,* 343 Sansome and Hoff's Store sites. The international range of these assemblages shows a global event—but it also shows how the flow of commodities was controlled and directed from entrepôt to entrepôt. Goods shipped from New York to Hong Kong, or London to Hong Kong, were rerouted to San Francisco, just as goods sent to the Chilean entrepôt of Valparaíso (such as Peruvian chocolate, Ecuadorian tobacco, Panama straw hats, or lumber from Australia) were transshipped to San Francisco.

These cargoes and assemblages reflect San Francisco's economy and its relationship to the regional and global processes in the world. But the cargoes sent to California between 1849 and 1851 not only reflect the global system of supply at sea, they also show that the system sent goods specific to San Francisco's and California's market needs. We can see this response in the luxury items sent to accommodate the conspicuous consumption of gold-dust–laden miners. Yet the majority of shipments and the dominant categories of items focused more on the actual needs of the growing city and region than on a gold-frenzied market of conspicuous consumers, as world perceptions of Gold Rush San Francisco might suggest. These goods were staples and basic commodities that spoke to the need for food, shelter, and clothing, as well as industry (table 17).

The consumables in the assemblages were largely mass-produced goods shipped from industrialized centers to build San Francisco. In each assemblage, and in the aggregate, the largest number of artifacts were building supplies, ranging from galvanized "zinc" plates to nails, tacks, bricks, white lead, and hardware. After this group, the next-largest group contained essential provisions and supplies, ranging from bulk goods like barley, beans, rice, coffee, and tea to provisions like hardtack, butter, salted pork, and bottled preserves. Only after these categories come personal-indulgence commodities, largely alcoholic beverages but also a few notable examples of luxury food items such as oysters and sardines (Hoff's Store) or truffle and paté sausages (*Niantic*).

The commerce of San Francisco and its port was less dependent on high-gain luxury items than on essential goods and building supplies. The

TABLE 17. COMPARISON OF ASSEMBLAGE COMMODITIES

Commodity	Niantic	Hoff's Store	343 Sansome	General Harrison
Essentials				
Barley		*		*
Beans	*	*		*
Bitters		*	*	*
Bricks	*			*
Butter		*		
Ceramics	*	*	*	*
Clothing	*		*	*
Coffee		*	*	
Dried fruits	*	*		Possibly
Firearms	*	*		*
Footwear	*	*	*	*
Malt beverages	*	*		*
Mess beef	Possibly	*		
Nails	*	*	*	*
Preserves	*	*	*	*
Rice		*		
Rope	*	*		*
Salt pork		*		
Sardines	*	*		
Tea		*		
Tin plates		*		*
Tobacco				*
Tools	*	*	*	*
White lead		*		
Wine	*	*	*	*
Luxuries				
Carpeting	*	*		
Champagne	*	*	*	*
Luxury fabrics				*
Madeira	*	*		
Oysters		*	*	
Port				*
Sherry	*	*		

world system's industrialized core produced these goods, the maritime system moved them to San Francisco, and the city used the goods to establish a more solid economic basis for its integration into the world system. The facility of the maritime system is also evident in the rapid integration of "the latest" or most desirable goods at the time, like cast-iron prefabricated houses, preserved foods in tin cans, and wire nails. In San Francisco, the system had a particularly American aspect, but it was nonetheless at a critical stage of incorporating the Pacific. The Gold Rush provided the means for expansion, but the maritime system provided goods for merchants intent on establishing an entrepôt that would both profit from and outlive Gold Rush consumers.

CHAPTER 8

San Francisco and the Nineteenth-Century World Maritime System

San Francisco's creation and development did not occur in a cultural or economic vacuum. The city's emergence was a mid-nineteenth-century manifestation of the expansion of European and American capitalism and creation of a world economy (Wallerstein 1974, 1980). This expansion is a significant illustration of Braudel's *longue durée,* in which "change is slow, a history of constant repetition, ever-recurring cycles" (Braudel 1972:20). European capitalism in the Pacific expanded and contracted in cycles known as Kondratieff waves, or K-waves (Kondratieff 1979), which correlate with Braudel's *conjunctures.* K-waves reflect alternating periods of economic stagnation/depression and booms that occur during the integration of new geographic areas and their commodities into the world system.

Kondratieff espoused three long waves or cycles. In the United States, the first cycle began to rise in 1790 and started its decline in 1814, hitting a "trough" in 1843. The California Gold Rush coincides with the next rise, Kondratieff's second cycle, which began in 1849 and peaked in 1864 (Kondratieff 1979:table 1). The Gold Rush provided surplus value in that its gold revived the core economies of Europe and the United States following decades of economic stagnation, especially in the United States following the economic depression known as the Panic of 1837. The Gold Rush was a "resuscitating process" (Groover 2003:11) that not only counteracted the previous decades' K-wave downswing but also allowed California to become a player in the world economy. This notion fits with Wallerstein's (1980) view that the world system's integration of new extractive areas (semiperipheries) was the main impetus for settlement and colonization.

However, a simple application of Wallerstein does not fully address the rise of San Francisco or the actual process of integration. Moreover, it does not offer a fully fleshed-out view of the rationale for the city's integration. A simple view of the process would characterize San Francisco as a frontier semiperiphery suddenly brought into the world system within the short period of the Gold Rush (1848–52). This perspective would fit with contemporary nineteenth-century views of San Francisco as an "instant city" that fulfilled the nation's manifest destiny, both of which are shortsighted and narrow interpretations. This interpretation also does not fit with a view in world systems theory that incorporating a new zone into the system takes decades, not years (Groover 2003:11).

San Francisco's integration had begun in the late eighteenth century when Spain established a military and religious outpost to control San Francisco Bay and counter rival, notably Russian aspirations. This process of colonization had coincided with rising European interest in the Pacific, particularly by Great Britain, and by the end of the eighteenth century, in establishing domination of the Northwest Coast's (including California's) maritime fur trade. These activities were in themselves part of an older, larger process in which Europe sought to incorporate China and greater Asia by dominating the trade to and from Asia.

The K-wave of expansion in the Pacific beginning in the last quarter of the eighteenth century contracted after 1814, and maritime trade remained stagnant until the 1840s. In that period of stagnation, however, an upswing began, thanks to the independence of Latin America and the subsequent opening of the region to free trade and establishment of a major entrepôt at Valparaíso. At the same time, the Opium Wars and the establishment of free zones (entrepôts) in Shanghai and Hong Kong and the rise of the Australian colonies as active traders contributed to the next rise in the K-wave. San Francisco was already undergoing integration, albeit slowly, through its participation in the hide and tallow trade of the 1830s and 1840s, which linked it to the industrialized shoe-manufacturing center of the United States and to the China trade. When gold was discovered in 1848, the rush of energy and capital propelled San Francisco toward integration.

THE MECHANISM OF INTEGRATION: THE MARITIME SYSTEM

The expansion of the world system in the past five hundred years has been a complex process of increased agricultural production, industrialization, the rise of extragovernmental bodies that control and expand trade, the extension of military force, colonization, and settlement (Wallerstein 1974, 1980). The connective link has been, at its simplest, the use of ships to carry goods and people and, at its most complex, the establishment of ports, shipping merchants' cooperatives and companies, and the use of surpluses and industrialization to create larger, more efficient, and faster ships, large and powerful naval forces, and larger port facilities to warehouse cargoes, load or off-load goods, and quickly transport goods intermodally to and from ports. The most effective port type has been the entrepôt, or zone of free exchange, where goods from various other ports could be collected for transshipment. These activities, centered on ships and shipping, formed a maritime system that proved to be the world system's most effective means of transporting flows of commodities to and from the core economy.

The maritime system was the primary engine for integrating the Pacific into the world economic system. Voyages of exploration and trade, the establishment of ports and fortified harbors, the creation of entrepôts, and the extension of regular maritime "trades" such as the China trade, the Northwest Coast maritime fur trade, and the South American trade all made this integration possible. The maritime system was global and multinational in its reach and connections, and despite the pitfalls of ocean transport (such as shipwreck), it was an increasingly fast, safe means of communication. Technological improvements in hull construction, propulsion, and navigation—especially those of the industrial revolution in the late eighteenth and early nineteenth centuries—shortened times at see and enabled ships to carry larger amounts of goods.

The maritime system provided a means for governments, corporations and companies, and individuals to participate in the growing global economy. The agents of this system were the merchants in key ports who established trade relationships in other ports to gain new items for trade and to control the flow of commodities. These relationships were regional, national, and in time global, as evidenced by China trade partnerships with partners and houses in New York, Boston, and Shanghai, or in London, Calcutta, and Hong Kong. Trading houses underscored the importance of such relationships by sending junior partners, employees, or family members to ports that presented desirable trade opportunities. This practice is clear in the large number of American and British merchants who established themselves as commission merchants in Valparaíso following Chile's independence from Spain. In time, several of these individuals or firms, like Mickle & Co., further extended their houses from Chile to California.

As I have sought to show here, the maritime system was the dominant factor in the rise of San Francisco. Merchants who saw an opportunity in Gold Rush San Francisco to create a permanent base in the northern Pacific in a sense hijacked the process of integration. They envisioned the city as a new entrepôt that could give them access to the Pacific Rim and provide an American outpost for the domination of Asian trade and perhaps, in time, the entire ocean. Their subsequent development of the city was instrumental in starting the gradual shift of the world system's core from Europe to the United States.

REDEFINING SAN FRANCISCO AS A FRONTIER

San Francisco does not fit the traditional pattern of frontier development in the United States. It started as an outpost on the maritime frontier, was created as an entrepôt, and demonstrated the world system's reliance on the maritime system to expand globally. This view fits with the most recent theoretical evaluations of San Francisco within the new western history. The concept of the American frontier has undergone a series of challenges and refinements since Turner's initial thesis, most dramatically beginning in the late 1980s with works by Limerick (1987, 1991), Gibson and Whitehead (1993), Robbins (1994), and White (1991). New western historians suggest that the West's history has been shaped by processes of "invasion, conquest, colonization, exploitation, development and expansion of the world market," the latter underlining the influence of Wallerstein (Limerick 1991). In the "new West," diverse peoples converged and interacted with each other as well as with the natural environment. This West was a place of moral ambiguity, where "heroism and villainy, virtue and vice, and nobility and shoddiness appear in the same proportions as in . . . any other subject in human history" (Limerick 1991:87). As I argue in this book, it was also a place with a coast that embraced the western ocean, as Gibson and Whitehead (1993) have emphasized by describing it as America's "maritime frontier."

The historians who originally examined San Francisco's history within the Turnerian framework saw the city's development as part of an inevitable progression of conquest by whites (Soulé, Gihon, and Nisbet 1855; Camp 1947). New western historians have since come to see San Francisco as a maritime-inspired outpost on the coast (Reps 1981:2; Gibson and Whitehead 1993:188). In their view, the city's emergence was not the result of a slow progression across the North American continent but a successful effort to leapfrog ahead, bypassing the intervening plains, mountains, and aboriginal peoples. In San Francisco, diverse cultures, including the native aboriginal and Hispanic cultures already in place on the coast, converged and met as part of the process of integration into the world economy. Though the city's integration had been under way for more than a decade, the Gold Rush accelerated the process. San Francisco was a cosmopolitan frontier, as Steffen (1979) asserts, far more than it was an "instant city," as Lotchin (1974) and Barth (1975) argue.

Not all historians have made this connection. Frost agrees with Barth's view that San Francisco was an "instant city" because of its rapid development "and relative absence of historical foundation" (Jones, Frost, and White 1993:19). However, this view does not take into account San Francisco's position within the *longue durée* of the Pacific (Jones, Frost, and White 1993; Perry 1994). Neither does it address the fact that the maritime system began to integrate San Francisco before the city achieved "critical mass" for extensive urban development through the Gold Rush and the influx of population, capital, and mass-produced consumer goods. New western historians assert that western expansion was closely linked to national and international economic systems. Robbins (1994:xi) and Gibson and Whitehead (1993) explicitly link these economic systems to maritime trade. Robbins notes that these links made San Francisco the "imperial heart of a vast trading network" that extended along the coast and into the interior (1994:173) and ultimately made it a peripheral center in a resource region linked by rail and sea to the manufacturing centers of the United States' eastern seaboard.

San Francisco fits this historical perspective as well as the archaeological view espoused by Hardesty (1988), in itself a reflection of the world system perspective. Hardesty views the mining frontier as a colony "financed, manned, and supplied from the urban centres of America and Europe. Despite . . . geographical remoteness and small sizes . . . linked to a vast transportation, communications, demographic, and economic network on a national and international scale" (1).

The key in this frontier model is the transportation and economic network that linked San Francisco to the rest of the world and why it did so. Though the central network elsewhere in the West was railroads, on the edge of the Pacific, San Francisco had unlimited access to world markets through the ocean. Its coastal location allowed commodities and labor to flow freely in and out and made it part of the interconnected processes that drove the rise of capitalism in the nineteenth century (Wolf 1982:4).

Access to San Francisco was via the maritime system, which offered a mode of efficient transport for all the commodities required to build urban centers; feed, clothe, and equip the miners; and transport gold to the national and international economy. Of course, San Francisco was not unique in having such access to the maritime system: Pacific entrepôts as diverse as Seattle, Vancouver, Honolulu, Lahaina, Levuka (Fiji), Sydney, Valparaíso, and Hong Kong were linked by the sea to the rest of the world and to each other and were emerging semiperipheral zones in the process of integration (Jones, Frost, and White 1993; Burley 2003).

THE ARCHAEOLOGY OF THE SAN FRANCISCO WATERFRONT AND THE MARITIME SYSTEM

The maritime system was and is more than an interconnected network of rivals and collaborators engaged in the business of ships and shipping. For archaeologists, it is a means of conceptualizing the integrated maritime activities of a region or a period and of assessing the relationship of maritime trade to the larger capitalist world system (Russell, Bradford, and Murphy 2004:101). My perspective in this book derives not from the traditional, particularistic approach of maritime archaeology but from the field's adoption of a regional approach, the *Annales* school, and world systems theory—in particular, the intersection of these theoretical approaches with urban and mining-site historical archaeology and with new western history.

The archaeology of the San Francisco waterfront served as a catalyst and focus for developing and illustrating this framework. The discovery of a buried ship and its assemblage was the starting point for detailed historical research. The resulting data and the discovery and analysis of other sites, culminating with *General Harrison* between 2001 and 2005, fed into a single understanding, revealing similarities, connections and an overall context. Coincidently, as new western history and historical archaeology provided a new context for the frontier, maritime archaeology shifted its focus from individual site study and particularism to a regional approach that examined wide areas and the interconnectivities of groups of shipwrecks (Murphy 1997; Gould 2000).

Global, regional, and local activities within the maritime system created a material culture in San Francisco culture that reflected an integrated maritime system. The maritime system included ships, shipyards, customhouses, storeships, outfitters, cargo and trade goods, regulations, rules, and the activities of individuals or groups such as boardinghouse keepers, salvagers, fishermen, and waterfront recruiters. All these features of the Gold Rush San Francisco waterfront are represented in the archaeological and archival record. The seemingly disparate elements of that waterfront's archaeological sites—two storeships, partially dismantled ships, the remains of wharves, a collapsed piling-supported series of stores, and cargoes stowed in the storeships—essentially form one site.

Not only was and is the San Francisco waterfront a maritime landscape, a material manifestation of the maritime system (Esser 1999; McCarthy 1999; Russell, Bradford, and Murphy 2004:101), it is also an example of Hardesty's (1988) features systems. The maritime activities of Gold Rush San Francisco left material remains and activity areas that were directly related even though they were several blocks or miles apart. To understand these features, one must not look at them in isolation but view them as separate pieces of an integrated whole (Hardesty 1988:9–11). In analyzing the material record of the waterfront, I have come to see the role of maritime trade and activities is the dominant factor. I first saw the value of this interpretive approach at Hoff's Store (Delgado 1990b), and the value is now more demonstrable with a look at other sites where earlier comparisons focused on similarities in artifacts and assemblages rather than on the nuances of the maritime system (despite an explicit recognition that these goods came to California by ship).

San Francisco's Gold Rush sites are ideal for assessing the concept of the maritime frontier. They represent a specific city/entrepôt with diverse and yet maritime-linked activities and infrastructure. Maritime archaeology provides a valid method to address the systemic behavior responsible for Gold Rush San Francisco's material record, namely the maritime system as a means of expanding the global economy. This framework fits with Staniforth's model of interpreting the material culture "in terms of the societies for which they were bound . . . [linking] maritime archaeology much more neatly to historical archaeology since it treats the transport of cargo as a single step in a wider trajectory or system of use" (2003:30–31). In chapter 2, I asked how we should characterize the San Francisco waterfront site(s): as urban, mining, or maritime sites? The answer is "maritime," if we consider not only the method of transportation but also the system's role in developing infrastructure, merchants' efforts to control flows of commodities through regular communication by ship, maritime partnerships and trade links, and warehousing in storeships until advantageous conditions existed for sale. The answer is also "maritime" when we take an integrated archaeological view that acknowledges the dominant role of the maritime system in the interpretation of the site(s).

San Francisco's Gold Rush waterfront and its assemblage of cargoes are artifacts not only of the city's development but of the worldwide development of capitalism. The commission merchants who created and managed the city were the successors of the eighteenth- and nineteenth-century merchants who added new peripheral zones to the world system through, as Wallerstein (Wallerstein 1980:129–130) notes, controlled production and merchandising decisions. He compared them to "what the French called *négociants* as opposed to *traitants* or *commerçants*" (153), who stationed themselves at bottlenecks of flows to adjust production to respond to market demands—or to limit flows to create demand. The merchants of Gold Rush San Francisco acted in just this way, using their networks and their warehouses and storeships to acquire, hold, and release goods.

The goods in the assemblages reflect a careful process of selection and commodity flow. The goal was not to make a quick profit from conspicuous consumers but to capitalize a city and port that would survive the inherent "boom and bust" of a mining town. Historical accounts emphasize the aspect of conspicuous consumption, perhaps because of the boisterous, colorful character of city life and an emphasis on this aspect in contemporary accounts by incredulous observers. The more mundane but important business of attending to housing, warehousing, feeding and clothing the denizens of San Francisco, and establishing a basis for industry and commerce did not often merit comment, but it is the reality reflected in the material record of the Gold Rush waterfront, with its trove of nails, tin plates, bricks, beans, and barley.

This reality also fits the theoretical perspective that casts San Francisco as part of a global system using maritime trade and connections—not just by sending hundreds of ships in an uncoordinated "rush" but by employing players, some with long-standing commercial maritime interests, to manage and control the influx of commodities to build a successful entrepôt.

The control of the flow is evident in the domination of trade into San Francisco by other key entrepôts—in 1849, by New York and Valparaíso; and in 1850, primarily by New York. Not only did these ports send more ships than other ones did, but the ships they sent carried cargoes of commodities that had been assembled from disparate international sources at New York and Valparaíso and then transshipped to San Francisco. Some of the goods that arrived at San Francisco were for use in building and sustaining the city; others were repackaged and transshipped to the interior of California and the gold mines. In this fashion, San Francisco grew into a sustainable port for ongoing trade with Asia and the wider Pacific.

For the above reasons, San Francisco fits Wallerstein's definition of the critical factors for hegemony, "dominance of the spheres of commercial distribution of world trade, with correlative profits accruing both from being the entrepôt of much of world trade and from controlling the 'invisibles'—transport, communications, and insurance. Commercial primacy in turn leads to control of the financial sectors of banking (exchange, deposit, and credit) and of investment (direct and portfolio); these superiorities are successive, but they overlap in time" (1980:38).

With hegemony came the ability to shift from the semiperiphery to the periphery and then to the core of the world system. San Francisco's rapid rise enabled it to integrate successfully into the core economies of Europe and the United States. The development of the port spurred the construction of the transcontinental railroad, completed in 1869, which joined the maritime system in merging San Francisco into the United States' core economy. The success of that merger played out in the late nineteenth century as American ambitions and economic interests joined forces with European interests to integrate the Pacific Rim more fully into the global economy. This process possible with the benefit of more bases of operation, some of them entrepôts, and the output of the industrial age, including massive steel-hulled, steam-powered ships that went even faster than earlier models, carried more freight and passengers, and reached hitherto-isolated regions.

Analysis of the material and archival records from a maritime-system perspective shows that 1849–56 San Francisco was no accident. The city and its port were neither an isolated frontier nor an instant city but rather key players in the Pacific's long processes of trade and the creation of the world economy. San Francisco was a critical player because it was America's principal port on the Pacific. The city's story is one of economic expansion that continues to this day. Maritime interests continue to play the critical role in the twenty-first century, moving containers, bulk freight, and petroleum by sea throughout the Pacific and around the world in a system that, even now, carries 90 percent of the world's goods by water.

TESTING THE MODEL: DAWSON CITY, THE
KLONDIKE GOLD RUSH, AND A FAILED ENTREPÔT

San Francisco came into its own in a century marked by several gold rushes, including ones in Australia, British Columbia, and Canada's Yukon/Klondike. The Klondike provides an instructive model for assessing the maritime system as a tool of integration and examining the system's ability to expand by creating entrepôts. As an outpost of the world system, the area also fits within the collaborative framework proposed by Lawrence (2003) for assessing the archaeology of the nineteenth century—in this case, allowing comparison with another outpost, San Francisco. Although Lawrence proposed her framework to analyze interrelated British Empire sites, it is applicable here because of the nature of the world and maritime systems.

The Klondike shared characteristics with the other nineteenth-century gold rushes, and the processes at work were the same as those that had shaped the West during the preceding fifty years, or to the time of the California Gold Rush (Brand 2003:3). I have selected the settlement of Dawson City to test the model I propose in this book. The town stood at the confluence of the Yukon and Klondike rivers at an important break in the transportation system to the Klondike mines—the "head of navigation," or the point at which steamboats could ascend no farther. (7). A community of 2,000 in 1897, it blossomed between 1898 and 1899 into the largest city in the Pacific Northwest after San Francisco and Canada's largest city west of Winnipeg, with a population of 16,000 (Fetherling 1997:152; Brand 2003:271). During that two-year period, it acquired modern amenities such as running water, steam heat, electricity, telephones, large stores, and government offices. In the rapidity of this rise, the "frontier outpost" of Dawson City was not unlike San Francisco five decades earlier.

The city was a riverine entrepôt in Canada that, like Gold Rush San Francisco, was dependent on the outside world for supplies like building materials, mining equipment, and food. In 1897 and 1898, Dawson City commission merchants, "dominated by large American mercantile firms . . . competed with other outfitters, wholesalers and distributors for a lasting slice of the Yukon trade. From this outfitting rush grew an enduring hinterland relationship between the Yukon and its primarily West-Coast suppliers . . . When these tons of goods had been redistributed by the end of the season a recognizable merchant element had emerged. Over the next season supply lines for a more stable market were established

and Dawson's merchant community became more specialized and so-
phisticated" (Archibald 1975:vii).

Dawson City thrived because of its ability to exchange gold for mass-
produced commodities. The initial rush by "Stampeders" in 1897 saw
most goods coming from Canadian sources by paddle wheeler from St.
Michaels (Archibald 1975). The volume of goods and the means of transport changed, however. Shipped from San Francisco, Seattle, Victoria,
and Vancouver, large amounts of goods and men were landed by ship on
the Alaska coast; hauled into the mountains on the Chilkoot Trail, at first
by mule and later by rail, to the rivers; and then run up to Dawson. The
role of the merchants in discharging tons of commodities at Dawson,
which were then redistributed to mining camps in the interior, also par-
alleled that of the merchants in San Francisco (Archibald 1975).

Linked to the world system, and with its own maritime system in play,
albeit a riverine one, Dawson City had every potential for success. However, by 1905, Dawson was a "well-appointed ghost town," with its population back to 2,000, many of its stores closed, and the city's commercial life "a shadow of its former self" (Archibald 1975:169). Why did
Dawson City fail to achieve critical mass as an entrepôt and as a sustainable
urban center? Obviously, the situation in the Klondike was far more lim-
iting than in California, particularly in its extreme winter conditions for
eight months of the year. Winter conditions notwithstanding, Dawson did
grow and prosper for a while. Brand (2003) argues that Dawson City and
the Klondike represent a study in transience, with prospectors and miners who fit White's definition of modern migration, moving temporarily
to obtain "property that could be transferred somewhere else," such as
gold, and then returning home (1991: 193). The transient community was
well served by the transportation network, and archaeological examination of the transient gold miners' district at Dawson City has documented
its extent, identifying manufacturers of commodities throughout eastern
Canada, the United States, and Europe (Brand 2003:271).

These transient miners were not the ideal population for either the
government or the mercantile establishment that formed the core of Dawson City and sought to establish a permanent community. Unlike San
Francisco, which had weak government control, Dawson City was under more stringent government regulation. Transients were not encouraged to settle permanently, and in time, the nature of the rush changed,
having fewer individual miners and more small groups who worked for
larger corporations and conglomerates (Brand 2003:272–273). This
change brought a concomitant shift from the trade of gold as a petty com-

modity to industrial production of gold and a decline in population. In addition, Dawson City's many stores and merchants gave way to two larger trade corporations, and then, after 1907, to direct supply to the major gold companies, which operated company stores and effectively bypassed the entrepôt (Archibald 1975:169).

Why did Dawson City decline and San Francisco not, especially after the California Gold Rush changed from a group of individual transient miners to a mechanized, industrial mining operation with large companies engaged in hydraulic extraction? Dawson City, despite its transportation links, was far more isolated and dependent on the mining and miners than was San Francisco. San Francisco's trade links shifted to a broader market after the Gold Rush; Dawson City's trade links rested solely on its gold mines.

San Francisco, on the coast, was readily accessible to ships, and these vessels could connect the city and its market far more rapidly to the rest of the world than Dawson City's location allowed. To reach Dawson City, one needed to take an ocean voyage to Alaska, a rail trip into the interior, and then a river voyage. The distance and the transportation breaks were too many, and Dawson City's relative isolation from the world market and system was overcome only by the demand of individual, transient consumers and the eagerness of the commission merchants to provide the goods to house, clothe, feed, and equip them. Once the miners left, the system retreated, leaving Dawson City high and dry. No amount of government support or capital could or did compensate for the lack of a direct connection by sea to the world system.

San Francisco's initial success lay in the economic energy of the California Gold Rush, but the merchants there were backed by larger national and international interests that saw in the port a future entrepôt not for mining-based regional trade but for trade via larger networks and for incorporation of a wider area of the Pacific Rim. The means to achieve this goal was the maritime system, a system that had ready access to San Francisco and only partial access to Dawson City.

The ultimate success of the maritime system in incorporating San Francisco into the world system made the city the world's principal Pacific entrepôt and a major player in the 1897–1900 supply system, transshipping goods north. After 1856, with many opportunities to participate in a variety of trades by sea, San Francisco expanded its ocean trade and secured its future with transpacific steamship lines to Hawai'i, the Society Islands, Asia, Australia, and South America. It did so through domination of North America's Pacific Coast trade and through global trade in lumber, coal, sugar, wheat, and oil trade, not to mention the pursuit of short-term but lucrative opportunities like the Klondike rush (Wright 1911). Without such links to the rest of the world by sea, Dawson City, isolated by land at the end of a river that froze up each winter, had but one opportunity to prosper. When the business of mining changed, Dawson City was finished as an entrepôt and as a growing concern because it could not access the ocean and diversified trade and therefore could not participate in the evolving global economy, which continued to use the ocean as its highway and means of expansion. Once again, we see that San Francisco's success, while initially fueled by the Gold Rush, was ultimately a result of the maritime system's role, not gold's.

A NEW LOOK AT THE MARITIME FRONTIER

This book is the summary of thirty years of performing fieldwork, excavating the buried Gold Rush waterfront of San Francisco, analyzing assemblages, and working in the archives. This work began in 1978 with the excavation and analysis of *Niantic* and continued with sites such as the buried *William Gray,* Charles Hare's shipbreaking yard, and Hoff's Store. The impetus for the book was the 2001 excavation of the storeship *General Harrison.*

Additional fieldwork as a maritime archaeologist on shipwreck sites during the intervening decades also played a role, especially when some of the projects and discussions with colleagues shifted my scholarly attention from individual sites to a regional approach adopted from historical archaeology. Similar insights into the maritime system have led archaeologists to accept and modify world systems theory. In recent years, several colleagues have led the way in this thinking and in demonstrating its application, especially through better integration of maritime archaeology into the mainstream of historical archaeology.

This work of colleagues with a focus on the maritime system, as well as that of western historical archaeologists whose world overlaps with the new western history, helped my thinking evolve. Instead of viewing ships in a particularistic way—as artifacts reflecting the practices and technologies of their construction and operation or mirrors of life on board—I see them as artifacts of a larger system. Just as new western historians argue that the West was defined by invasion, colonization, and the merging of diverse peoples, we can characterize the oceans and the maritime world, also mythologized as horrific and heroic but in reality places of moral ambiguity, as frontiers where the human experience in all its aspects has played out, albeit on a canvas far larger than any land-mass. Like other frontiers, the global span of the oceans has been a defin-ing factor in the development of the modern world's global economy.

Analyzing the rise and success of San Francisco as a maritime land-scape, as a group of interconnected features, and as a macroartifact of the maritime system has suggested that we can see the entrepôt as a model for settlement and integration on the maritime frontier. That model, I pro-pose, has applicability to other cities and ports, including not only those on ocean coasts but also those on major rivers or lakes that connect to the sea, like the Mississippi River or the Great Lakes. The key is to view these sites as places not where the land meets the sea but where the sea, not an obstacle but a readily traveled global highway, meets the land.

APPENDIX I

Commission Merchant Business Cards from the Supplemental *Daily Alta California,* October 4, 1849

Occasional special editions of the *San Francisco Daily Alta California* carried extensive business advertisements. The "supplemental" *Alta* of Thursday, October 4, 1849, lists a wide array of commission merchants. A number of their "business cards" appear below. The cards are illustrative, showing location of business, references (often the merchants' foreign partners or investors), and the status of some merchants as agents. The commission merchants who advertised in this edition provide a representative sample of the community and the connections that merchants had to the larger world at the beginning stages of San Francisco's development as an entrepôt.

Osborn & Brannan

COMMISSION MERCHANTS
Corner Montgomery and Sacramento sts., San Francisco
Jos. W. Osborn Saml. Brannan

McDonald, Reynolds & Co.

Shipping and Commission Merchants
Kearny street, 2 doors above Sacramento

Grayson, Guild & Co.

COMMISSION MERCHANTS
Corner of SACRAMENTO and MONTGOMERY sts.

Reference—Messrs. S. H. Williams and Co., in San Francisco and Honolulu

S. H. Williams & Co.

G. B. POST
Importers and Commission Merchants
San Francisco, A.C. Honolulu, Oahu, H.I.
S. H. Williams, Boston, Mass.
J. F. B. Marshall }
Honolulu, Oahu, H.I.
B. F. Snow }
Wm. Baker, Jr. }
San Francisco, A.C.
G. B. Post }

J. J. Chauviteau & Co.

COMMISSION MERCHANTS
Clay street, San Francisco, California
Bills of Exchange on New York, London and Paris.
Goods Received on Storage.

REFERENCES:
N. M. Rothschild & Sons, }
Darthez Brothers, London
De Rothschild Brothers, }
Green & Co. Paris
Bechet, Dethomas & Co. }
Hargous Brothers, }
New York
P. Harmony's Nephews & Co. }

Bleecker, Van Dyke & Belden

AUCTIONEERS
and General Commission Merchants
San Francisco.
The subscribers have leased the large and elegant store
and premises erected by Messrs. Mellus, Howard & co.
on Montgomery and Clay streets, for the purpose of conducting
the general auction and commission business.
An experience of many years in the conducting of this
business in the city of New York, will enable them to
render every satisfaction to those favoring them withtheir consignments.
Regular package sales will be held at least twice every week.
Shelf sales of assorted goods will be held as often as
Circumstances will admit.
Cargoes of merchandise, Vessels, and every description
of property will be sold on the usual terms.
To Let—Several stores, offices and vacant land for
building, being part of the above premises.
Storage—Heavy and light merchandise of every description
taken on storage, in store and yard.

BLEECKER, VAN DYKE & BELDEN

ANTHONY L. BLEEKER Auctioneers
RICHARD VAN DYKE, Jr. cor Montgomery and Clay sts.
ROBERT H. BELDEN

E. MICKLE & CO.

Importers and Commission Merchants,
San Francisco, Upper California.
E. MICKLE WM. H. TILLINGHAST

Messrs. Huttmann, Miller & Co.

COMMISSION MERCHANTS
At the Bee Hive, San Francisco.
E. HUTTMANN MORLEY E. MILLER
JOS. E. DALL H.S. AUSTIN

DALL & AUSTIN

GENERAL COMMISSION MERCHANTS
SAN FRANCISCO.
References————Messrs. Ward & Co. }
San Francisco.
Mellus, Howard & Co. }
Messrs. Turnbull, Dall & Slade }
Thomas Whitredge & Co. *Baltimore.*
Wm. Howell & son }
Stone, Slade & Farnham *Philada.*
Howell, Frazier & Co. *N. Orleans.*
Lawrence, Stone & Co. }
Waterston, Pray & Co. *Boston*
F. Skinner & Co. }
Wolcott & Slade }
Haggerty, Draper & Jones *N. York.*
Wm. Buckler, *Canton*

WARD & CO.,
(Late Ward & Smith,)

COMMISSION MERCHANTS,
SAN FRANCISCO, CAL.
GEO. A. WARD, FRANK WARD
{ J. H. Polhemus, Valparaiso, Chili
Agents
{ G. R. Ward, New York, U.S.

De Witt & Harrison

Importers, General Commission Merchants, and
Wholesale Dealers,
Sansome street, opposite Government Reserve
A. DE WITT H. A. HARRISON

Finley, Johnson & co.
Importers and Commission Merchants
Portsmouth House, Clay street,
San Francisco.

Pollard & Co.

Auctioneers and Commission Merchants,
CLAY STREET, SAN FRANCISCO.
A. POLLARD, A. G. RANDALL, T. CRUMMER.
Ref to—Messrs. Cross, Hobson & Co.,
William H. Davis, Esq.,
Robert A. Parker, Esq.
WM. CORNELL JEWETT CHARLES MELHADO

Jewett & Melhado,

AUCTION AND COMMISSION MERCHANTS,
(Successors to Capt. David Dring)
MONTGOMERY STREET.
Having arranged with Captain Dring, for his store and
entire stock of goods, we respectfully solicit the custom
of purchasers and holders of merchandise. Favorable
arrangements will be made with consignees, owners of
vessels, real estate, & c., for disposal of the same.
Regular sales Tuesdays and Fridays. Due notice of each
will be given. Gold Dust bought and sold, and remit-
ances, made to the United States and Europe. Consign-
ments entered at the Custom House, free of charge.
Refer to Gen. P. F. Smith,
Captain David Dring,
Ward & Co., *San Francisco.*
Moffat & Co.,
Burgoyne & Co.
Mason & Thompson,
B. H. Field, Esq. *New York.*
Hon. John M. Read,
Mulford & Alter, *Philadelphia.*
Wm. Mason & Son,
W. B. Ferguson & Co. *Baltimore.*
T. B. Wales & Co.,
Wm. Long, *Boston.*
Josiah Wills,
Jas. Gordon & Co. *Norfolk.*
Davenport, Allen & Co. *Richmond.*
J. W. Zacharie & Co. *New Orleans.*
J. B. Brown & Co. *Portland, Me.*
J. B. Fernand, Esq.,
Lewis Louis, Esq. *Panama.*
J. H. Smith
Lucas, Micholls Co. *London.*

Probst, Smith & Co.,

GENERAL COMMISSION MERCHANTS,
Washington street, San Francisco.

Robert Wells & Co.,
Merchants.

Robert Wells. James C. Ward.
SAN FRANCISCO.

James Creighton,
Commission Merchant.

*Sansome street, opposite the Government reserve, next
to the Warehouse of DeWitt & Harrison.*

Macondray & Co.

Commission Merchants and Bankers,
SAN FRANCISCO.
F. W. MACONDRAY, JAMES OTIS, R. S. WATSON

References:—
R. B. Forbes, W. S. Wetmore,
Sampson & Tappan, Cary & Co.,
Enoch Train & Co., A. A. Low and Brother,
Josiah Bradlee & co., Davis, Brooks & Co.,
Minot & Hooper, *Boston New York.*
Nye, Parker & Co.—*Canton,* Russell & Sturgis, *Manila.*

AGENTS:
Minot & Hooper, Boston / Peter Eddes, New York.
F. W. MACONDRAY, *Agent for the Boston Insurance
Companies.*
Insurance on treasure per steamer to New York and
Boston effected.
Exchange on New York, Boston, and London for sale.
Counting Room for the present at the Stockton Packet
Office, foot of Jackson st.

Woodworth & Morris,

COMMISSION MERCHANTS,
CLAY STREET WHARF.
FREDK. A. WOODWORTH, CHAS. A. MORRIS,
San Francisco New York
W. & M. will personally attend to the purchase or sale
of every description of merchandise, ships, launches,
ship's stores, and having their warehouse directly on the
wharf, consignees are saved all expense of cartage.
Merchandise forwarded to all the different embarcade-
ros on the bay and rivers in fast sailing launches at moderate rates of freight.
Goods received on storage, and lighters furnished for
discharging cargo.

Simmons, Hutchinson & Co.,

*EXCHANGE BROKERS AND COMMISSION
MERCHANTS.*
R. SIMMONS }
TITUS HUTCHINSON SAN FRANCISCO
JNO. F. POPE }
REFER TO
J. E. Thayer & Brother,
Thomas Lamb, *Boston.*
Weld & Minot,
D. & A. Kingsland & Co.
Hussey & Murray, *New York.*
Charles W. Morgan,
W. R. Rodman, *New Bedford.*
D. Sisson & Co., *Providence.*
C. Waln Morgan, *Philadelphia.*
Wood & Low *New Orleans.*

COOKE, BAKER & CO.,

General Shipping and Commission Merchants,
SAN FRANCISCO, UPPER CALIFORNIA.
JOSEPH J. COOKE, GEO. LEWIS COOKE, ROBERT B. BAKER.
References.—Barnard, Curtis and Co., Thatcher Tucker
and Co., Peck and Bloodgood, Amos R. Eno, Esq., *New
York;* E. D. Brigham and Co., *Boston;* I. H. Bartlett and
Son*, New Bedford;* Samuel Nightingale, Esq., *Provi-
dence;* Lemuel Goddard, Esq., *London;* Rawle, Drinker
and Co., *Hong Kong.*
C. B. & Co. will occupy the new building, nearly in
the rear of their permanent location, foot of Sacramento
street, until the erection of their own warehouse.

Starkey, Janion & co.,
Commission Merchants.

And Importers of Goods direct from England,
the Atlantic ports of the United States and China.
San Francisco.
W. M. Burgoyne, J. V. Plume.

BURGOYNE & CO.

BANKERS and COMMISSION MERCHANTS,
MONTGOMERY STREET,
San Francisco.
Exchange for sale. Gold dust bought.
REFERENCES:
Major General Persifor F. Smith, *San Francisco.*
Brig. Gen. B. Riley,——*Monterey.*
Major Washington Seawell,——*Benicia.*

Simmons, Lilly & Co.,

Importers and General Dealers in Merchandise.
W. SIMMONS
S. D. LILLY *San Francisco*
G. W. SIMMONS *Boston.*

W. H. Davis,

Wholesale and Commission Merchant
corner of Clay and Montgomery street,
San Francisco.

Salmon & Ellis,

COMMISSION MERCHANTS,
Pacific street, near the Buckland House.

Hopkins & Ela.

SHIP AND CUSTOM HOUSE BROKERS.
Office in Northam & Gladwin's building, opposite the
government cannon, and near the principal landing.
THOS. HOPKINS. JAMES M. ELA.
References.—Captain Edward A. King, Harbor-master;
Simmons, Hutchinson and Co., Cross, Hobson & Co.,
Cooke, Baker & Co.
N.B. Trunks and other goods taken on storage,

MEACHAM & TALLANT,

Auction and Commission Merchants,
Corner Montgomery and Clay streets, building of Mellus, Howard & Co., Cash advance made on consignments for auction sales.

Mack & Ovalle,

COMMISSION MERCHANTS.
Clay street, opposite Pollard & Co.

Godeffroy, Sillem & Co.,

Commission Merchants,
Sacramento street, San Francisco.
ALFRED GODEFFROY WILLIAM SILLEM.

Lovering & Gay,

Commission Merchants.
Montgomery street, opposite head of Central Wharf.
WM. LOVERING, JR. CHARLES GAY.

Mellus, Howard & Co.,

General Dealers and Importing Merchants.
HENRY MELLUS WM. D. M. HOWARD
TALBOT H. GREEN FRANCIS MELLUS
Montgomery street, San Francisco.

Blythe & Co.

SHIP BROKERS AND GENERAL AGENTS,
Corner of Pacific and Dupont streets.
Custom House business done.

The "Representative Storeship" of 1849–1851

Niantic, Apollo, and *General Harrison* are three of the hundreds of expedient "ship buildings" that merchants used in Gold Rush San Francisco. As we have seen, the template for the storeships was the earlier use of ships as structures in London, China, and other ports. The price of a storeship was not necessarily lower than that of a balloon-frame structure on piles. Storeships sold for some $2,500 to $5,000, as is evident from the sale of the ship *Rome* for $2,500 in June 1850 (Macondray and Co. 1850) and the auction of the 443-ton bark *Orion* for $5,000 in early July 1850 (*San Francisco Daily Alta California,* July 3, 1850).

Storeships were likely an attractive option because merchants could haul them in close to shore and easily use them as floating structures, or, as with *Niantic, Apollo, General Harrison,* and others, they could become permanently moored, housed-over buildings. Large, solid, equipped with pumps to combat flooding, ostensibly safer from fire than landlocked buildings, and movable (except for the three beached ships studied here) storeships were expensive, perhaps overcapitalized, but quickly installed investments for waterfront entrepreneurs.

Did merchants apply specific standards in selecting certain ships as storeships or ship buildings? The simple answer to this question is yes. Overwhelmed by the mass of crowded and ostensibly abandoned shipping in San Francisco's harbor, contemporary observers and later historians lumped together "abandoned ships" in one category, concluding that the vessels served "no better purpose" than to provide floating buildings. The use of ships as floating structures predated the California Gold Rush and was an expedient way either to make temporary use of active vessels or to give retired vessels one last function before their demise. In this fashion, entrepreneurs converted a number of vessels to "other uses" as floating or permanently moored structures in San Francisco.

Most vessels that served as floating warehouses did so only temporarily (for a few months to a few years), unlike *General Harrison, Niantic,* and *Apollo,* which were hauled in close to shore, hemmed in by pilings, and housed over, never again to go to sea. This latter form of storeship was the exception, although the unique nature of these more permanent structures and the frequent mention of them in contemporary accounts have led several historians to determine they were "representative" of most storeships in Gold Rush San Francisco. Analyzing available accounts of the storeships and the imagery of the waterfront of 1850–51, as well as later images through 1856, I can identify only a handful of housed-over vessels, and I estimate a total population of twelve to twenty vessels covered with "barns" or structures.

Archaeological excavation of two intact storeships, later scuttled and subsequently buried in landfill, has also been instructive. These vessels, *Rome* and *William Gray,* both spent years as storeships, and both, when excavated, had clear decks, including the intact bulwarks of *William Gray* and her lower rigging in the form of chain plates (Pastron and Pritchett 1979; William Self Associates 1996).

What type of storeship was representative of those on the San Francisco waterfront? Rather than work from a single example, *General Harrison,* I have first sought to determine how many storeships were on the waterfront and then selected a sample to analyze. According to Goodman's *Encyclopedia of the California Gold Rush Fleet* (1987), 762 ships sailed to San Francisco between December 5, 1848, and December 31, 1849. This number represents all vessels known to have sailed from American ports in that seminal Gold Rush year. Although it does not represent foreign (Canadian, Australian, New Zealand, South American, Asian, and European) vessels that also departed that year, or American clearances in 1850—a number equal to Goodman's tally—it provides a strong (54.4 percent) sample of the 1,400 vessels believed to have sailed for San Francisco in 1849 and 1850 and that arrived by the end of 1850 (Delgado 1990a:19). Of the Goodman listing of 762 vessels, 104, or 13.6 percent, are known to have served as or been converted to storeships. This sample represents just 7.4 percent of the estimated 1849 sailings; other vessels that sailed in 1850 from various ports were also converted to storeship use.

On July 17, 1852, the *San Francisco Daily Alta California* listed 164 storeships moored off San Francisco, 60 more vessels than Goodman accounted for. The *Alta*'s number does not include ships that had already cleared for sea after short-term use as storeships use and also omits the burned and sepulchred *Niantic, Apollo,* and *General Harrison.* The best conservative guess, therefore, is that 167 to 200 ships, of the population of 1,400 vessels, or 11 to 14 percent of all Gold Rush vessels, ended up as storeships. Based on this calculation, the Goodman listing, admittedly a selective sample, accounts for 52 to 62 percent of the storeship population—an exceptional sample of the vessels that served as storeships between 1849 and 1851.

I analyzed the following elements of the Goodman listing of vessels:

- ·   date of construction
- ·   relative size (based on the tonnage of cargo the vessel was registered to carry)
- ·   relative size (based on the vessel's rig)
- ·   place of construction.

My analysis yielded the results in table 18.

TABLE 18. PROFILE OF GOLD RUSH STORESHIPS
(number of vessels)

Sorted by Date of Construction

Before 1800	1
Before 1810	1
1811–20	5
1821–30	28
1831–40	45
1841–50	6

Sorted by Relative Size (tons)

Under 200	6
200–240	12
241–300	25
301–340	14
341–400	22
401–440	8
441–500	8
501–540	1
541–600	3
601–700	3

Sorted by Relative Size (rig)

Ships	56
Barks	34
Brigs	14

Sorted by Place of Construction

Connecticut	2
Delaware	1
Maine	28
Maryland	2
Massachusetts	29
New Hampshire	7
New York	11
Pennsylvania	2
Rhode Island	3
South Carolina	2
Unknown	16

SOURCE: Analysis of data in Goodman 1987.
NOTE: Totals do not match because of incomplete data for all ships.

Not all data fields were available for every vessel identified as a "storeship" in the database. However, the sample provided sufficient data to identify a "representative" storeship: a New England–built, 334-ton ship less than a decade old but generally no older than two decades. Thus, entrepreneurs tended to select relatively mature, but not too old or young, three-masted vessels with midrange stowage capacity—neither too small and hence overcrowded, nor too big and hence partially empty and unprofitable. Moreover, the vessels of choice were products of America's premiere wooden shipbuilders of the age in the shipbuilding centers of Massachusetts and Maine.

General Harrison, at 409 tons, and *Niantic,* at 452 tons, are larger than the average, but they are the right age (eleven and fourteen years old, respectively, when they arrived in San Francisco) and they were both New England built, although the Connecticut-built *Niantic* came from a state that produced only one other known storeship. Nonetheless, the profile of the representative storeship offers a yardstick; timing, availability, the right price, the relative desperation of buyer and seller—all nuances of individual circumstance—also played a role in creating San Francisco's Gold Rush storeships. The high cost of purchasing, converting, and operating a storeship on the San Francisco waterfront in combination with the high cost of wharves and other waterfront buildings offer material evidence of intensive overcapitalization by San Francisco's maritime mercantile community to ensure the success of its entrepôt.

Was the conversion of a vessel to a storeship a destructive, final use, or was it a form of recycling? The evidence suggests that storeship conversion was largely not a deliberate destructive use because approximately half of some 200 storeships went back to sea. The others were either broken up at Rincon Point or ended up sepulchred in the landfill that buried the Gold Rush waterfront in the throes of urban development (San Francisco Maritime Museum 1965). The ships broken up at Rincon Point were an older group of vessels; their presence in the point's ship graveyard and their ultimate dismantling indicates "natural" or deliberate selection of the older, less seaworthy craft for recycling. The use of a vessel as a storeship represented an adaptive reuse of the ship. After that use, a ship's ultimate disposition was as the source of raw metal and firewood to fuel forges and foundries from the broken up and recycled hulls.

Cargo Stored As Merchandise aboard the *General Harrison* Storeship

Below I have reconstructed the cargo stored as merchandise aboard the *General Harrison* storeship from Mickle & Co. advertisements in the *San Francisco Daily Alta California*, 1849–51. The terminology and quantities are based entirely on the advertisements. I have added explanatory notes identifying points of origin (of manufacture, growth, or shipment) and indicated which items are also evident in the archaeological record (as excavated in 2001). I have also compared the cargo described in the advertisements with the assemblages from *Niantic* and Hoff's Store.

ALCOHOL

"200 casks Scotch ale and porter" + "352½ dozen Scotch ale" + "Draft Ale in Casks"

> This large grouping of beverages is the most likely source of the black-glass malted-beverage containers and liquid samples excavated in 2001. The 200 casks were part of the cargo of *Pacific* from New York via Valparaíso advertised on July 10, 1850.

India pale ale

42 cases Tennent's ale

> These malted beverages made by John Tennent and Son of Glasgow were part of the cargo of *Oscar* that arrived from China on January 10, 1851, which means the ale was shipped to China and then to San Francisco. On February 9, Mickle & Co. advertised "20 casks Tennent's draught ale" for sale. Either this offering was a previously unadvertised lot of casks, or the "42 cases" were a misprint for "42 casks" and more than half the shipment had sold in the month since *Oscar*'s arrival.

33 dozen Arrak punch

> Also known as Arraks Punch Opium Drink, Swedish Punsch, and Caloric Punsch, this liqueur was made from "Batavia Arrak," a compound of rum and fermented Javanese rice, but despite the advertisement on some bottles, it contained no opium. The liqueur was part of the cargo of *Jackin* on April 5, 1851.

Brandy + Otard brandy

> Founded by a French nobleman of Scottish ancestry in Cognac in 1795, this cognac-producing house bears the family name. Otard still produces a variety of cognacs (www.otard.com).

400 cases champagne + Champagne (x2) + "200 cases superior champagne"

> This cargo item is the source of the bottles excavated in 2001. Then, as now, this sparkling wine came from the Champagne district of France near Reims, 90 miles (145 kilometers) northeast of Paris (Johnson and Robinson 2002:78–79). Without labels, one cannot determine which maison the wine came from; however, a crate from the *Niantic* excavation (1978) retains a fragmentary label that matches a contemporary mention of the wine that identifies its source as the maison of Jacquesson et Fils, one of the major champagne houses of Reims (Delgado et al. 1979; Smith 1981:145–147). The 400 cases were part of the cargo of *Pacific* from New York via Valparaíso advertised on July 10, 1850.

122 cases cherry cordial + "Cherry Cordial, in cases"

1000 cases claret wine + claret (x4) in casks and cases

> *Claret* is the nineteenth-century term for Bordeaux's red wines. In time, the term grew more generic and encompassed most of the heavier red wines (Johnson and Robinson 2002:82). The 1,000 cases were part of the cargo of the *Pacific* from New York via Valparaíso advertised on July 10, 1850.

cognac brandy, in 18 gallon casks + cognac + 2 kegs cognac

Hock

> *Hock* was the generic term for German white wines, usually Rieslings. The term comes from the Rheingau town and vineyards of Hockheim am Main (Johnson and Robinson 2002:226–227).

Madeira (x2)

> This fortified wine came from the Portuguese island of Madeira. Bottle fragments marked "Old Madeira" were recovered during the *Niantic* excavation in 1978 (Smith 1981:154).

"marsalla in casks"

> This item refers to the fortified white wine Marsala, which finds use today as a cooking wine but matched Madeira and sherry in popularity in the Gold Rush era. Like those wines, Marsala was particularly popular in the United Kingdom and the United States. The wine is produced at the western tip of Sicily near the port city of Marsala (Johnson and Robinson 2002:184).

50 cases "Paxarete (sweet sherry)"

Paxarete, or Pajarete, is a sweet sherry from Spain and is also made in Chile.

25 cases Frontignan

> This Muscat de Frontignan is a sweet dessert wine produced in southern France on the Coteaux du Languedoc. Located on the coast, west of Marseilles on the Golfe du Lion, the village of Frontignan has been a wine-producing center for more than two millennia. The Muscat grape, developed into a dessert wine around 1700 by the Marquis du Lur-Saluces (according to local lore) was a botryized (from the botrytis fungus) wine initially; it is now a fortified wine (Johnson and Robinson 2002:138–139). The wine arrived on *Jackin* on April 5, 1851.

60 cases brown Philadelphia stout

> This brew is another likely source of the black-glass malted-beverage bottles and liquid contents excavated in 2001. Despite its name, it may be the product of New York breweries, not Philadelphia ones. The 60 cases were part of the cargo of *John Marshall* from Baltimore via Valparaíso on September 26, 1850.

Port + "port wine, in 12 gallon casks" + "Port, in casks" + "10 cases old port"

> This fortified red wine is the product of the Portuguese Douro region near Oporto, which gives the wine its name (Johnson and Robinson 2002:207–211). An embossed

bottle label was excavated in 2001. The 10 cases were part of the cargo of *Pacific* from Valparaíso advertised on July 10, 1850.

Rum + 40 barrels of rum

Sherry (x4) + 80 cases + 20 cases sherry wine + 100 kegs sherry wine, 9 gals ea

Another dessert wine of the nineteenth century, sherry comes from Jerez de la Frontera on the southern coast of Spain. Served by the Port of Cadiz, Jerez has produced this white wine aperitif for centuries. The range of sherries in general goes from *finos* to *amontillados* and *olorosos* (Johnson and Robinson 2002:199). No known sherry bottles were excavated in 2001, but an embossed label marked "Xèrès" (the French name for Jerez) was excavated at the *Niantic* site in 1978 and may represent French sherry masquerading as Spanish wine (Smith 1981:154).

"Superior Wines, in cases"

This shipment is the likely source of the white wines excavated in 2001 with their liquid contents intact.

"casks sweet Malaga wine"

Malaga, in Andalusia, was the source of raisins that many people believed were the best available in the nineteenth century and it was also the source of rich, raisiny white dessert wines known locally as *vinos generosos*. Today the region produces Moscatel and Pedro Ximénez (Johnson and Robinson 2002:200).

"Mason's Vegetable Bitters"

The bitters were part of the cargo of *John Marshall* from Baltimore via Valparaíso, September 26, 1850. This shipment may be the source of bitters bottles excavated in 2001.

TOBACCO

30,000 first quality Havana cigars

The cigars were part of the cargo of *Pacific* from Valparaíso advertised on July 10, 1850.

22,500 superior Havana cigars + 58,000 superior Havana cigars

Havana and paper segars + 2 cases paper cigars

"Havana cigars"

"108 M Manila segars"

"segar paper"

100 bales of Virginia leaf tobacco + 30 ceroons tobacco, 2 cases cut tobacco

The 100 bales of Virginia leaf tobacco arrived on *Huntress* from Valparaíso on March 7, 1851. An advertisement on March 29, 1851 for 63 bales suggests that 37 of the bales had sold by that time.

"4 cases Bracamoro cigars"

These cigars contained South American tobacco from the Peruvian district of Jaen de Bracamoros, a center for tobacco production since colonial times. They were popular in the nineteenth century in Lima.

228 cases chewing tobacco

The tobacco was part of the cargo of *John Marshall* from Baltimore via Valparaíso, September 26, 1850.

PROCESSED FOODSTUFFS

360 14-lb. kegs "choice Dutch butter"

The butter was part of the cargo of *Pacific* from Valparaíso advertised on July 10, 1850. Two wooden cases containing six butter-filled salt-glazed stoneware crocks,

sealed with wooden stoppers, were excavated from the Hoff's Store Site in 1986.
No manufacturer's mark or point of origin was discernible (Hattori and Kosta
1990:92). Butter from Holland was considered to be of the highest quality (Tomlinson 1866;1:262).

currants

The currants were part of the cargo of *Pacific* from Valparaíso advertised on July 10,
1850.

"Chinese preserves"

This item was most likely jars of preserved ginger, kumquats ,and citron, as advertised (by another merchant) on March 15, 1851. The cargo of the Gold Rush wrecked
clipper brig *Frolic* included 100 boxes containing 6 jars each (2 jars of each type of
preserves) . The product was sold by a Chinese merchant, "Chyloong," for $4 per
box (Layton 2002:157).

35 bbls. Bordeaux wine vinegar

"sausages in lard"

1,109 lbs. dried apples

The wine vinegar, sausages, and dried apples were part of the cargo of *John Marshall*
from Baltimore via Valparaíso, September 26, 1850. The sausages and apples may be
Chilean.

"preserves"

This item was part of the cargo of *Oscar* from China, January 10, 1851. It may have
contained the same variety of "Chinese preserves" mentioned above.

3 kegs of Chile butter "in bladders"

Pigs' bladders (like modern sausage casings) provided an airtight package for the
shipping and long-term storage of butter in the era before refrigeration. The term
Chile butter, like *Dutch butter* above, refers to the country of origin, not a type.
This item was part of the cargo of *Pacific* from New York via Valparaíso advertised
on July 10, 1850.

American Chocolate + Spanish chocolate + Chocolate, Peruvian and Chile

The "American Chocolate" was part of the cargo of *John Marshall* from Baltimore
via Valparaíso, September 26, 1850.

"dried fruits"

Any variety of fruits could be dried, such as apples and peaches, and dried fruit was
easier to ship on a prolonged ocean voyage. The remains of crates "of spline and
glue construction" containing one scorched fig "in a desiccated condition" and fig
seeds were found in the *Niantic* assemblage in 1978. Painted a bluish green, the crates
had no identifying marks (Smith 1981:179–180).

"140 lbs superior fruit cake, in tins"

"preserved ginger"

The ginger was part of the cargo of *Sir George Pollock* from China on August 20,
1850.

40 cases ham + "10 barrels and 40 tierces hams"

The cases and tierces of ham (a tierce is a type of packing container) were part of the
cargo of *John Marshall* from Baltimore via Valparaíso, September 26, 1850.

580 cases fresh American lard + 356 kegs of lard + 25 cases lard + lard

This lard was rendered pork fat and was probably from Chile. The 580 kegs of fresh
American lard were identified as part of the cargo of *Pacific* from Valparaíso and
advertised on July 10, 1850. The 25 cases of lard were part of the cargo of *Huntress*
from Valparaíso on March 7, 1851. The simple listing of lard was part of the cargo
of *John Marshall* from Baltimore via Valparaíso, September 26, 1850.

35 casks molasses

The 35 casks of molasses were part of the cargo of *Oscar* from China on January 10, 1851.

Spanish olives

Seville olives

Spain continues to produce, as it has since antiquity, large green, brine-treated olives that are shipped, as they were in the nineteenth century, from Sevilla. The "Spanish olives" of Mickle & Co.'s advertisement of January 10, 1851, are also probably from Sevilla.

50 cases dried peaches + 147 cases dried peaches + 1458 lbs. dried peaches

A single, partial peach pit was recovered during the 2001 excavation. Like the "dried fruit" also advertised, this fruit was the likely product of Chilean orchards. Fruit seeds, including peach pits, presumably from dried fruit, were recovered from the Hoff's Store Site in 1986 (Hattori and Kosta 1990:89–90). The 1,458 lbs. of dried peaches were part of the cargo of the *John Marshall* from Baltimore via Valparaíso, September 26, 1850. The 50 cases were part of the cargo of *Pacific* from Valparaíso advertised on July 10, 1850.

25 cases assorted pickles in jars

The pickles were part of the cargo of *Pacific* from New York via Valparaíso advertised on July 10, 1850. Wide-mouthed jars holding pickled foods, including olives, were recovered from the Hoff's Store Site in 1986, many of them still packed in wooden cases (Hattori and Kosta 1990:90).

"50 barrels of mess beef"

163 cans oysters

The oysters were identified as part of the cargo of *John Marshall* from Baltimore via Valparaíso, September 26, 1850. A single embossed brass label from a tin can was recovered from the Hoff's Store Site in 1986. It was embossed with the legend ISAAC RECKHOW. OYSTERS 124 LIBERTY ST. NEW YORK (Hattori and Kosta 1990:91).

"prime pork" + pork

Packed in barrels or casks, like the Mess Beef, this was dried and salted meat. Collapsed barrels of this product were excavated at the Hoff's Store Site (Delgado 1990b:27; Hattori and Kosta 1990:83).

150 cases Malaga raisins + 1646 lbs raisins

These dried wine grapes (*Uvae malacenses* or *Uvae passae majoris*) are from Andalusia, Spain. They were dried in bunches and were considered the "finest" kind of raisin in the nineteenth century. The 150 cases were part of the cargo of *Pacific* from Valparaíso advertised on July 10, 1850.

sardines

Sardines were a common Gold Rush import. The 1925 recovery of a brass label from the *Apollo* site, marked J. COLIN A NANTES – SARDINES – J COBO HUILE – RUE DES SAR-R-S NO. 9 (Delgado 1986:116), was an early reminder of an emerging global industry, the canning industry—specifically the "sardine tin." Nantes, on the southern coast of Brittany and Anjou near the mouth of the Loire, gained an international market for sardines after 1824, when local confectioner Pierre-Joseph Colin invented the concept of sardines in a can. Colin's invention was inspired by the work of Parisian Nicolas Appert, who learned that cooking sealed vegetables in a tin can killed the organisms that led to spoilage, fermentation, and food poisoning ("Nicolas Appert" 2003). Adopting Appert's method, Colin (1786–1848) sealed the small fish in a flat tin, packing them in olive oil. The sealed tins were then cooked in boiling water. Sealed in oil, with no air reaching them, the sealed fish had an incredibly long shelf life, which enabled Colin to ship them around the world (Fichou 2004). The first major global market for the sardine tin came with the California Gold Rush. Two sardine-tin labels, embossed CHATONET JNE. FABRICT. DES CON-

SERVES ALIMENTAIRES SARDINES A L'HUILE QUAL. ST. NICOLAS NO. 54
LA ROCILELLE CHARPEVTIER A NANTES, were excavated at the Hoff's Store Site
(Hattori and Kosta 1990:91–92).

"Superior sugar house syrup"

"superior sweetmeats"

"sugars"

The sugars were part of the cargo of *Oscar* from China on January 10, 1851.

STAPLES

500 kegs barley + barley (x2) + 218 bags barley + 260 bags of barley + 49 bags barley

The 500 kegs were part of the cargo of *Pacific* from Valparaíso advertised on July 10,
1850. The 260 bags were part of the cargo of *Huntress* from Valparaíso on March 7,
1851. The 49 bags were part of the cargo of *Jackin*, arriving on April 5, 1851.

130 bags Chile beans + 360 bags of Chile beans + 187 bags beans

This item is the likely source of the beans excavated in 2001. Beans of undetermined
origin were excavated at the Hoff's Store Site in 1986 (Hattori and Kosta 1990:90).

cloves

A product of Indonesia (Ortiz 1992:84), the cloves were part of the cargo of *Oscar*
from China on January 10, 1851.

coffee + 50 sacks Central American coffee + 70 bags Java coffee

During the Gold Rush, coffee was one of the most valuable international trade com-
modities in the world. Originating in Ethiopia and then introduced to Yemen, coffee
traveled via Islamic merchants and later Dutch traders to Java, and then through
French traders to Martinique, the point of contact and divergence for subsequent Latin
American coffees. By 1850, Brazil produced half of the world's coffee. Although
Caribbean and other Latin American growers also participated in international trade,
their volume did not match that of European growers and Java (Topik 2003). The
"Central American" coffee imported by Mickle & Co. was either from Colombia or
Ecuador, and despite the identification of the other coffee as "Java," it may actually
have come from Brazil or Central America because until the twentieth century, most
Latin American beans were designated "Javas," "Bourbons," or "Mochas" because
the product from these early coffee-producing areas commanded the highest prices on
the market (Topik 2003). Nonetheless, the "69 bags Java coffee" presumably from
Java were part of the cargo of *Oscar* from China on January 10, 1851. Whole beans,
ground coffee, and coffee grinders were recovered from the Hoff's Store Site in 1986,
some in bags. No point of origin was discernible (Hattori and Kosta 1990:90).

"103 jars eggs"

Part of the cargo of *Oscar* from China on January 10, 1851, these "eggs" are likely
pidan, or preserved Chinese eggs, a commodity still available from China. Dating to
the Ming Dynasty, perhaps earlier, the practice of preserving eggs by coating them in
a mixture of lime, salt, charcoal, and black tea induces chemical changes that ensure
the longevity of the eggs. When coated with wax, eggs treated in this fashion last
over 200 days. Other preserved eggs known as *zaodan* were pickled in a fermented
grain mash. In both cases, duck eggs were (and are) preferred (Blunt and Wang 1918;
Hou 2005).

263 half bags Chile flour + 401 quarter bags Chile flour + Chile flour + 690 bags of flour
+ 300 half sacks flour

mace

This spice was part of the cargo of *Oscar* from China on January 10, 1851.

nutmegs

Both mace and nutmeg are products of the evergreen nutmeg tree *(Myristica fra-
grans),* originally confined to the Moluccas and the other "Spice Islands." Greatly

prized, they were a highly valuable commodity in the sixteenth and seventeenth centuries and were the cause of intense rivalry and war between Holland and England. By the eighteenth century, French and British entrepreneurs had broken the Dutch monopoly. British plantations in Asia and the West Indies (notably Grenada) provided supplied most of the British and American market demand by the mid-nineteenth century (Ortiz 1992:84, 88–89). The mace and nutmeg here, however, were part of the cargo of *Oscar* from China on January 10, 1851. Thus, the spices may have come from Indonesia via China.

oranges

The fruit was part of the cargo of *Sir George Pollock* from China on August 20, 1850.

potatoes

The potatoes were part of the cargo of the *Pacific* from Valparaíso advertised on July 10, 1850.

7000 lbs rice

The rice was part of the cargo of *Oscar* from China, January 10, 1851. Fragments of two burnt "mats" of rice were excavated from the Hoff's Store Site in 1986. They represented the remains of a long-grained, polished white rice, presumably from China, packaged in diagonally plaited matting, wrapped in a second layer of matting, and weighing approximately 100 to 200 pounds (fixed volumes). Rice from China dominated the Gold Rush market, as documented in contemporary references and in the Hoff assemblage (Hattori and Kosta 1990:88–89).

"spices"

This item was part of the cargo of *Oscar* from China, January 10, 1851.

sugar (x2) + 30 cases super loaf sugar + 25,000 lbs super loaf brown sugar + "Sugars, white and brown" + 1,119 bags of Brazil sugar

Brazil's sugar plantations, established in the sixteenth century, were the major source of quality sugar for the rest of Latin America in the nineteenth century, and sugar was also a prized commodity for international trade. The 30 cases super[ior] loaf sugar and 25,000 pounds of superior brown sugar were part of the cargo of *Oscar* from China on January 10, 1851.

249 boxes super Oolong tea + teas, superior, in 5 and 10 lbs. catties + superior black tea

The 249 boxes were part of the cargo of *Oscar* from China, January 10, 1851. The second shipment of teas, 5- and 10-pound catties (caddies), was part of the cargo of *Sir George Pollock* from China on August 20, 1850. The "superior black tea" was part of the cargo of *John Marshall* from Baltimore via Valparaíso, September 26, 1850. The Hoff's Store excavation of 1986 yielded chests and catties of Chinese tea, their contents preserved by the anaerobic conditions of their muddy burial (Pastron and Hattori 1990).

Vinegar in casks + 42 casks vinegar + vinegar

The "42 casks vinegar" were part of the cargo of *Oscar* from China, January 10, 1851.

1 box Tartaric acid

"A colorless and odorless substance" used in various preparations of alimentary products. Tartaric acid was "treated as a foodstuff" and stowed in barrels (Gavroche 1952:269).

CLOTHING AND FABRICS

Silks and satins

The fabrics were part of the cargo of *Oscar* from China on January 10, 1851. Layton describes the "visions of opulence" evoked by a detailed invoice of China cargo from the *Eveline*, sold at auction on November 22–24, 1849, which included silks and satins "some in ten choices of color combinations" (2002:160).

crepe shawls

white embroidered crepe shawls

colored embroidered crepe shawls

assorted damask embroidered crepe shawls

assorted damask scarfs

crimson cord sashes

"silks, satins and saranets of assorted colors and styles"

figured camlet

checked and satin gauzes

black silk and satin handkerchiefs

figured and checked handkerchiefs

> The preceding ten items were part of the cargo of *Sir George Pollock* from China on August 20, 1850. The white embroidered shawls, damask embroidered shawls, "silks, satins and saranets," and camlet were also listed on the *Eveline* invoice for the November 22–24, 1849, auction of its cargo. The "saranets" are actually "sarcenet" or "sarsnet," a thin silk fabric used as lining for women's fashions of the period. Camlet is a fine dress fabric made of silk and camel hair or of wool and goat's hair.

domestics, blue drills, ginghams & c.

> These fabrics are the most likely source of clothing "blanks" excavated at the *General Harrison* site in 2001. They were part of the cargo of *John Marshall* from Baltimore via Valparaíso, September 26, 1850.

black Levantine handkerchiefs

> The handkerchiefs were part of the cargo of *Sir George Pollock* from China advertised for sale by Mickle on August 20, 1850.

china shawls and silks

superior white satins and lute-strings

dress silks

saya saya

floss silk

> Mickle & Co. identified the preceding four items as "China goods" on December 31, 1850. I have not been able to identify "saya saya."

silks and satins

gunny bags

> One shipment of gunny bags was identified as part of the cargo of *Oscar* from China on January 10, 1851. Unused gunny bags were excavated in 2001.

undershirts

drawers

hose

towels

silks and domestics [fabric]

Panama hats, of all qualities

200 doz. Guayaquil hats

> Guayaquil, Ecuador, was another source for straw hats besides Panama. These hats were part of the cargo of *John Marshall* from Baltimore via Valparaíso, September 26, 1850.

four cases of straw hats

> 78Mickle & Co. advertised the hats as "China goods" on December 31, 1850.

SHOES AND LEATHER GOODS

"shoes and boots"

> This footwear was part of the cargo of *John Marshall* from Baltimore via Valparaíso, September 26, 1850.

English bluchers

> The "blucher" was a nineteenth-century laced boot made famous by Prussian field marshal Gebhard Leberecht von Blücher, who fought at Waterloo and was second only to Wellington as a popular figure of that battle. The "blucher" was (and is) a high shoe or half boot in which the vamp and tongue are made of one piece and the quarters lap over the top of the vamp (*History of Shoes* 2003).

winter boots

English pump leather

> Pump leathers are still manufactured and are leather gaskets for sprayers and hand pumps of various sizes. As their name suggests, they were made in England. As part of the cargo of the *Oscar* from China on January 10, 1851, the gaskets, like the Tennent's ale, were shipped from Great Britain to China and then to San Francisco.

5 cases brogans

> Brogans were the ankle-high work shoes of the period. The Hoff Store's excavation in 1986 yielded 1,131 footwear fragments with a minimum number of 420 shoes or boots, as suggested by the survival of 429 toe ends of boots (Huddelson and Watanabe 1990:96). Some of the brogans in the assemblage were stamped "F. DANE" (location unknown). Others appeared to be from a stack of shoes tied together with a leather tag embossed "BRAGDON BOSTON 13¼," which was linked them to William Bragdon, a Boston "leather measurer" and presumed shoe manufacturer at 19 Shoe and Leather Street between 1846 and 1862 (96–97). The cases of brogans imported by Mickle & Co. were part of the cargo of *Pacific* from Valparaíso that was advertised on July 10, 1850. They are presumably of American manufacture and may, like the Hoff assemblage, be from Massachusetts, the nineteenth century's "major shoe manufacturing center" in the United States and "responsible for much of the California trade" (98)

brogans

"2 cases gaiter boots"

FURNITURE AND FURNISHINGS

8 cases English prints

> The prints arrived on *Pacific* from New York via Valparaíso and were advertised on July 10, 1850.

20 cases paper hangings

camp couches

> The couches and paper hangings were part of the cargo of *Pacific* and were advertised on July 10, 1850.

"an assortment of lacquered ware"

> The assortment was part of the cargo of *Sir George Pollock* from China on August 20, 1850.

"table and hanging solar lamps"

> The lamps were part of the cargo of *Sir George Pollock* from China on August 20, 1850.

American rocking chairs

> Part of the cargo of *John Marshall* from Baltimore via Valparaíso, September 26, 1850.

prints

piano

4 bales Brussels carpeting

"furniture"

looking glasses

an assortment of book cases, counting house desks, side boards

rattan couches, settees, chairs and stools

extension dining tables

mosquito netting bandas

lacquered boxes

pictures

1 pair super ebony marble top tables

> The preceding items were part of the cargo of *Oscar* from China on January 10, 1851. The rattan furniture and lacquered boxes were also listed in the *Eveline* invoice for the November 22–24, 1849, auction of its cargo, and the ebony tables were listed as "Blackwood tables with marble tops."

1 pair super ebony sofas

Mosquito curtain, silk

oil cloth table covers

> The tablecloths were part of the cargo of *Oscar* from China on January 10, 1851.

oilcloths

Carpeting and Matting + 8 bales carpeting

straw mats

matting

> This item was part of the cargo of *Oscar* from China on January 10, 1851, and was listed as "straw table mats" on the *Eveline* invoice.

trunks

silk window curtains

> Mickle & Co. advertised the curtains as "China goods" on December 31, 1850.

BUILDING SUPPLIES

"50,000 front and hard red bricks" + 16,000 bricks

> The 50,000 bricks were part of the cargo of *John Marshall* from Baltimore via Valparaíso, September 26, 1850. The 16,000 bricks came from *General Harrison*'s shipment. Brick fragments found inside the hull of *General Harrison* in 2001 may be from these shipments.

"frame houses"

> These structures were prefabricated houses. "1 Frame house complete" was part of the cargo of *John Marshall* from Baltimore via Valparaíso, September 26, 1850.

"iron houses"

> These structures were also prefabricated houses.

130,000 feet of lumber + 100 dozen 3 inch planks + "spare timber"

"lime and hydraulic cement"

> These building supplies were part of the cargo of *John Marshall* from Baltimore via Valparaíso, September 26, 1850. The cement was probably packed in barrels.

22,800 shingles + 50,000 shingles

> The 22,800 shingles were part of the cargo of *John Marshall* from Baltimore via Valparaíso, September 26, 1850. An October 7 ad reported that the shingles had been loaded in Baltimore.

100 cases tin plates

> The plates arrived on *Pacific* from Valparaíso and were advertised on July 10, 1850.

10 cases zinc + "zinc"

> Zinc plates were galvanized precut sheets of metal for sheathing or shingling a building. The 10 cases were part of the cargo of *Pacific* from Valparaíso and were advertised on July 10, 1850.

iron (x3) + 21,000 lbs. Swedish bolt iron, from ½ "to 1"

> Some of the rod iron excavated in 2001 may be from this shipment from *Jackin*.

HARDWARE

brooms

> The brooms were part of the cargo of *Oscar* from China on January 10, 1851.

"assorted carpenters' tools"

> The tools were part of the cargo of *John Marshall* from Baltimore via Valparaíso, September 26, 1850.

Flint glass tumblers

> The tumblers were part of the cargo of *Huntress* from Valparaíso on March 7, 1851.

Collins's axes

> Collins axes were manufactured by the Hartford, Connecticut, firm of Collins & Co. Founded by brothers David and Samuel Collins in 1823, the company was the first firm in the United States to manufacture axes ready for use. The product was considered a superior axe and was highly desirable (Kauffmann 1972:41). The *Niantic* excavation of 1978 yielded one Collins axe, marked "COLLINS & CO. HARTFORD CAST STEEL WARRENTED NO. 3" (Smith 1981:104–105). The Mickle & Co. shipment was part of the cargo of *Oscar* from China on January 10, 1851. These Connecticut-made axes were therefore part of a cargo imported to China and re-exported to California from there.

"assorted hardware"

knives

> Mickle & Co. the knives as "China goods" on December 31, 1850.

oars

The oars were part of the cargo of *Oscar* from China on January 10, 1851.

Rope (x2) + "coir and Manila rope of all sizes, including hawsers"

> Coir is fiber from the husks of dry coconuts (Gavroche 1952:93). Manila, or Manila hemp, is Abacá, a textile fiber from the Philippine and East Indies banana tree (27). Both materials were used to make rope, so the advertisement offers rope made both fibers. Fragments of rope excavated in 2001 may be cargo rather than rope used on the ship. The "coir and Manila rope of all sizes, including hawsers" were part of the cargo of *Oscar* from China on January 10, 1851.

Tacks + "American tacks" + 38 cases tacks

> The 38 cases were part of the cargo of *John Marshall* from Baltimore via Valparaíso, September 26, 1850.

50 kegs white lead

> White lead is lead carbonate, usually shipped in the form of a heavy paste for use in paint manufacture (Gavroche 1952:288). Barrels of white lead were excavated at the Hoff's Store Site in 1986 (Delgado 1990b:27). The item is also listed in the *Eveline* invoice for the November 22–24, 1849, auction of its cargo.

locks, bolts, hinges, screws, cutlery etc.

> These hardware items were part of the cargo of *John Marshall* from Baltimore via Valparaíso, September 26, 1850.

10 white porcelain dinner services

wine and champagne glasses

> The porcelain china and glasses were part of the cargo of *Huntress* from Valparaíso on March 7, 1851.

EQUIPMENT

copper stills

"1 suction fire engine complete"

4 cases No. 3 cooking stoves + 140 boxes of stoves + "steel stoves"

"5 wagons with double setts harness"

"soda and mineral water apparatus complete"

> With the exception of the 140 boxes of stoves and steel stoves, the preceding four listings were part of the cargo of *John Marshall* from Baltimore, September 26, 1850.

OTHER

"artificial flowers"

> These decorative items were part of the cargo of *John Marshall* from Baltimore via Valparaíso, September 26, 1850.

"empty bags"

> The bags arrived on *Pacific* from New York via Valparaíso and were advertised on July 10, 1850.

boat spars

"drugs and medicines"

"books, 6 cases assorted"

> The preceding two items were part of the cargo of *John Marshall* from Baltimore via Valparaíso, September 26, 1850.

"Chinese fire crackers"

"Dry Goods"

"yellow soap and candles"

> These supplies were part of the cargo of *John Marshall* from Baltimore via Valparaíso, September 26, 1850.

48 bales pressed hay

> The hay arrived on *Pacific* from Valparaíso and was advertised on July 10, 1850.

ivory and tortoise shell combs

> Mickle & Co. advertised the combs as "China goods" on December 31, 1850. Tortoiseshell is the translucent covering on the carapace of turtles. Upon steaming, it becomes soft, and manufacturers molded it to make ornate combs and other items. The wreck of *Frolic* yielded fragments of tortoiseshell (Layton 2002:192), and the combs are listed in the *Eveline* invoice for the November 22–24, 1849, auction of its cargo.

market baskets

> The baskets were part of the cargo of *Oscar* from China on January 10, 1851.

paper

> Mickle & Co. advertised this paper as "China goods" on December 31, 1850.

"Peruvian bark"

> "Peruvian bark"—also "red bark," "Jesuits' powder," and "Chinchona bark"— comes from the evergreen trees *Chinchona succirubra* and *Chinchona officinalis*.

Found in the hottest climates of the world, it is widely cultivated in India. Introduced to Europe in 1640, the bark gained fame as a medicine in the seventeenth century, and it remains a medicinal botanical to this day. The bark has high alkaloid content and is used to make quinine (Duran-Reynals 1946).

fine sporting powder

This is gunpowder.

"1,500 canteens"

sheathing copper

whist counters

Mickle & Co. advertised the game pieces as "China goods" on December 31, 1850. The popular game of whist used counters or tallies made from a variety of materials, including ivory, wood, bone, and metal.

writing paper

"Indian Trade Beads"

Archaeologists have discovered a large quantity of "trade" beads from the Gold Rush period in Old Sacramento (Motz and Schulz 1980).

Sources Consulted and Cited

BOOKS, REPORTS, AND JOURNALS

Albion, Robert Greenhalgh. 1939. *The Rise of New York Port, 1815–1860*. New York: Charles Scribner's Sons.

Allan, James, Lori Harrington, and William Self. 1995. *Resource Recovery Report, Muni Metro Turnback Project*. Orinda, Calif.: William Self Associates.

Allendorfer, Harry. 1979. Letter of September 18 to David Nelson, Executive Director, San Francisco Maritime Museum Association. J. Porter Shaw Library, San Francisco Maritime National Historical Park.

Ambro, Richard D. 1988. Pre-Construction Archaeological Testing Program, 343 Sansome Street Project. Submitted by Mason Tillman Associates to Gerald D. Hines Interests. City and County of San Francisco, Department of Planning.

Andrews, Kenneth R. 1984. *Trade, Plunder, and Settlement: Maritime Enterprise and the Genesis of the British Empire, 1480–1630*. Cambridge: Cambridge University Press.

Apollo Warehouses. 1850. Illustrated broadsheet published by the *New York Sun*. California Historical Society collection, San Francisco.

Archeo-Tec. 1986. The Archaeology of 100 First Plaza, San Francisco. Submitted to Barker Interests Ltd. City and County of San Francisco, Department of Planning, and Archeo-Tec, Oakland, California.

———. 1987. Hills Plaza: Archaeological Data Recovery Program. Submitted to Mr. Gary Craft, BetaWest Properties. City and County of San Francisco, Department of Planning, and Archeo-Tec, Oakland, California.

Archibald, Margaret. 1975. *Grubstake to Grocery Store: The Klondike Emporium, 1897–1907*. Canadian Historic Sites: Occasional Papers in Archaeology and History, no. 26. Ottawa: Parks Canada.

Armstrong, John. 2004. The Role of Short-Sea, Coastal, and Riverine Traffic in

Economic Development since 1750. In *Maritime History as World History,* ed. Daniel Finamore, 115–129. Gainesville: University Press of Florida.

Arrighi, Giovanni. 1997. Capitalism and the Modern World-System: Rethinking the Non-Debates of the 1970s. Paper presented at the American Sociological Association Meetings, New York; www.uni-muenster.de/PeaCon/eliten/ arrighi1.htm.

Atherton, Lewis E 1971. *The Frontier Merchant in Mid-America.* Columbia: University of Missouri Press.

Ayers, Colonel James J. 1922. *Gold and Sunshine, Reminiscences of Early California.* Boston: R. G. Badger.

Bache, A. D. 1853. On the Tides of the Western Coast of the United States— Tides of San Francisco Bay, California. In *Report of the Superintendent of the United States Coast Survey, 1853,* 77–82. Washington, D.C.: United States Coast Survey.

Baird, Joseph M. 1967. *California Pictorial Lettersheets, 1849–1869.* San Francisco: David Magee.

Baker, William Avery. 1980. The *Niantic* Observed. *Sea History* 15:46.

Bancroft, Hubert H. 1888. *History of California.* Vol. 6, *1848–1859.* San Francisco: History Company.

———. 1890. *History of California.* Vol. 7, *1860–1890.* San Francisco: History Company.

Baron, Stanley Wade. 1962. *Brewed in America: The History of Beer and Ale in the United States.* Boston: Little, Brown.

Barreto, Luís Felipe, and José Manuel Garcia. 1990. *Portugal in the Opening of the World.* Lisbon: Comissão Nacional para as Comemorações dos Descobrimentos Portugueses.

Barry, T. A., and B. A. Patten. 1873. *Men and Memories of San Francisco in the Spring of '50.* San Francisco: A. L. Bancroft.

Barth, Gunther. 1975. *Instant Cities: Urbanization and the Rise of San Francisco and Denver.* New York: Oxford University Press.

Bass, George F. 1966. *Archaeology Under Water.* London: Thames & Hudson; New York: Praeger.

———. 1988. *Ships and Shipwrecks of the Americas: A History Based on Underwater Archaeology.* London: Thames and Hudson.

Bateson, Charles. 1963. *Gold Fleet for California: Forty-niners from Australia and New Zealand.* East Lansing: Michigan State University Press.

Bauer, K. Jack. 1969. *Surfboats and Horse Marines: U.S. Naval Operations in the Mexican War, 1846–48.* Annapolis, Md.: United States Naval Institute.

Bawlf, Samuel. 2004. *The Secret Voyage of Sir Francis Drake, 1577–1580.* Vancouver: Douglas & McIntyre.

Beach, Henry Day. 1850. Letters of January 12, December 15, 29, and 30 to Moses Sperry Beach. Beach Family Archive, collection of Cathy Solley, Waldport, Oregon.

———. 1851. Letters of January 29; February 13, 14, and 26; March 13 and 31; April 5, 13, and 29; May 29; August 29; September 13 and 27; October 28 and 30 to Moses Sperry and Alfred Beach. Beach Family Archive, collection of Cathy Solley, Waldport, Oregon.

Beechert, Edward D. 1991. *Honolulu: Crossroads of the Pacific.* Columbia: University of South Carolina Press.

Beilharz, Edwin A., and Carlos U. Lopez. 1976. *We Were 49ers! Chilean Accounts of the California Gold Rush.* Pasadena, Calif.: Ward Ritchie Press.

Belden, Josiah. 1849. Receipts from E. Mickle & Co. for auction goods purchased August 8. Josiah Belden Papers, Bancroft Library MSS C-B 878, University of California, Berkeley.

Benemann, William, ed. 1999. *A Year of Mud & Gold: San Francisco in Letters and Diaries, 1849–1850.* Lincoln: University of Nebraska Press.

Berry, Thomas S. 1984. *Early California: Gold, Prices, Trade.* Richmond, Va.: Bostwick Press.

Billington, Ray Allan. 1956. *The Far Western Frontier, 1830–1860.* New York: Harper and Bros.

Blanton, R. E., S. A. Kowalewski, G. Feinman, and J. Appel. 1981. *Ancient Mesoamerica: A Comparison of Change in Three Regions.* Cambridge: Cambridge University Press.

Blunt, H., and C. C. Wang. 1918. Chinese Preserved Eggs—Pidan. *National Medical Journal of China* 4:145.

Borthwick, J. D. 1857. *Three Years in California.* Edinburgh: William Blackwood and Sons.

Boxer, C. R. 1965. *The Dutch Seaborne Empire.* London: Hutchinson.

———. 1969. *The Portuguese Seaborne Empire.* London: Hutchinson.

Brand, Michael J. 2003. Transience in Dawson City, Yukon, During the Klondike Gold Rush. Ph.D. diss., Simon Fraser University.

Brandes, H. W. 2002. *The Age of Gold: The California Gold Rush and the New American Dream.* New York: Doubleday.

Braudel, Fernand. 1972. *The Mediterranean and the Mediterranean World in the Age of Philip II.* Trans. Siân Reynolds. New York: Harper and Row.

———. 1980. *On History.* Trans. Sarah Matthews. Chicago: University of Chicago Press.

Brown, John Henry. 1949. *Reminiscences and Incidents of "The Early Days" of San Francisco, by Actual Experience of an Eye-Witness, from 1845 to 1850.* Repr., Oakland, Calif.: Biobooks originally published San Francisco, Mission Journal Publishing Company, 1886.

Brown, Marley. 1979a. Assessing the Significance of Historic Sites: The Need for a Regional Approach to Historic Archaeology. Paper presented at the 12th annual meeting of the Society for Historical Archaeology, Nashville, Tennessee.

———. 1979b. Historical Archaeology and the Regulatory Context. In *Historical Archaeology at the Golden Eagle Site,* ed. Mary Praetzellis, Adrian Praetzellis, and Marley R. Brown III. Cultural Resources Facility, Anthropological Studies Center, Sonoma State University, Rohnert Park, California.

Bullen, Isabel. 1978a. *Niantic* Finds. J. Porter Shaw Library, San Francisco Maritime National Historical Park.

———. 1978b. Preliminary Report of an Excavation of the Gold Rush Ship *Niantic.* J. Porter Shaw Library, San Francisco Maritime National Historical Park.

———. 1979. A Glimpse into the *Niantic*'s Hold. *California History* 58 (4): 326–333.

Burley, David V. 2003. Toward the Historical Archaeology of Levuka, a South Pacific Port of Call: Historical Archaeology and Vernacular Archaeology at Levuka, Fiji. *International Journal of Historical Archaeology* 7 (4): 243–265.

Camp, William Martin. 1947. *San Francisco: Port of Gold.* New York: Doubleday.

Campbell & Hoogs, eds. 1850. *Campbell & Hoogs' San Francisco and Sacramento City Directory for March 1850.* San Francisco: Campbell & Hoogs, San Francisco.

Campbell, Charles F. 2001. *The Intolerable Hulks: British Shipboard Confinement, 1776–1857.* Tucson, Ariz.: Fenestra Books.

Canright, Stephen. 2001. Notes on Impressions of the *General Harrison.* September 11 memorandum/report from the curator of San Francisco Maritime National Historical Park to Archeo-Tec, Oakland, California.

Cantwell, Anne-Marie, and Diana diZerega Wall. 2001. *Unearthing Gotham: The Archaeology of New York City.* New Haven, Conn.: Yale University Press.

Capron, E. S. 1854. *History of California, From Its Discovery to the Present Time; Comprising Also Full Description of Its Climate, Surface, Soil, Rivers, Towns, Beasts, Birds, Fishes, State of its Society, Agriculture, Commerce, Mines, Mining, &c. with a Journal of the Voyage from New York, Via Nicaragua, to San Francisco, and Back, Via Panama.* Boston: John P. Jewett & Company.

Carlson, Jon D. 2002. The "Otter-Man" Empires: The Pacific Fur Trade, Incorporation and the Zone of Ignorance. *Journal of World-Systems Research* 8 (3): 390–442.

Caughey, John Walton. 1948. *The California Gold Rush.* Berkeley: University of California Press.

Childe, V. Gordon. 1928. *The Most Ancient East: The Oriental Prelude to European Prehistory.* London: Kegan Paul.

City and County of San Francisco, Department of Planning. 1978. Environmental Impact Report for 505 Sansome Street, San Francisco.

Cleland, Robert Glass. 1914. The Early Sentiment for the Annexation of California: An Account of the Growth of American Interest in California, 1835–1846. *Southwestern Historical Quarterly* 18 (July): 1–40, (October): 121–161.

———. 1915. The Early Sentiment for the Annexation of California: An Account of the Growth of American Interest in California, 1835–1846. *Southwestern Historical Quarterly* 18 (January): 231–260.

Cook, Warren. 1973. *Flood Tide of Empire: Spain and the Pacific Northwest, 1543–1819.* New Haven, Conn.: Yale University Press.

Cornejo, Roberto Hernandez. 1930. *Los Chilenos en San Francisco.* 2 vols., Valparaíso.

Coughlin, Magdalen. 1971. Commercial Foundations of Political Interest in the Opening Pacific, 1789–1829. *California Historical Society Quarterly* 50 (March): 15–33.

Curtin, Philip D. 1984. *Cross-Cultural Trade in World History.* Cambridge: Cambridge University Press.

Dames & Moore. 1989. Archaeological Investigations at an 1851 Commercial Site along Howison's Pier, San Francisco, 343 Sansome Street. D&M job no. 11188-019-109. City and County of San Francisco, Department of Planning.

Davis, William Heath. 1967. *Seventy Five Years in California.* San Francisco: Warren Howell Books.

Deetz, James. 1977. Material Culture and Archaeology—What's the Difference? In *Historical Archaeology and the Importance of Material Things,* ed. Leland Ferguson, 9–12. Ann Arbor, Mich.: Society for Historical Archaeology.

Delgado, James P. 1979. No Longer a Buoyant Ship: Unearthing the Gold Rush Storeship *Niantic. California History* 58: 316–325.

———. 1981a. Gold Rush Jail: The Prison Ship *Euphemia. California History* 60 (2): 134–141.

———. 1981b. What Becomes of the Old Ships? Dismantling the Gold Rush Fleet of San Francisco. *Pacific Historian* 25 (4): 1–9.

———, ed. 1984. *The Log of Apollo: Joseph Perkins Beach's Journal of the Voyage of the Ship Apollo from New York to San Francisco, 1849.* San Francisco: Book Club of California.

———. 1986. The Maritime Connotations of the California Gold Rush: National Register of Historic Places Thematic Group Study. Washington, D.C.: U.S. National Park Service, National Register of Historic Places.

———. 1990a. *To California by Sea: A Maritime History of the Gold Rush.* Columbia: University of South Carolina Press.

———. 1990b. "Ships Were Constantly Arriving. . . ." The Hoff Store Site and the Business of Maritime Supply and Demand in Gold Rush San Francisco. In *The Hoff Store Site and Gold Rush Merchandise from San Francisco, California,* ed. Allen G. Pastron and Eugene M. Hattori, 25–34. Ann Arbor, Mich.: Society for Historical Archaeology.

———. 1995. Ships as Buildings in Gold Rush San Francisco. *Mariners Museum Journal,* 2nd ser., I:4–13.

———. 2002. The Gold-Rush Storeship *Niantic. Maritime Life & Traditions* 13 (Winter): 34–51.

———. 2005. Documentation and Identification of a Stern Section of a Gold Rush-Era Vessel Recovered from the Charles Hare Shipbreaking Yard Site. Submitted to William Self Associates.

Delgado, James P., and Russell Frank. 1983. A Gold Rush Enterprise: Sam Ward, Charles Mersch and the Storeship *Niantic. Huntington Library Quarterly* 46:321–330.

Delgado, James P., J. Edward Green, David Hull, J. Phillip Langellier, John Martini, and Mary Hilderman Smith. 1979. Notes on a Crate of Champagne Found Inside the Hull of the Gold Rush Vessel *Niantic.* In the author's possession.

Delgado, James P., Allen G. Pastron, and Eugene M. Hattori. 1990. Civilian and Military Armament and Accoutrements from the Hoff Store Site. In *The Hoff Store Site and Gold Rush Merchandise from San Francisco, California,* ed. Allen G. Pastron and Eugene M. Hattori, 48–57. Ann Arbor, Mich.: Society for Historical Archaeology.

Delgado, James P., Allen G. Pastron, and Rhonda K. Robichaud, 2007. *"This Fine and Commodious Vessel:" Archaeological Investigation of the Gold Rush Storeship General Harrison.* Oakland, Calif.: Archeo-Tec.

Dellino-Musgrave, Virginia L. 2006. *Maritime Archaeology and Social Relations: British Action in the Southern Hemisphere.* New York: Springer.

DeWitt, Alfred. 1890. Reminiscence of the fire of May 4, 1851, dated June 19, 1890. Society of California Pioneers, San Francisco, California.

Díaz-Trechuelo, María Lourdes. 1988. The Philippines Route. In *Spanish Pacific: From Magellan to Malaspina,* ed. and pub. Ministerio de Asuntos Exteriores. Madrid.

Dmytrshyn, Basil, E. A. P. Crownhart-Vaughan, and Thomas Vaughan, eds. 1988. *Russian Penetration of the North Pacific Ocean: To Siberia and Russian America, Three Centuries of Russian Eastward Expansion.* Vol. 1. Portland: Oregon Historical Society Press.

Dow, Gerald R. 1973. Bay Fill in San Francisco: A History of Change. Master's thesis, California State University, San Francisco.

Duarte, Monica, and Francisco Requena. 1970. Valparaíso. Valparaíso: Ediciones Universitarias de Valparaíso, Universidad Catolica de Valparaíso.

Dudden, Arthur Power. 1992. *The American Pacific: From the Old China Trade to the Present.* New York: Oxford University Press.

Dudley, Josiah, and James C. Prince. 1850. Letter of February 28 from San Francisco to Messrs. Stone, Silsbee, Pickman & Co., Salem, Massachusetts. Robert J. Chandler Collection, Lafayette, California.

Dunbar, Edward E. 1867. *The Romance of the Age, Or, the Discovery of Gold in California.* New York: D. Appleton and Co.

Duran-Reynals, M. L. 1946. *The Fever-Bark Tree: The Pageant of Quinine.* New York: Doubleday & Co..

Dwinelle, John W. 1867. *The Colonial History of San Francisco; Being a Narrative Argument in the Circuit Court of the United States for the State of California, for Four Square Leagues of Land, Claimed by that City under the Laws of Spain, and Confirmed by That Court, and by the Supreme Court of the United States.* San Francisco: Towne & Bacon.

Early, Edwin, Elizabeth Baquedano, Rebecca Earle, Caroline Williams, Anthony McFarlane, and Joseph Smith. 1998. *The History Atlas of South America.* New York: Macmillan.

Easterby, Anthony. 1850. Letter of January 14 from San Francisco to Mr. Thomas M. Easterby, London Docks, or Barnet Town, Surrey, England. Robert J. Chandler Collection, Lafayette, California.

Eddy, Wm. M. 1849. *Official Map of San Francisco, Compiled from the Field Notes of the Official Resurvey.* New York: F. Michelin.

Eisenhower, John S. D. 1989. *So Far From God: The U.S. War with Mexico, 1846–1848.* New York: Random House.

Ekholm, K., and J. Friedman. 1979. "Capital" Imperialism and Exploitation in Ancient World Systems. In *Power and Propaganda: A Symposium in Ancient Empires,* ed. M. T. Larsen, 41–58. Copenhagen: Akademisk Forlag.

Elbert P. Jones Papers. 1846–52. C-B 464, Bancroft Library, University of California, Berkeley.

Eldredge, Zoeth S. 1912. *The Beginnings of San Francisco.* 2 vols. New York: John C. Rankine Co.

Esser, Kimberly. 1999. Inland Waterways of the California Delta: Identifying and Managing a Maritime Landscape. In *Underwater Archaeology, 1999,* ed. Adriane Askins Neidlinger and Matthew A. Russell, 17–20. Uniontown, Pa.: Society for Historical Archaeology.

Fardon, G. R. 1856. *San Francisco Album: Photographs of the Most Beautiful Views and Public Buildings of San Francisco.* San Francisco: Herre and Bauer.

Farrington, Anthony. 2002. *Trading Places: The East India Company and Asia, 1600–1834.* London: The British Library.

Faulkner, Alaric, Kim Mark Peters, David P. Sell, and Edwin S. Dethlefsen. 1978. *Port and Market: Archaeology of the Central Waterfront, Newburyport, Massachusetts. Submitted to the National Park Service /Interagency Archeological Services–Atlanta.* Newburyport, Mass.: Newburyport Press.

Fenenga, Franklin. 1967. Artifacts from the Excavation of Sutter's Sawmill. *California Historical Society Quarterly* 26 (2): 160–162.

Ferguson, Leland. 1977. *Historical Archaeology and the Importance of Material Things.* Columbia, S.C.: Society for Historical Archaeology.

Fernández-Armesto, Felipe. 2004. Maritime History and World History. In *Maritime History as World History,* ed. Daniel Finamore, 7–34. Gainesville: University Press of Florida.

Fetherling, Douglas.1997. *The Gold Crusades: A Social History of the Gold Rushes, 1849–1929.* Toronto: University of Toronto Press.

Fichou, Jean Christophe. 2004. Histoire du Mangeur de Sardines à l'Huile. Paper presented at the XVIIème congrès de l'AISLF (Association Internationale des Sociologues de Langue Francais), Tours, France.

Fifer, J. Valerie. 1998. *William Wheelwright, Steamship and Railroad Pioneer: Early Yankee Enterprise in the Development of South America.* Newburyport, Mass.: Historical Society of Old Newbury.

Finamore, Daniel, ed. 2004. *Maritime History as World History.* Gainesville: University Press of Florida.

Firth, Anthony. 1995. Three Facets of Maritime Archaeology: Society, Landscape and Critique. Paper presented at the TAG'93 Conference, Department of Archaeology, University of Southampton, England.

Fisher, Robin, and Hugh Johnston, eds. 1993. *From Maps to Metaphors: The Pacific World of George Vancouver.* Vancouver: University of British Columbia Press.

Folger & Tubbs. Circa 1851. Ship Chandlers, Catalogue. Unaccessioned document, Tubbs Cordage Company. J. Porter Shaw Library, San Francisco Maritime National Historical Park.

Frank, Andre Gunder. 1994. World System History. Paper presented at the annual meeting of the New England Historical Association, Bentley College, Waltham, Massachusetts; www.hartford-hwp.com/archives/10/034.htm.

———. 1998. *ReORIENT: Global Economy in the Asian Age.* Berkeley: University of California Press.

———. 1999. The Abuses and Some Uses of World System Theory in Archaeology. In *Practice Leadership, Production and Exchange,* ed. P. Nick Kardulias, 275–296. Boulder, Colo.: Rowman and Littlefield

Frank, Andre Gunder, and Barry K. Gills. 1993. *The World System: Five Hundred Years of Five Thousand?* London: Routledge.

Frost, Alan. 1988. Science for Political Purposes: The European Nations' Explorations of the Pacific Ocean, 1764–1806. In *Spanish Pacific: From Magellan to Malaspina*, ed. Ministerio de Asuntos Exteriores, Madrid.

Galantay, Ervin Y. 1975. *New Towns: Antiquity to the Present*. New York: George Braziller.

Gardiner, Howard C. 1970. *In Pursuit of the Golden Dream: Reminiscences of the Northern and Southern Mines and San Francisco, 1849–1857*. Ed. Dale L. Morgan. Stoughton, Mass.: Western Hemisphere.

Gavroche, Captain Pierre. 1952. *Dictionary of Commodities Carried by Ship*. Cambridge, Md.: Cornell Maritime Press.

Gebhardt, Charles L. 1955a. Preliminary Report of Archaeological Investigations at Sutter's Fort. No. 23. State of California, Division of Beaches and Parks, Sacramento.

———. 1955b. Sutter's Fort—A Study in Historical Archaeology with Emphasis on Stratigraphy. No. 25. State of California, Division of Beaches and Parks, Sacramento.

Gerstaeker, Freidrich. 1948. *California Gold Mines*. Oakland, Calif.: Biobooks.

Gibb, Daniel. 1850. Receipt from Whitehead, Ward & Co. dated June 22 for rent of rooms in the *Niantic*. Gibb Papers, no. 796. California Historical Society, San Francisco.

Gibson, Arrell Morgan, and John S. Whitehead. 1993. *Yankees in Paradise: The Pacific Basin Frontier*. Albuquerque: University of New Mexico Press.

Gibson, James R. 1992. *Otter Skins, Boston Ships, and China Goods: The Maritime Fur Trade of the Northwest Coast, 1785–1841*. Montreal: McGill-Queens University Press.

Gills, Barry K., and Andre Gunder Frank. 1991. 5000 Years of World System History: The Cumulation of Accumulation. In *Precapitalist Core-Periphery Relations*, ed. C. Chase-Dunn and T. Hall, 67–111. Boulder, Colo.: Westview Press.

Goodman, John B. III. 1987. *Goodman Encylopedia of the California Gold Rush Fleet*. 11 vols. Henry E. Huntington Library and Archives, San Marino, California.

Gough, Barry M. 1980. *Distant Dominion: Britain and the Northwest Coast of America, 1579–1809*. Vancouver: University of British Columbia Press.

———. 1992. *The Northwest Coast: British Navigation, Trade and Discoveries to 1812*. Vancouver: University of British Columbia Press.

———. 2004. *Britain, Canada, and the North Pacific: Maritime Enterprise and Dominion, 1778–1914*. Aldershot, England: Ashgate Publishing.

Gould, Richard A., ed. 1983. *Shipwreck Anthropology*. Albuquerque: School of American Research/University of New Mexico Press.

———. 2000. *Archaeology and the Social History of Ships*. New York: Cambridge University Press.

Groover, Mark D. 2003. *An Archaeological Study of Rural Capitalism and Material Life: The Gibbs Farmstead in Southern Appalachia, 1790–1920*. New York: Kluwer Academic/Plenum Publishers.

Hague, Harlan, and David J. Langum. 1990. *Thomas O. Larkin: A Life of Patriotism and Profit in Old California*. Norman: University of Oklahoma Press.

Halleck, Peachy and Billings Papers. 1852. CB-421. Bancroft Library, Berkeley, California.

Hamer, David. 1990. *New Towns in the New World: Images and Perceptions of the Nineteenth-Century Urban Frontier.* New York: Columbia University Press.

Hammond, George P., ed. 1967. *Digging for Gold without a Shovel: The Letters of Daniel Wadsworth Coit from Mexico City to San Francisco, 1848–1850.* Denver: Old West Publishing Company.

Hardesty, Donald L. 1980. Historic Sites Archaeology on the Western American Frontier: Theoretical Perspectives and Research Problems. Paper presented at the 13th annual meeting of the Society for Historical Archaeology, Albuquerque, New Mexico.

———. 1988. *The Archaeology of Mining and Miners: A View from the Silver State.* Special Publication Series, no. 6. Ann Arbor, Mich.: Society for Historical Archaeology.

———. 1993. *Archaeological Perspectives on Settler Communities in the West.* Paper presented at the Settler Communities in the West Symposium, Tacoma, Washington.

Harlow, Neal. 1982. *California Conquered: War and Peace on the Pacific, 1846–1850.* Berkeley: University of California Press.

Harmon, Albert. 1964. Gold Rush Panoramas, San Francisco—1850–1853. *Sea Letter* 2 (2–3).

Harris, J. P., Bogardus & Labatt, comp. 1856. San *Francisco City Directory for the Year Commencing October, 1856, Containing a General Directory of Citizens, a Street Directory and Appendix of all Useful and General Information Appertaining to the City.* San Francisco: J. P. Harris, Bogardus, and Labatt.

Hattori, Eugene M., and Bridgette M. Brigham. 1990. Construction Hardware from Gold Rush San Francisco. In *The Hoff Store Site and Gold Rush Merchandise from San Francisco, California,* ed. Allen G. Pastron and Eugene M. Hattori, 34–47. Ann Arbor, Mich.: Society for Historical Archaeology.

Hattori, Eugene M., and Jerre L. Kosta, 1990, Packed Pork and Other Foodstuffs from the California Gold Rush. In *The Hoff Store Site and Gold Rush Merchandise from San Francisco, California,* ed. Allen G. Pastron and Eugene M. Hattori, 82–93. Ann Arbor, Mich.: Society for Historical Archaeology.

Hawes, Dorothy Schurman. 1990. *To the Farthest Gulf: The Story of the American China Trade.* Ipswich, Mass.: Ipswich Press.

Hawgood, John A. 1958. The Pattern of Yankee Infiltration in Mexican Alta California, 1821–1846. *Pacific Historical Review* 27 (1): 27–37.

———, ed. 1970. *First and Last Consul: Thomas Oliver Larkin and the Americanization of California.* Palo Alto, Calif.: Pacific Books.

Heard, Kieron, and Damian Goodburn. 2003. *Investigating the Maritime History of Rotherhithe: Excavations at Pacific Wharf, 165 Rotherithe Street, Southwark.* London: Museum of London Archaeology Service.

Heizer, Robert F. 1947. Archaeological Investigation of the Sutter Sawmill Site. *California Historical Society Quarterly* 26 (2): 134–159.

———. 1948. Survey of Building Structures of the Sierran Gold Belt—1848–1870. State of California, Department of Natural Resources. *Division of Mines Bulletin* 141:91–166.

Helper, Hinton R. 1855. *The Land of Gold: Reality vs. Fiction.* Published for the author, Baltimore.

Hickman, Patricia Parker. 1977. Problems of Significance: Two Case Studies of Historical Sites. In *Conservation Archaeology: A Guide for Cultural Resource Management Studies,* ed. Michael B. Schiffer and George J. Gamesman, 269–275.New York: Academic Press.

History of Shoes (exhibit). 2003. Pair of Men's Military Lace Boots Found Under the Floor at Weedon Barracks, Northamptonshire, 1840–1850. Ref: 1955.56.1; www.northampton.gov/uk/museums/collections/boot_and_shoe/history_of-shoes.

Hittell, John S. 1878. *A History of San Francisco and Incidentally the State of California.* San Francisco: A. L. Bancroft & Company.

Ho, Kam-chuen, Ada K. Y. Lau Yau, Wing-see Ho, and Stoney L. C. Yeung. 1991. *Historical Pictures: Collection of the Hong Kong Museum of Art.* Hong Kong: Hong Kong Museum of Art.

Hodder, Ian. 1986. *Reading the Past: Current Approaches to Interpretation in Archaeology.* Cambridge: Cambridge University Press.

———. 1987. *The Archaeology of Contextual Meanings.* Cambridge: Cambridge University Press.

———, ed. 1987. *Archaeology as Long-Term History.* Cambridge: Cambridge University Press.

———, ed.. 1989. *The Meaning of Things: Material Culture and Symbolic Expression.* New York: Harper Collins.

———. 1992. *Theory and Practice in Archaeology.* London: Routledge.

Hodder, Ian, M. Shanks, A. Alexandri, V. Buchli, J. Carman, J. Last, and G. Lucas. 1995. *Interpreting Archaeology: Finding Meaning in the Past.* London: Routledge.

Holliday, J. S. 1981. *The World Rushed In: The California Gold Rush Experience.* New York: Simon and Schuster.

———. 1999. *Rushing for Riches: Gold Fever and the Making of California.* Oakland, Calif.: Oakland Museum/Berkeley: University of California Press.

Honeysett, Elizabeth, and Peter D. Schulz. 1990. Burned Seeds from a Gold Rush Store in Sacramento, California. *Historical Archaeology* 24 (1): 96–103.

Hou, Xiangchuan. 2005. Egg Preservation in China. Shanghai: Institute of Nutrition and Hygiene, Academy of Military Medical Sciences; www.unu.edu/unupress/food/83F032e/8F032E03.htm.

Howard, David Sanctuary. 1984. *New York and the China Trade.* New York: New-York Historical Society.

Howe, Octavius T., and Frederick C. Matthews. 1926. *American Clipper Ships, 1833–1858,* vol. 1. Salem, Mass.: Marine Research Society.

Huddleston, Julia E., and Mitsuru S. Watanabe. 1990. Pegged Footwear from 1851 San Francisco. In *The Hoff Store Site and Gold Rush Merchandise from San Francisco, California,* ed. Allen G. Pastron and Eugene M. Hattori, 94–100. Ann Arbor, Mich.: Society for Historical Archaeology .

Hugill, Peter J. 1993. *World Trade Since 1431: Geography, Technology and Capitalism.* Baltimore: Johns Hopkins University Press.

Hussey, John A. 1957. *The History of Fort Vancouver and Its Physical Structure.* Tacoma: Washington State Historical Society.

Hutchins, John G. B. 1941. *The American Maritime Industry and Public Policy, 1789–1914.* Cambridge, Mass.: Harvard University Press.

Igler, David. 2004. Diseased Goods: Global Exchanges in the Eastern Pacific Basin, 1770–1850. *American Historical Review* 109 (3): 693–719.

Irving, Washington. 1870. *Astoria, or Adventures of an Enterprise beyond the Rocky Mountains.* Philadelphia: J. B. Lippincott.

Jackson, Gordon. 1983. *The History and Archaeology of Ports.* Kingswood, England: World's Work.

James, Stephen R. Jr. 1986a. *Submerged Cultural Resources Survey, Sacramento Embarcadero, Sacramento, California.* Austin, Tex.: Espey, Huston & Associates.

———. 1986b. *Underwater Archaeological Investigations, "Docks Area," Sacramento, California.* Austin, Tex.: Espey, Huston & Associates.

Janzen, Olaf. 2004. A World-Embracing Sea: The Oceans as Highways, 1604–1815. In *Maritime History as World History,* ed. Daniel Finamore, 102–114. Gainesville: University Press of Florida.

Johnson, Drew Heath, and Marcia Eymann. 1998. *Silver and Gold: Cased Images of the California Gold Rush.* Iowa City: University of Iowa Press.

Johnson, Hugh, and Jancis Robinson. 2002. *The World Atlas of Wine.* London: Mitchell Beazley.

Johnson, Kenneth M., ed. 1964. *San Francisco As It Is: Being Gleanings from the Picayune, 1850–1852.* Georgetown, Calif.: Talisman Press.

Johnson, Robert Erwin. 1963. *Thence Round Cape Horn: The Story of the United States Naval Forces on Pacific Station, 1818–1923.* Annapolis, Md.: United States Naval Institute.

Johnson, W. Branch. 1970. *The English Prison Hulks.* London: Phillimore.

Jones, Eric, Lionel Frost, and Colin White. 1993. *Coming Full Circle: An Economic History of the Pacific Rim.* Boulder, Colo.: Westview Press.

Joyner, Tim. 1994. *Magellan.* Camden, Maine: International Marine Publishing.

Judd, Bernice, and Helen Yonge Lind. 1974. *Voyages to Hawaii before 1860.* Honolulu: University Press of Hawaii.

Justh & Co. 1851. The Morning After the Great Fire of May 4th, View Taken From the Corner of Broadway & Sansome Sts. San Francisco: Justh & Co..

Kauffman, Henry J. 1972. *American Axes: A Survey of Their Development and Their Makers.* Brattleboro, Vt.: S. Greene Press.

Keay, John. 1991. *The Honourable Company: A History of the English East India Company.* London: HarperCollins.

Kelly, William. 1950. *A Stroll Through the Diggings of California.* Oakland, Calif.: Biobooks. (Orig. pub. London, Simms & M'Intyre, 1852.)

Kemble, John Haskell. 1943. *The Panama Route, 1848–1869* Berkeley: University of California Press.

Kimball, Charles P., ed. 1850. *The San Francisco Directory.* San Francisco: Journal of Commerce Press.

King, Thomas F. 2004. *Cultural Resources Laws and Practice: An Introduction.* 2nd ed. Lanham, Md.: AltaMira Press.

Kohl, P. L. 1978. The Balance of Trade in Southeast Asia in the Mid-Third Millennium B.C. *Current Anthropology* 19:463–492.

———. 1979. The "World Economy" of West Asia in the Third-Millennium B.C. In *South Asian Archaeology,* vol. 1, ed. M. Taddei, 55–85. Instituto Universitario Orientale, Seminario di Stidui Asiatici, Naples, Italy..

———. 1987. The Ancient Economy, Transferable Technologies, and the Bronze Age World System, a View from the Northwestern Frontier of the Ancient Near East. In *Centre and Periphery in the Ancient World,* ed. M. J. Rowlands, 13–24. Cambridge: Cambridge University Press.

Kondratieff, Nikolai D. 1979. Review of *The Long Waves. Economic Life. Journal of the Fernand Braudel Center* II (4): 519–562.

Kristiansen, Kristian, and Jorgen Jensen. 1994. *Europe and the First Millennium B.C.* Sheffield Archaeological Series. Sheffield, England: Continuum International.

La Lone, Darrell. 1994. An Andean World-System: Production Transformations under the Inca Empire. In *The Economic Anthropology of the State,* ed. Elizabeth M. Brumfield, 17–42. Lantham, Miss.: University Press of America.

Landberg, Leif C. W. 1967. Problems of Post-1800 Urban Sites Archaeology at Old Sacramento, California. *Historical Archaeology* 1:71–78.

Lawrence, Susan. 2003. Exporting Culture: Archaeology and the Nineteenth-Century British Empire. *Historical Archaeology* 37(1): 20–33.

Layton, Thomas N. 1997. *The Voyage of the Frolic: New England Merchants and the Opium Trade.* Palo Alto, Calif.: Stanford University Press.

———. 2002. *Gifts from the Celestial Kingdom: A Shipwrecked Cargo for Gold Rush California.* Palo Alto, Calif.: Stanford University Press.

LeCount and Strong. 1854. *The San Francisco City Directory.* San Francisco: LeCount and Strong.

Leone, Mark, and Neil Asher Silberman, eds. 1995. *Invisible America: Unearthing Our Hidden History.* New York: Henry Holt.

Letts, J. M. 1853. *Pictorial View of California; Including a Description of the Panama & Nicaragua Routes. With Information & Advice Interesting to All, Particularly Those Who Intend to Visit the Golden Region.* New York: Henry Bill.

Lewis, Oscar. 1949. *Sea Routes to the Gold Fields: The Migration by Water to California in 1849–1852.* New York: Alfred A. Knopf.

———. 1966. *San Francisco: Mission to Metropolis.* Berkeley, Calif.: Howell-North Books.

Limerick, Patricia Nelson. 1987. *The Legacy of Conquest: The Unbroken Past of the American West.* New York: W. W. Norton.

———. 1991. What on Earth Is the New Western History? In *Trails: Toward a New Western History,* ed. Patricia Nelson Limerick, Clyde A. Milner II, and Charles Rankin, 81–88. Lawrence: University Press of Kansas.

Little, Barbara J., ed. 1992. *Text Aided Archaeology.* Boca Raton, Fla.: CRC Press.

Liu, Xinru. 1988. *Ancient India and Ancient China: Trade and Religious Exchanges. A.D. 1–600.* New Delhi: Oxford University Press.

Lockwood, Charles. 1978. *Suddenly San Francisco: The Early Years of an Instant City.* San Francisco: San Francisco Examiner Division, Hearst Corporation.

Lotchin, Roger W. 1974. *San Francisco, 1846–1856: From Hamlet to City.* Lincoln: University of Nebraska Press.

MacKay, David. 1985. *In the Wake of Cook: Exploration, Science, and Empire, 1780–1801.* London: Croom Helm.

Macondray & Company. 1850. Letter of May 31, from San Francisco to Messrs. Stone, Silsbee & Pickman, Salem, Massachusetts. Robert J. Chandler Collection, Lafayette, California.

Mahoney, J. Patrick, General Partner, MSC Associates. 1978. Letter from San Francisco to A. W. Gatov, President of the Board, San Francisco Maritime Museum, April 28. J. Porter Shaw Library, San Francisco Maritime National Historical Park.

Malloy, Mary. 1998. *Boston Men on the Northwest Coast: The American Maritime Fur Trade, 1788–1844.* Fairbanks: University of Alaska Press.

Mancke, Elizabeth. 2004. Oceanic Space and the Creation of a Global International System, 1450–1800. In *Maritime History as World History,* ed. Daniel Finamore, 149–166. Gainesville: University Press of Florida.

Marryat, Frank. 1855. *Mountains and Molehills; Or, Recollections of a Burnt Journal.* London: Longmans, Brown, Green and Longmans.

Marsden, Peter. 1994. *Ships of the Port of London: First to Eleventh Centuries A.D.* London: English Heritage.

———. 1996. *Ships of the Port of London: Twelfth to Seventeenth Centuries A.D.* London: English Heritage.

Mayo, John. 1987. *British Merchants and Chilean Development, 1851–1886.* Boulder, Colo.: Westview Press.

McCarthy, Celia. 1999. Training Walls and Ferry Slips are Not Sexy Lingerie. In *Underwater Archaeology, 1999,* ed. Adriane Askins Neidlinger and Matthew A. Russell, 11–16. Uniontown, Pa.: Society for Historical Archaeology.

McDougall, Dennis P. 1990. The Bottles of the Hoff Store Site. In *The Hoff Store Site and Gold Rush Merchandise from San Francisco, California,* ed. Allen G. Pastron and Eugene M. Hattori, 58–74. Ann Arbor, Mich.: Society for Historical Archaeology.

McGloin, John B. 1978. *San Francisco: The Story of a City.* San Rafael, Calif.: Presidio Press.

Mersch, Charles F. 1850. Letter of July 16 to "My Dear Friend," San Francisco. Manuscript RP52. Henry E. Huntington Library and Archives, Pasadena, California.

Meyer, David R. 2000. *Hong Kong as a Global Metropolis.* Cambridge: Cambridge University Press.

Miller, Robert Ryal. 1995. *Captain Richardson: Mariner, Ranchero and Founder of San Francisco.* Berkeley, Calif.: La Loma Press.

Milne, Gustav. 1992. *Timber Building Techniques in London c. 900–1400: An Archaeological Study of Waterfront Installations and Related Materials.* Special paper 15. London: London & Middlesex Archaeological Society.

———. 1998. *Nautical Archaeology on the Foreshore: Hulk Recording on the Medway.* Swindon: Royal Commission on the Historical Monuments of England.

———. 2003. *The Port of Medieval London.* Stroud, England: Tempus Publishing Ltd..

Ministerio de Relaciones Exteriores Del Ecuador. 2005. *Relacion Historica de Ecuador y Europe: Dinamarca*; www.mmrree.gov.ec/mre/documentos/pol_internacional/bilateral/europa_dinamarca

Monaghan, Jay. 1966. *Australians and the Gold Rush: California and Down Under, 1849–1854*. Berkeley: University of California Press.

———. 1973. *Chile, Peru, and the California Gold Rush of 1849*. Berkeley: University of California Press.

Monkkonen, Eric H. 1988. *America Becomes Urban: The Development of U.S. Cities and Towns, 1780–1980*. Berkeley: University of California Press.

Morgan, A. W. 1852. *A. W. Morgan & Co.'s San Francisco City Directory, September 1852*. San Francisco: F. A. Bonnard.

Morgan, Dale L., and James R. Scobie, eds. 1964. *Three Years in California: William Perkins' Journal of Life at Sonora, 1849–1852*. Berkeley: University of California Press.

Morris, Don, and James Lima. 1996. *Channel Islands National Park and Channel Islands National Marine Sanctuary, Submerged Cultural Resources Assessment*. Santa Fe, N.Mex.: National Park Service.

Motz, Lee, and Peter D. Schulz. 1980. European "Trade" Beads from Old Sacramento. In *Papers on Old Sacramento Archeology*, ed. Peter D. Schulz and Betty J. Rivers, 49–68. California Archaeology Reports, no. 19. Sacramento: Cultural Resources Management Unit, Department of Parks and Recreation.

Mrozowski, Stephen A. 1987. Exploring New England's Evolving Urban Landscape. In *Living in Cities: Current Research in Urban Archaeology*, ed. Edward M. Staski, 1–9. Special Publications Series, no. 5. Ann Arbor, Mich.: Society for Historical Archaeology.

Muckelroy, Keith. 1978. *Maritime Archaeology*. Cambridge: Cambridge University Press.

Mulford, Prentice. 1889. *Prentice Mulford's Story*. San Francisco: F. J. Needham.

Mulhern, Thomas D., Chief, Cultural Resources Management. 1978. Report on Meeting, Gold Rush Ship *Niantic*, May 8, 1978, San Francisco, California. Memorandum of May 9 to Regional Director, Western Region. National Park Service, San Francisco.

Murphy, Larry E., ed. 1984. *Submerged Cultural Resources Study: Portions of Point Reyes National Seashore and Point Reyes-Farallon Islands National Marine Sanctuary: Phase 1—Reconnaissance, Sessions 1 and 2, 1982*. Santa Fe, N.Mex.: National Park Service.

———, ed. 1993. *Dry Tortugas National Park: Submerged Cultural Resources Assessment*. Southwest Cultural Resources Center Professional Papers, no. 45. Santa Fe, N.Mex.: National Park Service.

———. 1997. Regional Approach. In *British Museum Encyclopaedia of Underwater and Maritime Archaeology*, ed. James P. Delgado, 339–340. London: British Museum Press.

———, ed. 1998. *H. L. Hunley Site Assessment*. Santa Fe, N.Mex.: National Park Service.

Nasatir, A. P., ed. and trans. 1935. *The Inside Story of the Gold Rush, by Jacques Antoine Moerenhout, Consul of France at Monterey*. San Francisco: California Historical Society.

————, ed. 1964. *A French Journalist in the California Gold Rush: The Letters of Etienne Derbec.* Los Gatos, Calif.: Talisman Press.

National Oceanic and Atmospheric Administration (NOAA). 1841. Navigation Chart of the Sacramento River and the Bay of San Pablo and the Harbor of San Francisco. chart no. 161. NOAA, Washington, D.C.

Neasham, Aubrey. 1947. Sutter's Sawmill. *California Historical Society Quarterly* 26 (2): 109–133.

Ngo, Tak-Wing. 1999. *Hong Kong: A History.* London: Routledge.

Nicolas Appert. 2003. In *Hutchinson Dictionary of Scientific Biography.* N.p.: Helicon Publishing. Repr. AccessScience@McGraw-Hill, Companies, 2000–03.

Nugent, Walter. 1994. Western History, New and Not So New. *OAH Magazine of History* 9 (1): 5–9.

Ogden, Adele. 1941. *The California Sea Otter Trade, 1784–1848.* Berkeley: University of California Press.

Olmsted, Nancy, and Adrian Praetzellis. 1993. The Archaeology of Buried Ships and Wharves. In *Tar Flat, Rincon Hill and the Shore Mission Bay: Archaeological Research Design and Treatment Plan for SF-480 Terminal Separation Rebuild,* vol. 2, ed. Adrian Praetzellis and Mary Praetzellis, 349–364. Oakland, Calif.: Caltrans District 04; Rohnert Park, Calif.: Sonoma State University.

Olmsted, Roger, Nancy Olmsted, and Allen G. Pastron. 1977. *San Francisco Waterfront: Report on Historical Cultural Resources.* San Francisco: San Francisco Clean Water Program.

————. 1978. Levi's Plaza: Report on Historical and Archaeological Resources, app. B. San Francisco Office of Environmental Review.

Olmsted, Roger, Nancy Olmsted, Jack Prichett, and Allen G. Pastron. 1981. The King Street Ship. In *Behind the Seawall: Historical Archaeology along the San Francisco Waterfront,* ed. Allen G. Pastron, Jack Prichett, and Marilyn Zeibarth, 107–250. San Francisco: San Francisco Clean Water Program

Olsen, William H. 1959a. Archaeological Investigations at Sutter's Fort S.H.M. 1959. State of California, Division of Beaches and Parks, Sacramento.

————. 1959b. Second Preliminary Report on the 1959 Archaeological Investigations at Sutter's Fort. State of California, Division of Beaches and Parks, Sacramento.

————. 1961. Archaeological Investigations at Sutter's Fort 1960. State of California, Division of Beaches and Parks, Sacramento.

Ordinances and Joint Resolutions of the City of San Francisco. 1851. San Francisco: Monson and Valentine.

Ortiz, Elizabeth Lambert. 1992. *The Encyclopedia of Herbs, Spices and Flavouring.* London: Dorling Kindersley.

Ostrogorsky, Michael. 1987. Economic Organization and Landscape: Physical and Social Terrain Alteration in Seattle. In *Living in Cities: Current Research in Urban Archaeology,* ed. Edward M. Staski, 10–18. Special Publications Series, no. 5. Ann Arbor, Mich.: Society for Historical Archaeology.

Pagden, Anthony. 1995. *Lords of All the World: Ideologies of Empire in Spain, Britain and France, c. 1500- c. 1800.* New Haven, Conn.: Yale University Press.

Parker, James M. 1852. *The San Francisco Directory for 1852–1853.* San Francisco: Monson, Haswell and Co..

Pastron, Allen G. 1980. Gold Rush Hulks: Archaeology on a Grand Scale along San Francisco's Waterfront. Paper presented at the 13th annual meeting of the Society for Historical Archaeology, Albuquerque, New Mexico.

———. 1985. *Rincon Point—South Beach: Report on Historical Cultural Resources*. San Francisco: San Francisco Redevelopment Agency.

———, ed. 1987. Hills Plaza: Archaeological Data Recovery Program. Archeo-Tec, Oakland, California, and City and County of San Francisco, Department of Planning.

———. 1988. William C. Hoff's Gold Rush Emporium: Bonanza from Old San Francisco. *Archaeology* 41 (4): 32–39.

———. 1989. On Golden Mountain. *Archaeology* 42 (4): 48–53.

———. 1990. Historical Background of the Hoff Store Site and an Overview of Gold Rush Archaeology in Downtown San Francisco. In *The Hoff Store Site and Gold Rush Merchandise from San Francisco, California*, ed. Allen G. Pastron and Eugene M. Hattori, 4–18. Ann Arbor, Mich.: Society for Historical Archaeology.

Pastron, Allen G., and James P. Delgado. 1990. Archaeological Investigations of a Mid-19th Century Shipbreaking Yard, San Francisco, California. *Historical Archaeology* 25 (1): 61–77.

Pastron, Allen G., and Eugene M. Hattori, eds. 1990. *The Hoff Store Site and Gold Rush Merchandise from San Francisco, California*. Special Publication Series, no. 7. Ann Arbor, Mich.: Society for Historical Archaeology.

Pastron, Allen G., Eugene M. Hattori, Michael R. Walsh, and James P. Delgado. 1990. Some Observations and Concluding Remarks: The Hoff Store Site. In *The Hoff Store Site and Gold Rush Merchandise from San Francisco, California*, ed. Allen G. Pastron and Eugene M. Hattori, 101–105. Ann Arbor, Mich.: Society for Historical Archaeology.

Pastron, Allen G,. and Jack Prichett. 1979. The Ship at Levi's Plaza: Archaeological Investigations on San Francisco's Northeastern Waterfront. San Francisco Office of Environmental Review.

Pastron, Allen G., Jack Prichett, and Marilyn Zeibarth, eds. 1981. *Behind the Seawall: Historical Archaeology Along the San Francisco Waterfront*. 3 vols. San Francisco: San Francisco Clean Water Program.

Paul, Rodman Wilson. 1963. *Mining Frontiers of the Far West, 1848–1880*. New York: Holt, Rinehart and Winston.

Payen, Louis A. 1960. Preliminary Report No. 2 of Archaeological Investigations at Sutter's Fort. No. 86. State of California, Division of Beaches and Parks, Sacramento.

———. 1961. Excavations at Sutter's Fort 1960. State of California, Division of Beaches and Parks, Sacramento.

Payen, Louis A., Lyle R. Scott, and J. M. McEachern. 1969. Archaeological Reconnaissance in the Melones Reservoir, Calaveras and Tuolumne Counties, California, 1968 Season. Central California Archaeological Foundation, Sacramento.

Peregrine, Peter. 1992. *Mississippian Evolution: A World-System Perspective*. Madison, Wisc.: Prehistory Press.

Perry, John Curtis. 1994. *Facing West: Americans and the Opening of the Pacific.* Westport, Conn.: Praeger Publishers.

Philbrick, Nathaniel. 2003. *Sea of Glory: America's Voyage of Discovery, the U.S. Exploring Expedition, 1838–1842.* New York: Viking.

Phillips, Stephen Willard, ed. 1937. *Ship Registers of the District of Newburyport, Massachusetts, 1789–1870.* Salem, Mass.: Essex Institute.

Pitt, Leonard. 1966. *The Decline of the Californios: A Social History of the Spanish-Speaking Californians, 1846–1900.* Berkeley: University of California Press.

Pomerantz, Kenneth. 2000. *The Great Divergence: Europe, China, and the Making of the Modern World Economy.* Princeton, N.J.: Princeton University Press.

Potter, Parker B. Jr. 1990. An Envelope of Questions That Count in Underwater Archaeology. In *Underwater Archaeology 1990,* ed. Toni Carrell, 34–38. Tucson, Ariz. Society for Historical Archaeology.

Praetzellis, Mary, Adrian Praetzellis, and Marley R. Brown III, eds. 1980. Historical Archaeology at the Golden Eagle Site. Report submitted to the Redevelopment Agency of the City of Sacramento. Cultural Resources Facility Anthropology Studies Center, Sonoma State University, Rohnert Park, California.

Price, Glenn W. 1967. *Origins of the War with Mexico: The Polk-Stockton Intrigue.* Austin: University of Texas Press.

Purser, Margaret. 2003a. Professor of Anthropology, Sonoma State University, Rohnert Park, California. Personal communication (e-mail), June 16.

——. 2003b. Plats and Place: The Transformation of 19th Century Speculation Townsites on the Sacramento River. Paper presented at the annual meeting of the Society for Historical Archaeology, St. Louis, Missouri.

Rasmussen, Louis J. 1965. *San Francisco Ship Passenger Lists,* vol. 1. Colma, Calif.: San Francisco Historical Records.

——. 1966. *San Francisco Ship Passenger Lists,* vol. 2. Colma, Calif.: San Francisco Historical Records.

——. 1970. *San Francisco Ship Passenger Lists,* vol. 3. Colma, Calif.: San Francisco Historical Records.

Registry for *General Harrison.* 1840. Port of Newburyport, Massachusetts, April 28. Record group 41. Washington, D.C.: National Archives.

——. 1850. Port of San Francisco, no. 71, March 7, surrendered at San Francisco, September 24, 1851. Record group 41. Washington, D.C.: National Archives.

Renfrew, A. C., and S. Shennan, eds. 1982. *Ranking, Resource and Exchange: Aspects of the Archaeology of Early European Society.* Cambridge: Cambridge University Press.

Renfrew, Colin, and Paul Bahn. 1996. *Archaeology: Theories, Methods and Practice.* 2nd ed. London: Thames and Hudson.

Reps, John W. 1965. *The Making of Urban America: A History of City Planning in the United States.* Princeton, N.J.: Princeton University Press.

——. 1981. *The Forgotten Frontier: Urban Planning in the American West before 1890.* Columbia: University of Missouri Press.

Rich, E. E.,ed. 1941. *The Letters of John McLoughlin from Fort Vancouver to the Governor and Committee, 1825–1838.* Hudson's Bay Company Series, vol. 4. Montreal: Champlain Society.

———, ed. 1943. *The Letters of John McLoughlin from Fort Vancouver to the Governor and Committee, 1839–1844.* Hudson's Bay Company Series, vol. 6. Montreal: Champlain Society.

———, ed. 1944. *The Letters of John McLoughlin from Fort Vancouver to the Governor and Committee, 1844–1846.* Hudson's Bay Company Series, vol. 7. Montreal: Champlain Society.

Richards, Benjamin B., ed. 1956. *Gold Rush Merchant: The Journal of Stephen Chapin Davis.* Pasadena, Calif.: Huntington Library.

Riess, Warren. 1987. The Ronson Ship: The Study of an Eighteenth-Century Merchantman Excavated in Manhattan, New York, in 1982. Ph.D. diss., University of New Hampshire.

———. 1989. Design and Construction of the Ronson Ship. In *Proceedings of the International Symposium on Boat and Ship Archaeology, Amsterdam, 1988,* 176–183.

———. 1997. Ronson Ship. In *British Museum Encyclopaedia of Underwater and Maritime Archaeology,* ed. James P. Delgado, 349–350. London: British Museum Press.

Ringgold, Cadwallader. 1850. *Series of Charts, with Sailing Directions.* Washington, D.C.: U.S. Coast and Geodetic Survey.

Ritter, Eric. W., ed. 1970. Archaeological Investigations in the Auburn Reservoir Area, Phases II-III. National Park Service, San Francisco.

Robbins, William G. 1994. *Colony and Empire: The Capitalist Transformation of the American West.* Lawrence: University Press of Kansas.

Robinson, Eugene. 1978. A Gold Rush Ship Is Dug Up Downtown. *San Francisco Chronicle,* May 4.

Robinson, J. P. 1859. *Report upon the Condition and Requirements of the City Front of San Francisco Made to the San Francisco Dock and Wharf Co.; January 25, 1859.* H. S. Crocker & Co., Sacramento. Bound into the report is the *Map of City Front and Profiles of Wharves Showing the Progress of Filling,* lithographed by Geo. H. Baker, Sacramento.

Rohrbaugh, Malcolm J. 1997. *Days of Gold: The California Gold Rush and the American Nation.* Berkeley: University of California Press.

Rosato, Joe. 1978. Remembering the *Niantic:* FSU Professor's Special Cameras Will Preserve Hulk of Gold Rush Ship. *Fresno Bee,* June 2.

Roske, Ralph J. 1963. The World Impact of the California Gold Rush. *Arizona and the West,* Autumn (5):187–232.

Russell, Matthew A., James E. Bradford, and Larry E. Murphy. 2004. *E. C. Waters* and Development of a Turn-of-the-Century Tourist Economy on Yellowstone National Park. *Historical Archaeology* 38 (4): 96–113.

Sahlins, Marshall, and Patrick Kirch. 1992. *Anahulu: The Anthroplogy of History in the Kingdom of Hawaii.* 2 vols. Chicago: University of Chicago Press.

San Francisco Maritime Museum. 1965. Gold Rush Vessels Beached, Scuttled and Broken Up. J. Porter Shaw Library, San Francisco Maritime National Historical Park.

Scherer, James A. B. 1925. *The First Forty-Niner and the Story of the Golden Tea Caddy.* New York: Inton, Balch & Company.

———. 1939. *The Lion of the Vigilantes: William Tell Coleman and the Life of Old San Francisco.* Indianapolis: Bobbs-Merrill Company.

Schulz, Peter D., and Betty J. Rivers, eds. 1980. *Papers on Old Sacramento Archeology.* California Archeology Reports, no. 19. Cultural Resources Management Unit, Department of Parks and Recreation, State of California, Sacramento.

Schulz, Peter D., Betty J. Rivers, Mark M. Hales, Charles A. Litzinger, and Elizabeth A. McKee. 1980. *The Bottles of Old Sacramento: A Study of Nineteenth-Century Glass and Ceramic Retail Containers,* part 1. Cultural Resources Management Unit, Department of Parks and Recreation, State of California, Sacramento.

Schurz, William Lytle. 1939. *The Manila Galleon.* New York: E. P. Dutton.

Schuyler, Robert L., ed. 1975. *Historical Archaeology: A Guide to Substantive and Theoretical Contributions.* Farmingdale, N.Y.: Baywood Publishing Company.

Shanks, Michael, and Christopher Tilley. 1990. *Re-Constructing Archaeology: Theory and Practice.* London: Routledge.

Shaw, Carlos Martínez. 1988. *Spanish Pacific: From Magellan to Malaspina,* ed. the Ministerio de Asuntos Exteriores. Madrid: Ministerio de Asuntos Exteriores.

Shaw, William. 1851. *Golden Dreams and Waking Realities: Being the Adventures of a Gold-Seeker in California and the Pacific Islands.* London: Smith, Elder & Company.

Singletary, Otis A. 1960. *The Mexican War.* Chicago: University of Chicago Press.

Smith, Mary Hilderman. 1981. An Interpretive Study of the Collection Recovered from the Storeship *Niantic.* Master's thesis, San Francisco State University.

Smith, Philip Chadwick Foster. 1984. *The Empress of China.* Philadelphia: Philadelphia Maritime Museum.

Smith, Sheli O., Stephen R. James Jr., James P. Delgado, Jack Hunter, and Monica Reed. 1988. *La Grange: A California Gold Rush Legacy: A Report Prepared for the California Department of Parks and Recreation.* San Pedro, Calif.: Underwater Archaeological Consortium.

Soulé, Frank, John H. Gihon, and James Nisbet. 1855. *The Annals of San Francisco.* New York: D. Appleton.

Spate, Oscar. 1988. The Spanish Lake. In *Spanish Pacific: From Magellan to Malaspina,* ed. Ministerio de Asuntos Exteriores. Madrid: Ministerio de Asuntos Exteriores.

Staniforth, Mark. 1997. The Archaeology of the Event: The *Annales* School and Maritime Archaeology. In *Underwater Archaeology, 1997,* ed. Denise C. Lakey, 17–21. Uniontown, Pa.: Society for Historical Archaeology.

———. 2003. *Material Culture and Consumer Society: Dependent Colonies in Colonial Australia.* New York: Kluwer Academic/Plenum Publishers.

Stanton, William. 1975. *The Great United States Exploring Expedition of 1838–1842.* Berkeley: University of California Press.

Staski, Edward, ed. 1987. *Living in Cities: Current Research in Urban Archaeology.* Special Publication Series, no. 5. Ann Arbor, Mich.: Society for Historical Archaeology.

Steffen, Jerome O. 1979. Insular *v.* Cosmopolitan Frontiers: A Proposal for the Comparative Study of American Frontiers. In *The American West: New Perspectives, New Dimensions,* ed. Jerome O. Steffen. Norman: University of Oklahoma Press.

———. 1981. *Comparative Frontiers: A Proposal for Studying the American West.* Norman: University of Oklahoma Press.

Stein, Gil. 1999. *Rethinking World Systems: Diasporas, Colonies, and Interaction in Uruk Mesopotamia.* Tucson: University of Arizona Press.

Stillman, J. D. B. 1877. *Seeking the Golden Fleece; A Record of Pioneer Life in California: To Which is Annexed Footprints of Early Navigators, Other than Spanish, in California; with an Account of the Voyage of the Schooner Dolphin.* San Francisco: A. Roman & Co.

Street, Franklin. 1851. *California in 1850, Compared With What it Was In 1849, With a Glimpse At Its Future Destiny.* Louisville, Ky.: R. E. Edwards & Co..

Taylor, Bayard. 1850. *Eldorado; Or, Adventures in the Path of Empire.* 2 vols. New York: George P. Putnam.

Terrey, Paula B., and Allen G. Pastron. 1990. Chinese Export Porcelain in Gold Rush San Francisco. In *The Hoff Store Site and Gold Rush Merchandise from San Francisco, California,* ed. Allen G. Pastron and Eugene M. Hattori, 75–81. Ann Arbor, Mich.: Society for Historical Archaeology.

Thomsen, Fonda Ghiardi, Laboratory Manager, *Bertrand* Conservation Laboratory. 1978a. Trip Report/Log of Activities at *Niantic* Site, May 5–10, 1978. Memorandum of May 16 to Chief of Museum Services, National Park Service, Harpers Ferry Center, Harpers Ferry, West Virginia. National Park Service, San Francisco, California.

———. 1978b. Comments on the "Excavation of the Historic Ship *Niantic,*" May 5–10, 1978. Memorandum of May 17 to Chief of Museum Services, National Park Service, Harpers Ferry Center, Harpers Ferry, West Virginia. National Park Service, San Francisco, California.

Todd, John. 1978. Gold Rush Sailing Ship Destroyed at Building Site. *San Francisco Examiner,* May 11.

Tomlinson, Charles. 1866. *Cyclopaedia of Useful Arts.* 2 vols. London: Virtue & Co.

Topik, Steven. 2003. The World Coffee Market in the Eighteenth and Nineteenth Centuries, from Colonial to National Regimes. Paper presented at the first Global Economic History Network Conference, Bankside, London.

Trigger, Bruce. 1989. *A History of Archaeological Thought.* Cambridge: Cambridge University Press.

Turner, Frederick Jackson. 1894. *The Significance of the Frontier in American History.* Madison: State Historical Society of Wisconsin.

U.S. Secretary of State. 1851. *Report on Consulate at Valparaiso.* 31st Cong., 1st sess. Senate Exec. Doc. 16. Viola, Herman J., and Carolann Margolis. 1985. *Magnificent Voyagers: The U.S. Exploring Expedition, 1838–1842.* Washington, D.C.: Smithsonian Institution Press.

Waley, Arthur. 1958. *The Opium War Through Chinese Eyes*. London: George Allen & Unwin.

Wall, Diana DiZerega. 1987. Settlement System Analysis in Historical Archaeology: An Example from New York City. In *Living in Cities: Current Research in Urban Archaeology*, ed. Edward M. Staski, 65–74. Special Publications Series, no. 5. Ann Arbor, Mich.: Society for Historical Archaeology.

Wallerstein, Immanuel. 1974. *The Modern World System: Capitalist Agriculture and the Origins of the European World-Economy in the Sixteenth Century*. New York: Academic Press.

———. 1980. *The Modern World System II: Mercantilism and the Consolidation of the European World-Economy, 1600–1750*. New York: Academic Press.

———. 1989. *The Modern World System III: The Second Era of Great Expansion in the Capitalist World-Economy*. New York: Academic Press.

Walsh, Michael R. 1990. Field Methods for the Hoff Store Site. In *The Hoff Store Site and Gold Rush Merchandise from San Francisco, California*, ed. Allen G. Pastron and Eugene M. Hattori, 19–24. Ann Arbor, Mich.: Society for Historical Archaeology.

Ward, Christopher. 1993. *Imperial Panama: Commerce and Conflict in Isthmian America, 1550–1800*. Albuquerque: University of New Mexico Press.

Watson, Graham E. 2001. *Royal Navy Hulks Overseas, 1800–1976, and England's Hulks*. Published online at Emp-Comm-Forces@tropica.com and subsequently republished at www.ku.edu/~kansite/ww_one/naval/rnhulks.htm.

Westerdahl, Christer. 1992. The Maritime Cultural Landscape. *International Journal of Nautical Archaeology* 21 (1): 5–14.

Wheeler, Alfred. 1852. *Land Titles in San Francisco, and The Laws Affecting the Same, with a Synopsis of All Grants and Sales of Land Within the Limits Claimed by the City*. San Francisco: Alta California Steam Printing Establishment.

White, Katherine A., comp. 1930. *A Yankee Trader in the Gold Rush: The Letters of Franklin A. Buck*. Boston: Houghton Mifflin Co..

White, Richard. 1991. *"It's Your Misfortune and None of My Own": A New History of the American West*. Norman: University of Oklahoma Press.

Whited, Warren. 2004. The Great San Francisco Bottle Dig; http://members.tripod.com~WaipahuHaole1/SanFrancisco.html.

William Self Associates. 1996. Down She Went: A Report on the Excavation and Analysis of the Gold Rush-Era Ship Rome, San Francisco, California. Report submitted to City and County of San Francisco, Department of Planning.

———. 2006. Final Archaeological Resources Report, 300 Spear Street Project, San Francisco, California. Submitted to City and County of San Francisco, Department of Planning.

Wills, John E. Jr. 1993. Maritime Asia, 1500–1800: The Interactive Emergence of European Domination. *American Historical Review* 98:83–105.

Windeler, Adolphus. 1969. *California Gold Rush Diary of a German Sailor*. Ed. W. Turrentine Jackson. Berkeley, Calif.: Howell-North Books.

Wiren, John. 1910. Letter of December 24 to Mr. Gilliland, San Francisco, with copper spike from *Apollo* attached. In the author's possession.

Wolf, Eric R. 1982. *Europe and the People Without History.* Berkeley: University of California Press.
Woodward, Daniel, ed. 1992. *The Key to the Goodman Encyclopedia of the California Gold Rush Fleet.* Los Angeles: Zamorano Club.
Wright, Benjamin C. 1911. *San Francisco's Ocean Trade: Past and Future.* San Francisco: A. Carlisle & Company.
Wylie, M. A. 1993. Invented Lands/Discovered Pasts: The Westward Expansion of Myth and History. *Historical Archaeology* 27(4): 1–19.

NEWSPAPERS

Albany (N.Y.) Evening Atlas. June 23, 1849.
El Mercurio del Valparaíso. Biblioteca Nacional, Santiago, Chile. May 8, 1854.
Gleason's Pictorial Drawing Room Companion (Boston). July 12, 1851.
Illustrated London News. July 5, 1851; July 12, 1851.
Monterey Californian. April 17, 1847.
Neighbor (Valparaíso). Biblioteca Nacional, Santiago, Chile. November 29, 1848; December 1, 1848; December 3, 1848; December 5, 1848; December 21, 1848; January 29, 1849; February 13, 1849; March 1, 1849; March 23, 1849; April 29, 1849; June 29, 1849; December 5, 1849.
New York Herald. January 18, 1848; April 14, 1852.
Nytt Allvar och Skämt (Sundsvall, Sweden). September 5, 1850.
San Francisco Bulletin. May 10, 1912; May 5, 1925.
San Francisco Call. April 6, 1884; January 1, 1889; July 16, 1895.
San Francisco Chronicle. June 9, 1890; March 28, 1907; January 15, 1921.
San Francisco Daily Alta California. January 18, 1849; January 25, 1849; January 28, 1849; February 5, 1849; February 8, 1849; February 23, 1849; March 22, 1849; April 5, 1849; April 12, 1849; May 7, 1849; May 23, 1849; June 21, 1849; June 28, 1849; August 9 1849; August 16, 1849; August 23, 1849; August 24, 1849; August 31, 1849; September 6, 1849; September 20, 1849; September 27, 1849; October 4, 1849; October 9, 1849; October 29, 1849; November 1, 1849; November 7, 1849; November 8, 1849; November 15, 1849; December 6, 1849; December 10, 1849; December 14, 1849; December 15, 1849; December 24, 1849; December 29, 1849; January 2, 1850; January 7, 1850; January 11, 1850; January 18, 1850; January 21, 1850; January 28, 1850; January 30, 1850; January 31, 1850; February 2, 1850; February 7, 1850; February 9, 1850; February 18, 1850; February 21, 1850; February 23, 1850; March 9, 1850; March 11, 1850; March 15, 1850; March 19, 1850; April 10, 1850; May 1, 1850; May 4, 1850; May 9, 1850; May 11, 1850; May 15, 1850; May 16, 1850; May 30, 1850; June 14, 1850; June 18, 1850; June 22, 1850; June 28, 1850; July 3, 1850; July 4, 1850; July 9, 1850; July 10, 1850; July 23, 1850; July 26, 1850; July 30, 1850; August 3, 1850; August 5, 1850; August 6, 1850; August 7, 1850; August 10, 1850; August 13, 1850; August 14, 1850; August 16, 1850; August 20, 1850; August 23, 1850; August 24, 1850; August 28, 1850; September 1, 1850; September 6, 1850; September 19, 1850; September 21, 1850; September 26, 1850; September 27, 1850; September 28, 1850; September 29, 1850; Octo-

ber 1, 1850; October 4, 1850; October 5, 1850; October 7, 1850; October
10, 1850; October 11, 1850; October 20, 1850; October 29, 1850; November 1, 1850; November 3, 1850; November 4, 1850; November 5, 1850; November 7, 1850; November 19, 1850; November 25, 1850; December 12,
1850; December 14, 1850; December 19, 1850; December 31, 1850; January 1, 1851; January 2, 1851; January 3, 1851; January 9, 1851; January 10,
1851; January 20, 1851; January 27, 1851; February 8, 1851 February 18,
1851; February 20, 1851; February 26, 1851; March 1, 1851; March 7, 1851;
March 21, 1851; March 25, 1851; March 29, 1851; April 5, 1851; April 12,
1851; May 4, 1851; May 7, 1851; May 13, 1851; May 24, 1851;May 20,
1851; May 31, 1851; October 5, 1851; October 6, 1851; October 7, 1851;
October 26, 1851; November 1, 1851; January 9, 1852; July 10, 1852; July 17,
1852; July 19, 1852; August 25, 1852; August 2, 1872; May 22, 1882; May 29,
1882; June 5, 1882.
San Francisco Daily Examiner. September 26, 1865.
San Francisco Daily Herald. December 12, 1850; February 20, 1851; March 31,
    1851; May 8, 1851; February 2, 1855; February 11, 1857.
San Francisco Evening Picayune. August 29, 1850; September 9, 1850; September 30, 1850; October 23, 1850; June 16, 1851; September 24, 1851.
San Francisco Prices Current and Shipping List. July 7, 1852; February 9, 1853.
Santa Rosa Press Democrat. August 20, 1972.

Index

Text:	10/13 Sabon
Display:	Sabon
Compositor:	Integrated Composition Systems
Printer and binder:	Thomson-Shore, Inc.